DEDICATED

TO THE MEMORY OF

BOB CUMMINGS

CONTENTS

Preface 1

Introduction: Sorry, We're Still Open *by Terry Glavin* 2

PART ONE 1967–1972

Bad Trips and Bum Raps

Great Bus Stop Bust 10
Café Intimidates Straights 11
Green Thumb 11
Letters 12
Excerpts from Dr. HIPpocrates *by Dr. Eugene Schoenfeld* 12
Victoria Report *by Tom Berger* 13
Coffee Burns Holes in Genes: Danger Greater Than LSD *by Eric Sommer* 14
Who Killed Gordon Massie? *by Barry Cramer* 15
Bay Day in the Hosery Department *by Bob Cummings* 16
The Hudson's Bay Treaty 1968 *by Stan Persky* 16
The Addled Retirwepyt *by Bob Cummings* 17
What Do You Want Me to Arrest You For? *by Dan McLeod* 19
Straight Awards OAFS *by Bob Cummings* 20
Can You Dig It? *by Bob Cummings* 21
Acidman in Contempt 23
Almost Anonymous *by Stan Persky* 23
The Town Gossip *by Paul Tarasoff (AKA Dan McLeod)* 24
Ginsberg and Webster 24
Myth Shattered: We Win One! *by Stephen Brown* 25
Cynthia to Cast Prosecutor? 26
Gastown: On Being Saved, or Any More Progress Like This and We'll All Be Done In *by Bert Hill* 26
Sorting It Out from Canada *by Ken Lester* 27
Occasional Nothings *by Wanis Kouri (AKA Bob Cummings)* 27
Let It Breed *by Engledink Birdhumper (AKA Brad Robinson)* 27
Start Walking All Over People—Final Solution for Gastown? *by George Stanley* 28
Operation Whirlwind: Who Are the Criminals? 29
How Not to Get Busted at the Grasstown Smoke-in 29
Muzzle the Mayor *by Alderman Harry Rankin* 31
Power and the Open Mike *by Mason Dixon* 31
High Fashion 32

There Goes the Neighbourhood

Inaugural Column *by Milton Acorn* 33
Impo 67 or the Importance of Being Foolish *by Rick Kitaeff* 34
A Fool and His Asses Departed 35
The Ugliest City *by John Mills* 35
New Psyche Shops *by mouse (AKA Nancy Taylor)* 37
Occasional Nothings *by Wanis Kouri (AKA Bob Cummings)* 37
Ecology Happening *by J. Arthur* 38
Greenpeace 38
Greenpeace Is Beautiful *by Irving Stowe* 38
Shitpower Gives Birth to Shitcar! *by Jeannine Mitchell* 39
Everywhere We Went We Spread the Plague, *interview with Bob Hunter* 39
Rapid Transit System *by Estevan Pardo* 42
Viaduct Opens *by Sylvia Hawreliak* 42
Just Another Polluter 43
Kitsilano: Oceanside Sketches of a Doomed Village *by Michael Wallis* 43
$30,000 for This? *by Daniel Wood* 43
Patching Up the World *by Gary Gallon* 45
Free Mattress *by Butch* 45

Communication Breakdowns

Letters 46
What Makes a Hippie? *by Alderman Harry Rankin* 47
Turn On, Tune In, Take Over!!! 47
Book Review *by Ian Wallace* 48
Fellatio Rock #1 *by George Bowering* 49
Lennon Lie-in, *interview by Fred Latremouille and Dan McLeod* 50
Sun Writers Smoke Pot: 33 Fail to Turn on Publisher *by veritas (AKA Stephen Brown)* 50
Dr. Spong Wails, *interview by Lanny Beckman and Stan Persky* 51
Letters 52
Street Communication: Turn Over a New Leaf *by Muz Murray* 52
Letters 53
Implosion *by Lanny Beckman* 53
Occasional Nothings *by Wanis Kouri (AKA Bob Cummings)* 54
Let It Breed *by Engledink Birdhumper (AKA Brad Robinson)* 54
Face the Moussaka 54
Sex Ads Found Wanting *by Lani* 55
Listen, Hippies 56
Holy Shrist! 56
Women's Occupation Issue Introduction 56
The Failure of the *Georgia Straight* 57
Occasional Nothings *by Wanis Kouri (AKA Bob Cummings)* 58
No (FLASH in the PAN) 58
The Continuing Saga… 58
So, What's New? *by Wanis Kouri (AKA Bob Cummings)* 59

All in a Day's Work *by Wanis Kouri (AKA Bob Cummings)* 59
Benevolent Dictator Talks, *interview with Dan McLeod* 60
A Short Vocabulary Lesson *by George Peabody* 61
Be-in a Love-in 61
And Now for Something Completely Different *by Daniel Wood* 62
News Item: The *Grape* 65
A Mother's Lament 65

Chronology 1967–1972 67

PART TWO 1973–1985

Walking on the Wild Side

20th-Century Amazons: Ike and Tina at Baceda's *by Rob Geldof* 76
SFU Prof in Sex Play? *by John L. Daly* 77
Reading Between Those Classified Lines! 78
Vancouver's Male Strippers Let It All Hang Out *by Dona Crane* 78
Attempted Murder on the Ice *by Paul Watson* 80
Andy Bruce Trial Opens: Convicts Are Fuel for "Justice" Industry *by Tom Shandel* 84
The Kiss *by Britt Hagarty* 85
D.O.A. Alive or Dead? *by Alex Varty* 87

Altered States

Drama *by Tom Crighton* 90
Catnapping at the All-Canadian Drive-in *by John Haslett Cuff* 91
They Got Plenty of Nothin' *by Ted Laturnus* 92
The Nights Before Christmas *by D.M. Fraser* 92
Workers Rejoice for TV Listings! 95
bill bissett, *interview by Alan Twigg* 95
Artists Are Bums *by Doug Collins* 97
Sunstroke *by Tom Shandel* 98
It's a Bird! It's a Plane! No, It's the Maharishi! *by Bob Mercer* 99
Spotting Trends: Time for a New Highway into the '80s, an Energy Lifestyle Exposition at the PNE *by Donna Sturmanis* 99
Out Tramping Where the Runways Were Never Built *by George Woodcock* 100
Al Neil: Music at the Centre, *interview by Alex Varty* 103

Living in a Material World

They're Abuildin' at The Creek, Ma! *by Daniel Wood* 104
Working for the Government *by Kerry Banks* 107
What Makes Bruce Eriksen Run? *by John Faustmann* 110
Time to Say Good-bye to the Angus Garage *by Fred Pear* 114
Let Them Eat Concrete *by Bob Mercer* 115

Chronology 1973–1985 119

PART THREE 1986–1996

Truly Vulgar Cowboy Shirts
User-Friendly Expo Guide *by Dave Watson* 128
Nightshift *by John Armstrong* 130
Twig Art, Grey Bacon, Talking Heads *by Oraf* 131
Dave Crosses Over *by Dave Watson* 131
The Socred Stonehenge *by Dave Watson* 131
Dave Goes Skiing *by Dave Watson* 132
Of Taxidermy, Gospel Tents, and Dixieland Bands *by James Barber* 133
Of Punks, Peach Crumble, and Pitiful Puns *by Ian Gill* 136
Here We Are Now, Entertain Us *by Dave Watson* 140
White Peril *by Taras Grescoe* 142
Letters 143
When Will the Mayhem End? *by Ken Hegan* 144
Peach of a Dream Leads to a Trinity of Messiah Tests *by Bill Richardson* 145

Health and Welfare
The Greenpeace Giant *by Martin Dunphy* 148
PR Giants, President's Men, and B.C. Trees *by Ben Parfitt* 150
How Should We Police the Police? *by Martin Dunphy* 153
Is Logging Threatening Our Water? *by Ben Parfitt* 155
The Fight for Fish *by Terry Glavin* 156
River of Doubt *by Dirk Beck* 157
An Ancient Enigma and a Death on the River *by Terry Glavin* 159
Stupidville *by John Masters* 160
The Green Shadow *by Andrew Struthers* 163
War Without Winners *by Daniel Wood* 168
An Insatiable Emptiness *by Evelyn Lau* 169
The Road Never Travelled *by Shawn Blore* 171
Infernal Voice Mail Plays Grave Reminder *by Bill Richardson* 173

Everything Old
People Make Market Work *by Sean Rossiter* 175
Phantom Will Haunt Orpheum Birthday *by Sean Rossiter* 177
Stadium Distorts Time-Space Continuum *by Verne McDonald* 179
Another Country Lies Across the Lions Gate *by James Barber* 181
Remembering Woodward's *by John Lekich* 182
The Bridge of Our Dreams *by Sean Rossiter* 183
Closing a Door to the Past *by James Barber* 185
The Ballroom's Modest Prince *by John Lekich* 187

Chronology 1986–1996 193

Photo & Illustration Credits 199

STRAIGHT
SUN WRITERS
SMOKE POT

PREFACE

Condensing 17 boxes holding 30 years' worth of *Georgia Straights* into the slim volume you now hold in your hand was a really daunting job. It took twice as long as it should have, and four times as long as we expected. It involved as many capricious, arbitrary decisions as the average newspaper editor makes in a lifetime.

Many worthy contributions to the *Straight* have been excluded. Many mainstays of the paper don't have a word in this book. The arts and entertainment coverage that is now the backbone of the publication has been given short shrift. Almost nothing that doesn't relate specifically to Vancouver has made the cut. Some fairly ordinary stories have been included because of what they tell us about a particular time and place, or because they represent the recurrence of a familiar theme in a new context.

Nevertheless, we're happy with the result. We think that *What the Hell Happened?*—which consists entirely of excerpts from the *Straight*, save for the five years we've added to the chronology that appeared in our 25th-anniversary issue—manages to tell a few good stories. It offers a picture of '60s excess collapsing in on itself. It offers some insight into the idealism that persisted. It shows how ideas that were once considered extreme have become mainstream. And it suggests that we still have a long way to go to effectively meet the challenges that confront us. It also offers perspectives on life in Vancouver that could only have come from the pages of the *Georgia Straight.* In assembling the material, we've tried to keep each section as chronological as possible. We have attempted to make it stylistically consistent without removing all the idiosyncrasies of presentation that give the material character. We have indicated substantive omissions, but not every cut or word change made for accuracy, clarity, or length is apparent.

On the matter of thanks, it's not possible to acknowledge all the people who have contributed to the book, because everyone who has worked for or assisted the *Straight* can claim a share of the credit. Help in assembling the book came from Dave Watson, Gail Johnson, Lorée Campbell, Allison Buchanan, June Epp, Joan Szewczyk, Kevin Statham, Brigit Goldammer, and—especially—Douglas & McIntyre's incredibly patient Saeko Usukawa.

We hope you enjoy *What the Hell Happened?* We certainly had a hell of a time putting it together.

CHARLES CAMPBELL & NAOMI PAULS

INTRODUCTION

Sorry, We're Still Open

BY TERRY GLAVIN

For much of its life, alone among Canada's newspapers and magazines, the *Georgia Straight* has been consistently identified with and defined by the circumstances of its birth. The Summer of Love and all that. In 1997 the *Georgia Straight* turned 30, an event that demanded that its staff bear the unavoidable observation made by stupid people in the 1960s: You can't trust anybody over 30.

Here's the thing. It has never been possible to trust the *Georgia Straight*. The newspaper cannot be trusted to behave properly or respectably, the way a newspaper is expected to behave. According to American intellectual and media critic Noam Chomsky, late-20th-century newspapers are specifically designed and intended to "induce conformity to established doctrine" and engage in "the regurgitation of welcome pieties." For 30 years, the *Georgia Straight* has refused to do these things. This much has not changed.

In 1971, hippie journalist Pierre Coupey, recalling events surrounding the *Georgia Straight*'s conception in the spring of 1967, described the foundation of the newspaper as a direct response to a "campaign against the youth culture" mounted by Vancouver's two daily newspapers, the *Sun* and the *Province*. In Coupey's version of events, the two dailies were deliberately terrifying the public about the revolutionary spirit of the age in order to provide "a cover for police suppression," and the *Georgia Straight* was launched in order to expose all of this. It was to serve as a forum for the besieged youth culture and to provide a flag for the resistance. For the times, there was nothing particularly outlandish about such a purpose. These were the days of the Retinal Circus, My Indole Ring, the Seeds of Time, Allen Ginsberg, Mock Duck, Orange Sunshine, and the Easter Be-in at Stanley Park. Hundreds of thousands of 18-year-olds were on the loose.

The precise circumstances of the *Georgia Straight*'s birth, however, remain the subject of grave dispute and much conjecture. Poets were involved in it. There was Milton Acorn, Pierre Coupey, Stan Persky, Gerry Gilbert, Peter Hlookoff, Rick Kitaeff, and others. Dan McLeod was there from the beginning—he argued for the name *Georgia Straight*, became its proprietor, and remained publisher 30 years later. The whole thing might have arisen from a discussion that followed a reading by Leonard Cohen at the University of B.C. in February 1967. Some early stalwarts point to a handbill—printed by bill bissett's blewointment press—advertising an open meeting for April 2, 1967, that resulted in serious plans for the foundation of a radical newspaper. Drugs were involved. Confusion persists to this day.

Whatever the case, the *Straight*'s first editorial package was stitched together in McLeod's Kitsilano apartment. The paper itself was laid out in a Prior Street warehouse studio. The result was Volume 1, Number 1, the *Georgia Straight*, May 5–18, 1967. It was a 12-page, tabloid-sized newspaper. It cost a dime.

On May 12, the newspaper moved into an old office building at 432 Homer Street. That same day, McLeod spent three hours behind bars for "investigation of vagrancy," which was enough to impute sinister motives on the part of the authorities. There wasn't a single web press in Vancouver willing to print the second issue (which featured all the juvenile boisterousness one might expect from a newspaper produced by boisterous juveniles, but nothing libellous or obscene), so Number 2 and Number 3 were printed, with difficulty, on a flatbed press owned by someone's dad. Then the paper found a printer in Victoria.

Vancouver Mayor Tom Campbell pulled the *Straight*'s business licence; McLeod had the suspension overturned in court. Other municipalities prohibited the sale of the newspaper on their streets; McLeod and the *Straight*'s vendors sold the paper openly and courted arrest. For poking fun at a judge, the *Straight* was charged with criminal libel, sparking a legal battle that lasted years. For the ribald humour of its comics pages, the *Straight* fought nine obscenity charges. For printing instructions on marijuana-growing, the *Straight* was charged with "inciting to commit an indictable offence." A sex-advice column from a hippie doctor brought four separate obscenity charges. For running an excerpt from a novel, the *Straight* faced another obscenity charge. All this took place within two years of May 5, 1967. "Being charged with an offence, taken to court, locked up in prison, is a constant possibility for everyone who publishes or writes for an underground newspaper," *Straight* editor Bob Cummings observed in 1968. It wasn't until December 14, 1973, that Allan Fotheringham offered this, in the *Vancouver Sun*: "Someday some scholar interested in the law and its abuse is going to do a serious study of how authorities in this town have attempted to intimidate and bust the *Straight* by persistent harassment and prosecution.... Everyone will ask what the rest of us were doing—including the newspapers—while this was going on."

From reading the pages of the newspaper down through the years, it is difficult to say when it was, exactly, that the *Georgia Straight* ceased to be an "underground" newspaper and became an "alternative" newspaper. It was an event that simply occurred during a transition of sorts that roughly coincided with the wilting of hippie sensibilities and the rise of punk nihilism, sometime between the U.S. withdrawal from Vietnam and the day Mary Steinhauser was shot to death at the B.C. Penitentiary. What followed was a succession of editors, and one generation of writers gave way to another, and there were various changes in focus and format. At some point—here, again, there is no identifiable threshold—the *Georgia Straight* matured from its posture as an alternative weekly to become what can be reasonably described as a publication that, at its best, is one of the most intelligent weekly newsmagazines in the English-speaking world. In the three years preceding its 30th birthday, the *Georgia Straight* garnered 65 nominations and 31 awards for editorial excellence, including five

National Magazine Awards, three other national awards for science and health writing, and one award for best feature reporting in print, radio, or television in British Columbia. The awards came in categories that include travel, humour, food, culture, business, columns, news, and innovation.

To be fair, a staggering amount of horrible and preposterous material has found its way into the pages of the *Georgia Straight*, and no amount of excuses about the youthfulness or exuberance of the newspaper's editors and writers can explain it all away. Perhaps the only honest explanation is to concede that, well, stuff like that happens. A lot can happen in 30 years. One thing that has not happened is the *Straight*'s death, which is saying something: the *Straight* is the only "underground" publication from the 1960s to have survived in Canada. From that era, the *Straight* is one of only a handful of such publications (most notably *Rolling Stone*, a few months younger than the *Straight*) still with us anywhere in the world. Some credit rightfully belongs to McLeod's good business sense, but there are other reasons.

Among them is the *Georgia Straight*'s strategic position on the margins of the mass media (and its interest in what the rest of the media tend to treat as marginal issues), which has allowed the *Straight* to provide something distinct from the mainstream noise the mass media increasingly produces. The *Straight*'s corporate independence has helped make room for this distinctiveness. Since the late 1960s, the story of North America's news and entertainment media has been one of franchises—newspaper chains and media companies—displacing local and independent companies. Corporate mergers and takeovers have produced a kind of integration in which the producers of various goods and services—the purchasers of advertising space and advertising time—are in many cases one and the same as the companies that own the media. The line between what was formerly known as "advertising" and what was formerly known as "news" has become blurred; in some cases, that line has disappeared entirely. One might say that the outrageous things *Straight* writers used to allege about the mass media 30 years ago are, in fact, closer to reality in the 1990s than they were back then.

The *Straight*'s persistent posture as Vancouver's free press is no less significant than its corporate independence. In 1967, the *Georgia Straight* subtitled itself "Vancouver's Free Press" (for a brief time, the name *Georgia Straight* gave way entirely to the *Vancouver Free Press*), and although the *Georgia Straight* describes itself modestly in 1997 as "Vancouver's News and Entertainment Weekly," the newspaper, at 30, is published as the product of the Vancouver Free Press Publishing Corp. It might be this persistent notion of itself as Vancouver's "free press" that lies at the heart of what distinguishes the *Georgia Straight* and accounts for its survival and its success. Whatever the case, all this has resulted in a magazine that continues to make room for writers whose work would not otherwise be considered acceptable to "mainstream" magazines and the daily newspapers. The *Georgia Straight* has tended to break "news" that the other media either can't or won't handle, and it has made a nuisance of itself by going further than the dailies in exploring the underlying issues. Sometimes, the *Straight*'s success has been a simple matter of identifying what other media don't provide and making it available to the public, even if that is as obvious as a useful events calendar. It has also meant covering the gay community with respect, which until recently no "mainstream" newspaper in Canada had the guts to do. And it has meant covering "environmental issues" seriously and consistently, which the *Georgia Straight* began doing about a decade before the mainstream media.

After the strange cohesion of the 1960s gave way, *Straight* music editor Bob Geldof (now "Sir Bob," formerly of the Boomtown Rats) observed that music and the arts were a source of unity among the *Georgia Straight*'s traditional readership. As it turned out, the *Straight*'s cultural coverage generally continues to sustain loyal readers and bring in new ones every year. Consistent, intelligent coverage of art, literature, dance, music, film, and theatre, which so many newspapers seem to regard as practices no less antiquated than blacksmithing or coopering, has become the *Georgia Straight*'s mainstay. In an age in which the printed word is said to be dying, when the attention span of the "average" newspaper reader is said to be rapidly diminishing, and virtual reality is taking over from reality itself, the *Georgia Straight* has pursued increasingly complex questions that demand more and more of the reader's attention. There are—God forbid—long stories. Cover essays of 3,000 words or more are the rule, rather than the exception.

Meanwhile, since 1967, the rest of the media in Canada have become increasingly captive to companies like WIC Western International Communications Ltd., Southam Inc., Thompson Corp., and Sterling Newspapers Ltd., corporations that rely on a value system that demands consumption. We oblige. Despite the media caricature of British Columbians as inordinately sensitive to "environmental" concerns, British Columbians produce more garbage than any other people in Canada or on the planet—about twice the amount that people throw away in the Netherlands, Sweden, or the United Kingdom. British Columbians also consume more energy per person than in any region on the planet: about one-third more than Americans, about twice as much as Scandinavians, and almost three times as much as the Japanese. The Lower Mainland is growing at a pace that adds a population equal to that of New Westminster every year. Overnight, subdivisions bloom. Every year, there are new suburbs, new roads, new malls, and new real estate.

The Southam corporation, which owns dozens of newspapers in the region, mainly weeklies and real-estate flyers, as well as the *Vancouver Sun* and the *Province*, props up that value system. By the time I left the *Vancouver Sun* in 1993, the newspaper's weekend editions contained the Homes section, the New Homes section, "home-improvement" pages, real-estate supplements, and so on, stuffed between advertisements and advertising supplements from Home Hardware, Lumberland, garden-shop franchises, and page after page of real-estate listings, real-estate showcases, and on and on and on.

In general, the number of advertising executives, middle-management "editors," and marketing specialists in the media has grown while newsrooms have shrunk. Increasingly, news organizations rely upon prepackaged news and features, along with the dispatches of pooled reporters and syndicated movie reviews, columns, book reviews, and political commentary. Reporting is being replaced by stenography. Reporters are harried, pretending to be well informed when they are, in reality, bounced from one assignment to another, from the news release to the news conference, from one media availability session to some other staged media event. The media have become little more than a conduit for private media strategies that have been designed to form and shape public opinion. Of course, it's not always that bad. Sometimes it's just people who don't know what they're talking about interviewing people who don't know what they're talking about.

So there is this strange reality, and a widening chasm between what happens in the real world and what ends up on television or in the newspapers or on the radio. It is noise, the sound of a thousand axes grinding. It is ridiculous. The *Georgia Straight* has remained on the margins of all of this, and in this strange way, it has been possible for the *Straight* to remain true to its original ideals of journalistic principle over slavish conformity. As a result, the *Straight* has become one of the most old-fashioned newspapers in the country: it honours the traditional journalistic methodologies—independent investigation, independent confirmation of facts, and the presentation of the results in a comprehensible and engaging way—that are disappearing elsewhere. The *Straight* has done this without losing its sense of humour and without taking itself too seriously. The *Georgia Straight* has defied all conventional wisdom about the direction journalism must take in order to survive in the late 20th century. It remains fiercely loyal to the highest standards of English-language journalism.

In its earliest days, the *Georgia Straight* was a writer's newspaper. Today, the *Georgia Straight* is a writer's newspaper.

I wrote my first story for the *Straight* the summer I got out of high school. I wanted to write a piece about how kids could use the B.C. government's new human-rights legislation to protect themselves against discrimination. The story was for Chinatown kids, Sikh kids, Indian kids, and Quebec farmworker kids in the Okanagan. I was a bit timid about it, but I reckoned that if I dressed the part, maybe then the *Georgia Straight* would be more interested in my story. In my boots, my jean jacket (with a little red Mao pin on it), and straggly hair, I took the bus from Burnaby to the *Straight*'s old offices on Powell Street. A sign in the glass door proclaimed "Sorry, We're Open" (its flip side: "Yes, We're Closed").

The place smelled like a patchouli-oil factory. Everything was in boxes or piled in heaps on the floor. There were "black light" posters and everything. A big-haired guy, leaning over a mess of typewritten sheets on a desk, listened to my story idea. He finally looked up from whatever he was doing and said "Sure." I went home and started writing. That was almost a quarter-century ago. I have never stopped writing. I've written five books. I spent more than 15 years working for daily newspapers. I've written reams of copy for the *Georgia Straight*, not all of it bad, and I still write for the *Georgia Straight* from time to time. Its editors are the sharpest, the most demanding, and the best a writer could ever hope for.

As for the importance of the circumstances of the *Georgia Straight*'s birth, *Straight* editor Bob Cummings got it right back in 1968 when he observed, "Underground papers are the bastard sons of a free society."

The *Georgia Straight* is still a bastard of a newspaper. Vancouver is all the better for it. So is the country.

FACING PAGE: Dan McLeod selling the *Straight*, June 1968.

georgia straight
Keep Bay Rum
Legal
music

ADVANCE MATTRESS FOOL'S ASSES

RAZZ JOBS AND HIPPY-CRYTES

BATHING'S BEAUTY JIGGY-JIGGY

PINKERTONS AND INDIANS MRS.

SCHROTCH SPREAD THE PLAGUE

PART ONE

1967–1972

BASTARD SONS CAN YOU DIG IT

ACIDMAN OD'D DRAG QUEENS

RIPPED OFF GASSY'S HEAD

SOME PRETTY HEAVY ACTION

AND OPERATION DUSTPAN

NO WAY WAS I RESPONSIBLE

georgia straight

•MISSION FAIR GOES AHEAD

•STREET SINGERS ARRESTED

25¢ Vol 5 No 194 TWO ISSUES PER WEEK FRIDAY-MONDAY Aug 20-23, 1971

UNDERGROUND FILMS SEIZED

BAD TRIPS AND BUM RAPS

Great Bus Stop Bust

MAY 5–18, 1967

Picture a sunny spring afternoon at 4th and Arbutus, and the B.C. Hydro bus stop during rush hour with its dozens of people standing or sitting on the grass or vacant lot behind.

Substitute 30 of the Vancouver diggers and replace the bus with a paddy wagon and you have the scene as it was Monday, April 24, when the fuzz picked up four digger passengers for "vagrancy." It proved to be the most spectacular "vagrancy" bust since several people were arrested last summer in front of the Vancouver Public Library during business hours, for loitering. That case was thrown out in a hearing, and the victims were given a "stern reprimand." This time, the much-harassed hippies were not so lucky.

The diggers had gathered at the Phase 4 behind the bus stop, so as not to disturb the customers or passers-by. The diggers watched the cops approach slowly. All then moved off the lot except for Victor Avery, Roger Mantle, Julius Coutu, and Elaine Silzer. As they explained to The Man, they were not harming the owner's lot. Nor were they sleeping on it, as told in the *Sun.*

The very next morning, Elaine was brought before a magistrate and, too confused to attempt to seek legal counsel, was given a suspended sentence (hence a criminal record) and ordered to post a $100 bond. She was finally forced to leave town the following Friday midnight.

The remaining three retained counsel and got their cases remanded. They were scheduled to appear on May 5.

Police harassment increases, and the war between the young hip and creeping old fogeyism is being escalated.

Café Intimidates Straights

MAY 19, 1967

The sign on the door of the Arbutus Café at 4th and Arbutus read "We do not serve hippies or beatniks." The owner was advised by two cops (who will remain numberless) to put up the sign, some weeks ago.

It was there, Wednesday afternoon on May 10, when *Straight* editors Pierre Coupey and Dan McLeod and three friends were refused service and accused of belonging to "that gang that hangs around here."

An hour later, Dan returned from City Hall with a copy of City Bylaw #3846, which prohibits discriminatory business practices.

The waitress remembered him as one of the persons she had intimidated an hour earlier. He then read the bylaw and demanded that all discrimination cease by noon the next day, under penalty of hippie sit-in action, beginning at 3:00 p.m. These sit-ins would be legal, under Bylaw #3846 and the B.C. Public Facilities Act.

Later that evening, the owner, Mrs. Schrotch, took the sign down on the advice of—guess who?—#523. Pierre talked with Mrs. Schrotch the next morning, and she promised not to discriminate again.

Have you had any trouble in cafés lately? A Discrimination-End-It-Yourself-Provo-Kit will be published in the next issue.

Green Thumb

MAY 19, 1967

The opinion is current, among certain criminal elements, that local marijuana is excellent. In order to stamp out the cultivation and preparation of this illegal substance, it is desirable that the techniques used be widely known.

First, the seeds are soaked in water for a couple of days. Next, they are stored between moist tissue paper for a few more days. This helps them to germinate. These germinated seeds are planted in good loose soil, at a depth of about ½ inch, either in window boxes, or else in the ground, someplace where they can be watered until they are firmly established.

For maximum yield, the seeds are planted in groups of about six, at a distance of about 1 ½ feet apart. In this way, the lawbreakers practise selective

McGeer Irresponsible see p.4

FREE PRESS VANCOUVER'S georgia straight 10¢

VOL 1 NO 1 / MAY 5-18 1967

great BUS STOP BUST

Picture a sunny spring afternoon at 4th and Arbutus, and the B.C. Hydro busstop during rush hour with its dozens of people standing or sitting on the grass or vacant lot behind.

Substitute 30 of the Vancouver Diggers and replace the bus with a paddy wagon and you have the scene as it was Monday, April 24, when the fuzz picked up 4 Digger passengers for "vagrancy". It proved to be the most spectacular "vagrancy" bust since several people were arrested last summer in front of the Vancouver Public Library during business hours, for loitering. That case was thrown out in a hearing, and the victims were given a "stern reprimand". This time, the much-harassed hippies were not so lucky.

The diggers had gathered at the Phase 4 behind the bus stop, so as not to disturb [illegible] or [illegible]-by. The diggers watched the cops approach [illegible]. All then moved off the lot except for Victor Avery, Roger Mantle, Julius Coutu, and Elaine Silzer. As they explained to The Man (see photo), they were not harming the owner's lot. Nor were they sleeping on it, as told in the Sun.

The very next morning, Elaine was brought before a magistrate and, too confused to attempt to seek legal counsel, was given a suspended sentence (hence a criminal record) and ordered to post a $100 bond. She was finally forced to leave town the following Friday midnight.

The remaining three retained counsel and got their cases remanded. They were scheduled to appear on May 5.

Police harassment increases, and the war between the young hip and creeping old ogeyism is being escalated.

Police harassment is on the rise in the Kitsilano area. These people were busted at the bus stop on 4th and Arbutus, when police acted on an irate but mistaken lot-owner's complaint. Imposing figure in center is Vic Avery

WAR Crimes Tribunal

TORONTO——The first meeting of the International War Crimes Tribunal ends May 6. It's purpose: to investigate U.S. violation of the principles established by the Nuremberg trial and rules fixed by international agreements.

Georgia Straight is now gathering material on the Tribunal for the next and future issues.

Meanwhile, a Canadian Committee has been set up to collect evidence, distribute information, and to accept donations for the Tribunal. They are: The Canadian Committee for the International War Crimes Tribunal, 6-758 Yonge St., Toronto 5, Ontario.

PROVOS PROVOKE POLICE

—— CANADIAN FREE PRESS (Ottawa)

".....AMSTERDAM IS A SWINGING TOWN.... peopled by DEPENDABLE, honest DUTCHMEN. .....It has a matchless cleanliness, a wide open 'something for everybody' nightlife, Rembrandt paintings, battalions of bicycles, and so many arteries of canals winding through the city that it overshadows even Venice. It is a throbbing, modern-day business wonder coupled with culture and old world charm in amazing abundance. The old and the new and the unusual sweeping you along in a present-dat riot of traveller delights. And you get your money's worth in a very literal sense. The prices are among the lowest in Europe. DUTCH FRIENDLINESS is a big national product and they pass the time of day with you in your own language almost as if they never spoke any other. So come on down, up or over to Amsterdam and start making memories ...this is the place where the ACTION is...

BIGGEST SURPRISE OF ALL" THE PROVOS! The provokers, who are the grooviest anywhere. Now! There is no doubt. In the first issue of Provo they call on the 'provotariat' of the world "beatniks, pleiners, nozems, teddy boys, blousons noirs, gammler, raggare, stiljagi, mangupi, mods, students, artists, rockers, delinquents, anarchists, ban-the-bombers, misfits...those who don't want a career, who lead irregular lives..."Increasingly the youth of first Holland, then Belgium, France and England has risen with them against mediocrity, the self and soul destruction of our times. Comes Canada. But we have no traditions like this.

WE WILL START ONE!
IN THE STREETS!
SOON!

Free Press initiates and will continue a far-ranging analysis and report on this new front against the spectacularly well-packaged creeping death. For starters, a few Provo exploits from various sources...

Discontent is ready to explode in a great number of places; in Amsterdam it was largely due to the fantastic energy of one man, the artist Robert

cont. page 5

The first issue of the *Georgia Straight*.

breeding, allowing only the strongest one in each group to grow. There is no wastage, because the sicklier plants are still smoked. The plant may attain a height of eight feet, making it easy to spot from the air. To combat this, illegal cultivators in Mexico grow it between corn plants. The conditions that corn thrives under are also the best for hemp cultivation. They consider it desirable that the plants be permitted to flower. The flowers and pollen are the stuff that hashish is made of. The ripe seeds are saved, to plant the following season.

These criminals dig the plants out by the roots. Then they cure them, by immersing the roots in boiling water for a couple of hours. This causes the sap to rise to the leaves, saturating them with cannabinol, the active ingredient. The plants are then hung upside down, until they dry. Then the leaves and flowers are harvested. In a very small space, these criminals can grow enough marijuana to keep themselves, and all their friends, breaking the law for an entire winter.

There are some who plant under more desperate circumstances, like on the courthouse lawn. These lawbreakers strip off the leaves as soon as they appear. They claim that these are powerful enough to get them "high," which is a very illegal state of mind. They also claim that marijuana is virtually indestructible. They have actually dried wet stashes in ovens, claiming that this makes it stronger.

This practice is deplorable, in view of the fact that marijuana, although harmless, is illegal. Under no circumstance should this article be construed as an encouragement to those who would cultivate this substance....

Letters

JUNE 28, 1967

I have a high regard for publications such as *Georgia Straight*, and stalked your last issue with the zeal of a hunter.

I found it interesting, informative, and, in part, very amusing.

I particularly enjoyed "Green Thumb" & have enclosed a small gift for its editor.

Wendy
Victoria, B.C.

Editor's Note: wow!!! (A plant-in was held at Victory Square. Thanks, Wendy.)

Excerpts from Dr. HIPpocrates

BY BERKELEY'S DR. EUGENE SCHOENFELD (A SYNDICATED COLUMN)

NOVEMBER 10–23, 1967

Question: Is masturbation physically harmful if I do it once a day?

Answer: There is a story about a little boy who was found masturbating and told that he would go blind unless he stopped. "Well," he pleaded, "can I do it until I need eyeglasses?"

There is no evidence that masturbation is physically or mentally harmful whatever its frequency.

JANUARY 12–25, 1968

Question: Have you ever heard of something called a "hum" job? During fellatio or cunnilingus one vigorously hums a tune such as "Jingle Bells." What do you think of this?

Answer: Hmm. Merry Christmas.

FEBRUARY 2–22, 1968

Question: To attempt to become an auto-fellatioist—would this be stretching things too far?

Answer: I think it may be stretching narcissism too far.

Question: The reader who wrote you about the "hum-job" divulged a rare and beautiful secret indeed; but have you heard of a razzberry-job? It is similar to the hum-job (humming during fellatio and/or cunnilingus), but instead of humming one executes a loud and vibratory "razzberry" at the appropriate moment—which is determined by individual experimentation.

It is important to maintain good contact while "razzing" so that the vibrations are not all lost to the air.

Answer: I think a "razzberry" is the same as a "Bronx cheer." But are you giving us a snow job?

MAY 28–JUNE 1, 1971

Dear Dr. Schoenfeld,

My old lady and I are having a huge hassle over what she calls my "unsanitary" body. I used to take a shower every day until I realized how stupid it was. Now I take a bath about once a month.

I don't see what's so unhealthy about it, but my old lady says it's unhealthy. Which of us is right? If she is, how often should I take a bath? Doesn't soap wash away the organic body oils?

Answer: Bathing is very healthy, natural, and organic. In primitive cultures, the only people who don't bathe regularly are those who haven't ready access to water. I've noticed that people on communes who have insufficient bathing facilities have many skin infections.

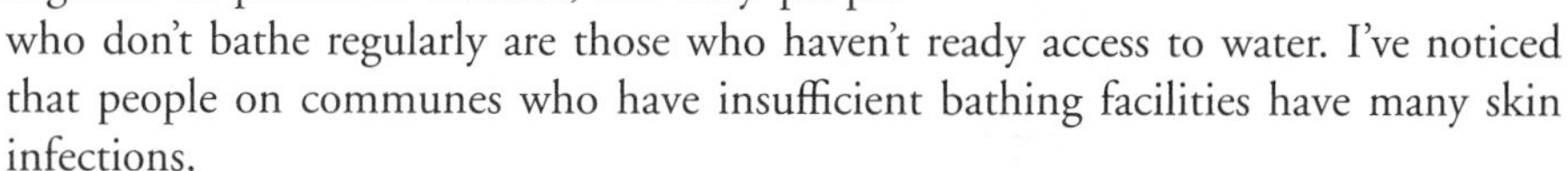

How often you should bathe depends upon your individual body chemistry, the amount of physical work you do, the weather, how close you want to be to strangers, and your old lady's sensibilities. Your friends and neighbours suggest twice a week for a start.

Victoria Report

BY TOM BERGER, MLA (NDP, VANCOUVER-BURRARD), MARCH 1, 1968

Some of our legislators are consumed with interest about so-called psychedelic drugs.

This may be the reason why Les Peterson, the Minister of Education, announced that the House Committee on Social Welfare and Education would examine the extent to which "marijuana, LSD and other lysergic drugs are available to our young people, study the causes and effects of such drugs, and report their observations and opinions thereon."

What is this study in aid of? Does the minister contemplate a serious scientific and sociological study of the problem? If so, the place to begin is the study made by Miss Ingebor Paulis for the Narcotic Addiction Foundation last year. After all, the provincial government subsidizes the foundation with a quarter of a million dollars a year. Why not get the foundation to do the job?

But the minister has made it clear what he has in mind. He told the *Victoria Times* that he wanted the committee to find out how many professors have led their students astray. This is obviously intended to be an intellectual witch-hunt.

What kind of hearings does the minister have in mind for the committee? Well, the chairman of the committee will be obliged "to draw to the attention of any witness his right to claim the protection of the Evidence Act of the province and of Canada." Does he want university students to come before the committee, to confess to their use of illegal drugs, and then to implicate their teachers at the university? Sad to say, the answer seems to be yes. Sad because a minister of the Crown has already found our university teachers guilty of encouraging the use of illegal drugs, when there is no evidence at all of this. Sad because the spectacle of young people implicating themselves will accomplish nothing, except to mark them for life with the taint of crime.

Coffee Burns Holes in Genes: Danger Greater Than LSD

BY ERIC SOMMER, MAY 17–30, 1968

Caffeine damages chromosomes!

So says Dr. W. Tagart in a well-documented report in the *Journal of Mutation Research*. Dr. Tagart, a member of the Institute for Human Genetics at the University of Munster in West Germany, studied the effect of caffeine on cultures of human tissue.

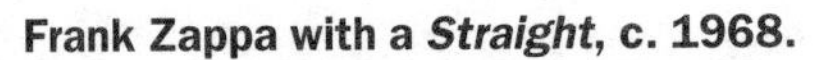

Frank Zappa with a *Straight*, c. 1968.

His conclusion: One cup of coffee damages your chromosomes approximately as much as .01 roentgens of radiation.

He also reported that doubling the dose of caffeine doubles the damage. So drinking an average of four cups of coffee a day for a year will damage your chromosomes as much as 14.6 roentgens of radiation.

UBC genetics expert David Suzuki evaluated Dr. Tagart's findings in an exclusive interview with the *Georgia Straight*. He estimated from the Tagart study that four cups of coffee a day causes more than 150 times as much chromosome damage as one day of the fallout which occurred during the period of atomic testing in the atmosphere.

"One of the direct consequences of chromosome breakage this extensive," Dr. Suzuki told the *Georgia Straight*, "is an increase in the probability of cancer."

Suzuki also pointed out that caffeine works on your chromosomes only while the DNA is duplicating itself in preparation for cell division. "The caffeine effect," he said, "would tend to zero in on the sex cells—for they reproduce the most often."

Comparing the effect of caffeine with LSD, Suzuki stated: "Chromosome damage due to caffeine is quite well established; chromosome damage due to LSD is not. In any case, the breakage due to caffeine is much, much greater than anything ever attributed to LSD."

Who Killed Gordon Massie?

BY BARRY CRAMER, MARCH 8–21, 1968

On January 24th of this year, 29-year-old Gordon Arthur Massie choked to death while resisting the efforts of two dope-squad men who were trying to make him throw up a balloon they believed to contain dope. (Later a balloon was removed from the dead man's windpipe which contained 20 caps of heroin valued at $300 on the illicit dope market.)

Did the two dope-squad men kill Gordon Massie? They were merely following the established procedure of using brute force to secure evidence from a suspected dope pusher. They did nothing out of the ordinary; it just happened that this particular suspect up and died on them during the course of their regular duties.

Did the chief of police kill Gordon Massie? He has stated that his men are expected to use all reasonable means to secure evidence. His dope squads work with the RCMP dope squads, who in turn work with the American Bureau of Dope Squads, and they all approve of the tactics that apparently must be used in order to get evidence.

Did the *Vancouver Sun* kill Gordon Massie? They headlined the heroic efforts of the dope-squad men to revive the "victim." However, their second report on the incident, in which the wife of the "victim" gave evidence, was at least twice as short as the first. (Presumably, as more facts about the tragedy were revealed, the story became less interesting.) Who developed these barbaric procedures; who teaches them; who approves of them? The *Sun* questions no one.

Did the magistrates kill Gordon Massie? They are too busy giving jail terms to young and old male and female citizens who have been convicted of possession of marijuana (instead of legal dope) with the same zeal as they have been for years sentencing dope pushers (who are providing dope, at enormous personal profit, to sick people). Massie certainly could expect no mercy from them, and the dope squad men knew that their savage behaviour would be ignored as the magistrate scratched the conviction into his record book.

Did Wilfred Heffernan kill Gordon Massie? He wouldn't want to because, as Special Crown Drug Prosecutor, he makes his living from getting convictions of live dope pushers. He knows of the inhuman methods used to get evidence, but that is secondary to the ultimate conviction. Could there be anything lower in his mind than dope pushers and what could be harsh enough punishment for them?

Did the knowledgeable doctors and lawyers and psychologists and pharmacologists and sociologists and psychiatrists and nurses and politicians kill Gordon Massie? They are aware of the mass of researched evidence that supports a more humane and just approach to the problems of drug addiction, and yet they remain remarkably silent.

Stay silent, good people; watch the lunacy of a 57-year-old woman jailed for smoking pot and a 64-year-old junkie with a chronic brain condition jailed for possession of pain-relieving dope. The paranoia of "dope" in our city is reaching out way beyond the "criminal fringe" of society, but don't say anything and turn your eyes away...it can't happen to you...those brutal dope-squad men won't break into your home and grab you by the throat and punch you in the kidneys. After all, they respect you for your silence, don't they?

Okay, one more time: who killed Gordon Arthur Massie? I did. And so did you.

Bay Day in the Hosery Department

BY BOB CUMMINGS, MARCH 8–21, 1968

The Hudson's Bay Company has instituted a "No 'Hippies' Allowed" policy in its Round Table restaurant and Malt Bar areas. Uniformed guards are barring the entrance of any person with long hair or a beard. To prevent "hippies" from congregating around the corner of Georgia and Granville, the Bay has a workman constantly washing the windows with a hose.

This action followed an item by *Sun* minimalist Denny Boyd in which he bewailed the fact that "hippies" occupied the same city as himself. In the column he labelled himself a bigot by claiming that his rights superseded the rights of what he considers to be an inferior class of citizen. The amount of dirt he professed to see on the "hippies" was more than matched by the insular vomit he spewed out in the paper. A large part of his diatribe was on "hippies" who frequented the Bay basement.

Aside from Boyd, the Bay's action was partially justified, although not to the extent to which it has been carried. For several months, a group of longhaired people has congregated in the Round Table and surrounding areas. Often they occupied tables for prolonged periods, buying the bare minimum and preventing other people from using the facilities. They often blocked aisles, inconveniencing store shoppers. This inconsideration for other people was unjustified and exhibited a selfish attitude.

The important question is whether the Bay took its action because some people acted in bad taste or because of the discriminatory group classification suggested by Boyd. If it was the latter, the move should be fought on the grounds that group intolerance is no more permissible than racial intolerance.

It is unfortunate that the Bay could not have settled the matter by speaking to the group involved and depending on mutual goodwill to solve the problem. Personal communication is always preferable to thoughtless retaliation.

The Hudson's Bay Treaty 1968

BY STAN PERSKY, MARCH 22–APRIL 4, 1968

It's the 300th anniversary of the first ship to sail into Hudson Bay to trade for furs and now we're riding up five floors of escalators through a maze of junk to negotiate with Mr. Buckley, general manager of the western empire. We're the Indians, sort of....

The people have fur hats, beads, vests, cowboy hats, necklaces, buttons with words and signs, long hair, etc., looking, I suppose, pretty much like the Hudson's

Bay men who came pouring down these rivers westward to the Pacific a hundred and sixty years ago.

Mr. Buckley's executive office is located behind the lamp department. Tucked inside my copy of Mr. Pinkerton's history of the HBC I'm carrying a proposed agreement I had just drafted and read to my friends at the free school.

The agreement says Hudson's Bay will stop discriminating, that the city government will get people off the street corner, that the real problem is civic centres—there's no place for young people to publicly gather, we urge the city council to recognize the problem and act constructively, we note that when people gather at the courthouse fountain (a monstrous chunk of rock bathed in geysers of water) they're harassed by the police, we propose that within the concept of youth centres (which, while nice airy ugly modern shells, are largely unused) it might be a good idea to spawn some coffeehouses which would provide places to meet and at the same time be something that is credible within the cultural context of the people who are now seen as undesirables and a problem, and that Hudson's Bay, who once gave the Indians beads and trinkets which now appear...on the bodies of the young [causing] fright and hostility...would give some free coffee to the project....

Ed and I tread a path carpeted by the pelts of a million beavers.

Mr. Buckley isn't going to sign the agreement. "Could we agree to disagree?" he asks. We get a truce. Quietly, tomorrow, the Bay will stop discriminating. We'll quietly disperse the street-corner conglomeration (which will be simplified because everyone will be in courthouse square).

There are a few other quiet details.

Mr. Ross, the personnel manager, is there too. He's a bright, pale man. Everything about him is pastel faded: his hair, his suit, his new tie. He wants to know if the kids think of himself and Mr. Buckley as Nazis. He wants us to know that the Hudson's Bay is not opposed to anyone's philosophy of life. Both he and Mr. Buckley use the word *philosophy* in the same way they use the term *three-piece-sectional couch.*

We're told a modern-day anecdote about the Hudson's Bay department store in Calgary, the point of which is two kids were found making it, of all places, on the roof....

The Addled Retirwepyt

FROM "THE ADDLED TYPEWRITER" OF BOB CUMMINGS, APRIL 19–MAY 2, 1968

This exclusive column will regularly rape your mind in future issues of the *Georgia Straight.*

It was almost noon on an August morning and throngs of people passed the corner of Dunsmuir and Granville where two strangers stood. He was a man in an establishment suit and tie, waiting for some friends. She was in her late teens, with a soft, almost childlike face formed into a teardrop shape by long blonde hair. She was wearing a loose sweater, tight jeans, and a string of bright beads. Her smile reflected the fun of being, and she gave it to each passing person, whether they bought a copy of the *Georgia Straight* or not. It was a sunny day with a fresh breeze coming in off the sea that made even Dunsmuir and Granville smell fresh and alive.

They were an anachronism to a summer day... a pair of blue uniforms walking down the street watching cars and people... looking for crime, criminals, or reasonable suspicion. Black belts, guns, handcuffs. The older one, tall with a slight paunch, was obviously the leader of the pair. They crossed Dunsmuir and approached the corner. The sun was a glare on their eyes.

The girl "hippie" smiled. "*Georgia Straight*?"

The leader-cop snapped, "Get that garbage out of my way!"

Like most straight people, the man in the establishment suit had an innate fear of the police uniform. However, he also had a point of sensitivity that had just been jabbed. He heard himself react to the leader-cop, "What gives you the right to talk to her that way? She's not hurting anybody!"

He was suddenly bracketed between two hovering uniforms. The leader-cop glared down and commanded, "This is police business! I advise you to keep your mouth shut unless you want to be arrested for obstructing a police officer!"

The younger cop held out his hand. "Let's see some identification!"

Establishment suit was shocked. "I haven't committed any crime. I just objected to the way you spoke to..."

The leader-cop interrupted, "We're checking you under the Vagrancy Act! If you resist we can take you in for 24 hours on suspicion!" It was a bluff but one that always worked on people unfamiliar with the law.

Angry, nervous, and embarrassed, the man in the establishment suit handed over his wallet and answered questions while passers-by stared at him as though he was a criminal. The leader-cop pulled photos and papers out of the wallet while his partner took notes. Handing back the wallet, the leader-cop pointed to the man's briefcase. "What's in that?"

"Just business papers..."

"Open it up!" When the man showed signs of objecting, the leader-cop said, "We're checking it under the Narcotics Control Act!" It was another bluff. To make such a search legally, they would have to produce a Writ of Assistance. But the man in the suit didn't know this and opened his case.

Finishing the search, the leader-cop grinned. "Maybe next time you'll be smart enough to mind your own business!" His partner added, "It's part of our job to deal with these hippies for the public good!"

When the police left, the man in the establishment suit looked at the girl and mulled the words *for the public good* over in his mind. He remembered newspaper articles about *filthy hippies, police action,* and *irate merchants*... and he began to wonder.

The girl smiled. "Don't let it bother you. It's just a Vag check. They do it all the time." She explained that a "Vag" check was a form of harassment used by some members of the police against those they disliked.

And the man in the establishment suit went to lunch wondering about the qualities of freedom in a country that not only condoned this police persecution but legalized it.

Like most Canadians, he had always assumed that this was a free country, that justice and law were equally applied to all citizens, that a person's right to differ and be different would be protected by every level of authority.

Like most Canadians, he was repelled by the conditions in Communist and Fascist dictatorships and disgusted by the police brutality and bigotry against minorities in many parts of the United States. While not a communist or hippie, he was proud that in his country, Canada, a person could be a communist or hippie or anything else with impunity and freedom.

When the police stopped him on the street, they robbed him not of his dignity as a man, but of his pride as a Canadian. In removing the illusion of equality from a hippie, they cast doubts into the meaning of an anthem, the symbolism of a flag, and the truth of national myth woven in the name *Canada*.

In a country based on equality, justice, and freedom, the persecution of one human being, no matter how small or insignificant, is a cancerous blemish that marks every citizen and blots the memory of every man or woman who ever died in the country's name. One cop using one law to persecute one hippie casts a shadow on 20 million people.

The man in the establishment suit was just another face in the mass of a large city. He was moderately successful, moderately happy, and moderately sure of what he was and where he was going... Until he spoke out in defence of a hippie girl at Dunsmuir and Granville.

Three months later I joined the staff of the *Georgia Straight*.

What Do You Want Me to Arrest You For?

BY DAN McLEOD, JUNE 28–JULY 12, 1968

Last Friday I decided to brave the ban on *Georgia Straight* on the streets of New Westminster imposed by the local Gestapo. Armed with a hundred copies of the last issue, I stood on a corner on Columbia Street until they were all gone.

The only unhappy incident of the day came when a police officer approached me and asked for ID. Not wishing to embarrass him by telling him he had no legal right to ask for it, I produced my press card.

He asked me if I was the one who was arrested for disturbing the peace a few months ago; I said yes.

Straight **staffer Julie Palmer.**

He asked me if I knew it was illegal to display papers on the street; I asked him if I was under arrest.

"What do you want me to arrest you for—disturbing the peace?"

"No—I want you to arrest me for whatever I'm doing that's illegal. But before you do maybe you had better go up to the Municipal Hall and look up the law for what I'm doing that's wrong; then come down and charge me under that law."

He then jumped into his police car and drove away. I stood there for an hour and a half and he never came back.

The point that it *is* legal to sell papers on the street even *without* a city licence derives from our Canadian Bill of Rights and so-called freedom of the press. This point will eventually have to be established in the courts. This is not what I was trying to do on Friday.

Friday I was giving away papers and collecting donations, in the same way that the Jehovah's Witnesses collect donations for *Awake!* and *Watchtower.*

Dan McLeod in New Westminster.

Straight **Awards OAFs**

THE ADDLED RETIRWEPYT, BY BOB CUMMINGS, JULY 26–AUGUST 8, 1968

Displaying the aplomb of a diarrhea victim at the end of a long line in front of a faulty pay toilet, Mayor Campbell recently put his foot into it up to the groin by predicting: (a) The imminent demise of the *Georgia Straight* due to a lack of sales, and (b) The evaporation of the hippies within two or three weeks.

Whereas the paper's sales are on a sharp increase and have been for several issues and whereas the city's hip population has shown no tendency to vanish, it might be wise to question Campbell's source of information. If he gets it through the grapevine, the age of his facts would imply that someone along the line has been making a vintage wine. If he consults a soothsayer, the seer should give up examining the entrails of chickens bought on sale at the Safeway frozen-food counter. If it is astrology, somebody has been making a Pisces (the fishes) out of a Libra (Campbell's sign) by giving him a line of Taurus (the bull).

Inspired by His Worship's penchant for getting his left shoe on his right hand while eating, his fervent desire for publicity, and his talent for creating verbal catastrophes, the *Georgia Straight* is delirious to announce the formation of the "Order of the Abundant Flatulence" in order to recognize such men as he....

The selection committee makes no apologies and commands to your attention the 1968 recipients of the Order of the Abundant Flatulence (OAF).

CAMPBELL, Mayor Thomas J. The Happy Crapshaw Memorial Trophy. (Crapshaw was the man who, between 1927 and 1934, predicted the end of the world 72 times and who made his views known by threatening to jump off bridges unless given newspaper space.)

The citation reads: *"To Thomas CAMPBELL, who has proven that the lip is faster than the mind, and who embodies that sense of delivery and natural flair that changes a simple error in judgement into an insoluble blunder. BY YOUR IMAGE MEN SHALL KNOW YOU—on both channels as often as you can arrange it."*

FISK, Police Chief John. The Heinrich Himmler Humanitarian Award. (While accused of certain irregularities in connection with his work, Himmler was known to be an efficient police officer, a loving family man, and uncommonly gentle with animals, especially chickens.)

The citation reads: *"To John FISK, who has striven, despite the terrible restriction of the Canadian Legal Code, to maintain the splendid police tradition established in Germany, Russia, South Africa, and Selma, Alabama. YOU HAVE WITHSTOOD THE ENEMY—such as progress, civil liberties, and legal equality."*

ECKHARDT, Magistrate Lawrence. The Pontius Pilate Certificate of Justice. (Unfairly maligned by critics, Pilate upheld the highest traditions of a judge by placing law and order above human considerations and by helping to clear the streets of Jerusalem of degenerate nonconformists.)

The citation reads: *"To Lawrence ECKHARDT, who, by closing his mind to justice, his eyes to fairness, and his ears to equality, has encouraged the belief that the law is not only blind, but also deaf, dumb, and stupid. LET HISTORY JUDGE YOUR ACTIONS—then appeal."*...

Can You Dig It?

THE ADDLED RETIRWEPYT, BY BOB CUMMINGS, AUGUST 16–22, 1968

And so now it begins! Detectives, polite and correct, asking questions; a blue piece of paper commanding attendance in the name of the Queen; names and words on the radio; a nervous discomfort that lives in the guts like a ball of squirming larvae; and waiting.

Being charged with an offence [for criminal libel of a magistrate], taken to court, locked up in prison, is a constant possibility for everyone who publishes or writes for an underground newspaper. Every week you are aware of other newspapers that don't arrive on schedule and letters stating that they have been "busted"—"... is in jail and we are trying to raise the bail."—"They seized our papers and records."—"We are charged with...." And then it is you!

Underground papers are the bastard sons of a free society. They exist by grace of freedom of expression. Freedom of speech and freedom of the press. And they exist as a test of those freedoms, to remind a monolithic society of its flaws and to remind it, sometimes at the price of the death of an underground paper, that the realities of freedom are still a long way from the words in patriotic songs and political speeches.

Underground papers are not, and do not see themselves, as perfections. They are often wrong, sometimes they are mostly wrong—they are the products of minds that are often too critical or enthusiastic, depend too much on feelings over cold reason, go too far in quest of what they believe in, or strike too hard at what they oppose. And yet, they are the honest expressions of free minds trying to communicate their beliefs to a free society.

Underground papers conscientiously attack many parts of the capitalistic system and yet are some of the greatest examples of practical free enterprise. They arose at a time when the term *newspaper* meant multimillion-dollar enterprise and even the publishing giants were suffering from financial and circulation losses. Rarely do they have financial backing or even credit privileges. They get no preferential treatment by governments, no tax concessions, no immunities or assistance. In fact, the authorities usually apply every restriction, law, and bylaw in an attempt to contain or destroy these dissident bastards of print. Often, special laws are scraped up and enforced, or obviously discriminatory regulations placed on them. What no government would even consider doing to a major paper, they do with impunity to the underground press—banning distribution, arresting salesmen, cancelling licences.

The financial success of most underground papers depends on selling one edition in order to pay for the printing of the next. As they will not be controlled or cowed by their advertisers or mass public opinion, both circulation and advertising revenue are undependable. This is what is meant by the term *free press*—the expression of free thoughts and ideals as the highest, and only, consideration in deciding the content and direction of the paper.

The need for a "free press."

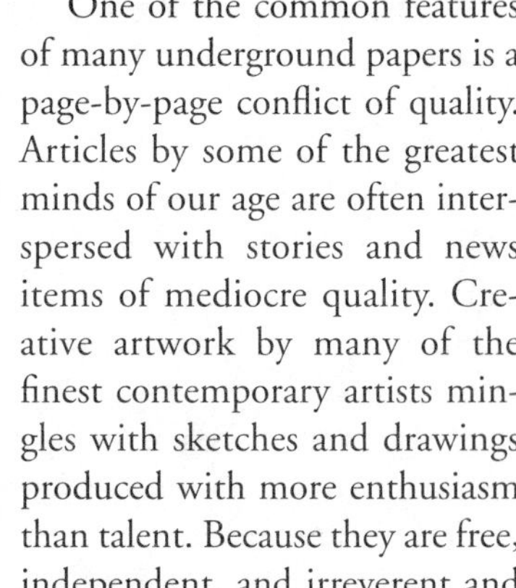

One of the common features of many underground papers is a page-by-page conflict of quality. Articles by some of the greatest minds of our age are often interspersed with stories and news items of mediocre quality. Creative artwork by many of the finest contemporary artists mingles with sketches and drawings produced with more enthusiasm than talent. Because they are free, independent, and irreverent and recognize no social icons, underground papers like the *Georgia Straight* make many enemies. Because they choose to battle with the most entrenched and powerful establishment institutions, those enemies often appear to be society itself. And yet, the basic credo of the *Straight* and other similar papers is social justice, human rights, and freedom. This is humanity; humanity is people; and people are society.

Attacks on the underground press and its people are often contradictions. Young people are told that if they disagree with the system, they should fight to change it instead of dropping out. And then they see those who are fighting, including underground papers, under vehement attack, with demands for their destruction.

The question now is: Despite its shortcomings, will it really be a better society without a *Georgia Straight*?

PRAY FOR *G.S.*, BABY!

Acidman in Contempt

SEPTEMBER 27–OCTOBER 3, 1968

Last week's edition of the *Georgia Straight* did not appear for a number of reasons beyond our control, having to do with editors in jail, editors running away from jail, and the Tiny Tom show on Friday's TV.

In addition, ACIDMAN does not appear this week because it comments on a case which is now before the courts and could be in contempt of court, even though it was drawn before the court action was started.

Almost Anonymous

BY STAN PERSKY, SEPTEMBER 13–19, 1968

Vincent is dead from an OD of schmeck.

Bilingual translation for all you nice folks who work in the B.C. Hydro Building, go to pleasant middle-class universities like UBC, shoot in the low 90s at the Shaughnessy Golf Club, etc.: Vincent was a drag queen who drank in the New Fountain pub on Cordova St. Last Saturday night, she shot some heroin on top of beer, whiskey, and pills, maybe.

Somebody says it was only a skin-pop, no more than half a cap. Today they're waiting to ship the body, tracked and with a rotted liver and a stopped heart, back to New Brunswick.

Vincent was part of the neighbourhood where men dress in women's clothes, where underground papers get produced and print obituaries for the almost anonymous, where, like in the grocery store next door [where] I'm buying cigarettes, fat drunk Indian women with bashed-up faces eat frosted doughnuts for dinner.

Right now it's raining slowly on Cordova St., on Carrall, on Hastings. And when you buy this story from the beautiful hippie on Georgia and Granville, it might be sunny.

Vincent did one thing before she died that took a kind of courage. She came and told me that cops on the beat were harassing drag queens in the pub where she drank. She knew there might be some shit as a result of telling the story to us. But in some crazy way she figured that drag queens had the right to do their thing.

She tried to get some of the others to tell me about the scene. A couple did, but a lot of people were scared to talk. And after the story came out, she got some of the heat. Other people on the scene put her down. Saturday afternoon there was a kind of crazy scene in the pub, with people cursing at her, shouting at each other, etc. For everybody on the scene it was real; for us freaks it was strange. (I mean, if the drag queens are a kind of scene, and if we're the freaks, what does that make those of you who need this explained?)

She got drunk and depressed. She went home with a lesbian friend. Then she cranked it. Then the friend called emergency rescue. A trip for them for nothing. And called more friends. They called the coroner. Funeral parlour. Relatives who live at the other end of this mouldy maple leaf.

I'm not too interested in coming on bitter with this. I'll leave it to her friends to hold the wake. But I'm impressed that death is pretty mechanical. At least in our part of town. Maybe everywhere.

So it's a suicide. Maybe. That's one version. Then there are darker rumours. We'll never really know. In whodunits, knowing who is the point, without sentimentalizing it, is how things are here.

In our shop, the radio plays revolutionary music. My longhaired friends put the filthy rag to bed. I'll talk to some more people on tape recorders as I become a master of sociology or a poet. Maybe I'll go back to the pub for a beer and see how things go with the young queen I was digging in there a couple of hours ago. I don't feel sorry about Vincent, but I feel something.

The Town Gossip

BY PAUL TARASOFF (AKA DAN McLEOD), SEPTEMBER 27–OCTOBER 3, 1968

The *Straight* is now banned in Haney! We got a phone call this week from a salesman in Haney who had his papers seized by the local RCMP. The cop acted illegally, but who's going to tell *him* that? It's the easiest way to ban a paper, other than breaking the presses. So add Haney to the list (hmm, let's see: New Westminster, Surrey, White Rock, North Vancouver, West Vancouver, Squamish, etc., etc...).

Ginsberg and Webster

EXCERPTS FROM JACK WEBSTER'S MARCH 11TH CKNW INTERVIEW WITH ALLEN GINSBERG, APRIL 4–10, 1969

Webster: I'm saying that many of my listeners will think that free press is a bad cause.
Ginsberg: Oh, listeners, you don't really think free press is a bad cause, do you?
Webster: No, but it's been in all kinds of trouble with the law.
Ginsberg: Free press has been in all kinds of trouble with the law...
Webster: Well, talking about the *Georgia Straight*, yes, it has been in all kinds...
Ginsberg: Isn't that a press?
Webster: Oh yes, it's a free press, and there are some things I like about it. I myself from the old square position think it's been a little bit immature at times, but...
Ginsberg: Well, just like any of the other newspapers around, I suppose...
Webster: But I'm open to be converted.
Ginsberg: Yes, well, I'm not going to convert you about its maturity. I'm just interested in the question of freedom.
Webster: Total freedom?
Ginsberg: No, a free press.
Webster: But a total free press.
Ginsberg: Free press, like they have for the other newspapers, like they have for you to speak your mind on the air, or for me to speak my mind on the air.
Webster: But of course if I insult a magistrate to his face, or if I commit a criminal libel, I've got to take the punishment.
Ginsberg: Well, of course if the magistrate doesn't quite obey the proprieties of free

men's laws; like, why was the free press bugged by the law? Because the free press criticized the courts for saying that Stan Persky, who is a poet, could not sit in the park. In other words, a citizen couldn't sit in the park. So we have a problem here not only of free press, but also of free persons.
Webster: But Allen Ginsberg, I don't want to get bogged down in technicalities…
Ginsberg: Into the technicalities of sitting in the park and of publishing a newspaper. BUT IT'S NOT VERY TECHNICAL. (Webster tries to butt in.) Either you sit in the park and you publish a newspaper, or the city comes along and says you *can't* sit in the park and you *can't* publish a newspaper.

Myth Shattered: We Win One!

BY STEPHEN BROWN, SEPTEMBER 24–OCTOBER 1, 1969

We won—at last.

Judge Bernard Isman dismissed three out of three obscenity charges (nine counts in all) against the *Georgia Straight* after a three-hour trial Tuesday.

This is the first time the courts have dismissed any of the long series of charges laid on the *Straight* by the police and other authorities.

Isman dismissed the first obscenity charge, for a syndicated interview with "Cynthia Plastercaster," a Los Angeles chick who makes statues of penises, on the grounds that this one article did not render the whole publication obscene. "I cannot possibly deem the whole publication to be obscene, because the dominant character of the newspaper is not undue exploitation of sex," he said in his decision.

The judge dismissed the obscenity rap for a back-cover drawing of Acidman showing his genitals, because "while the picture offends my sense of what may be proper," judges are not entitled to decide what is obscene on the basis of their personal opinion.

The other half of the charge, against a cartoon showing a dog pissing on a fire hydrant, was also dismissed. He dismissed the charge against a classified ad by a guy who wanted a girl for muffdiving on the basis that he has never heard of the word, that it is not in general use as an expression for cunnilingus, and therefore is not obscene.

Isman said of the charges: "It is common knowledge that there are publications sold in every newsstand and grocery full of nothing but obscene matter; it has always been a puzzle to me why some publications are singled out for charges."

Lawyer John Laxton, defending the *Straight*, called the charges "patently absurd" and urged that a full inquiry be held to discover why the police laid the charges in the first place.

Cynthia to Cast Prosecutor?

MARCH 4–11, 1970

LOS ANGELES—Cynthia Plastercaster, the famous underground caster of rock stars' phalluses, announced Monday that she may visit Vancouver soon in an attempt to cast members of the city prosecutor's office.

The announcement came when she was told of the *Georgia Straight's* second obscenity acquittal on Monday morning. In court, County Court Judge Darling said the "Penis de Milo" article on Cynthia was a satire on the adulation of rock stars by our society.

"The serious side of my work has finally been recognized," said Cynthia. "Now I would like to poke fun at the establishment.

"Casting is exciting and lots of fun—but it's lots of work too. So why should I travel around casting rock stars for next to nothing, when I can cast the people THEY (the establishment) worship—the prosecutors, mayors—and get a lot more money for it?"

But did she really think the establishment heroes would go for it?

"Of course they would," she explained. "If they didn't, then everybody would know it was a cop-out. They would have to prove their masculinity."

Chief Prosecutor Stewart McMorran was not available for comment.

Gastown: On Being Saved, or Any More Progress Like This and We'll All Be Done In

BY BERT HILL, MAY 14–20, 1969

Gastown was named for Gassy Jack Deighton, who opened this town's first saloon. Later the high-handed CPR turned a sleepy little milltown into the railroad terminus and named it after a British sea captain—Vancouver.

Ninety years later the good citizens of Vancouver are looking back at the old townsite (Water, Carrall, Hastings, Cambie) and are about to rescue it from Indians, drunks, the aged, the poor, the prostitutes, drug addicts, and last and certainly not least the hip community.

In the modern, fast-moving, fast-changing, technologically revolutionized, upward-mobilized, gross national product–conscious, welfare-state, liberal-capitalist, trendy, and switched-on Just Society, can the plastic be far behind?

The do-gooder/investor complex (equally insidious as the military-industrial complex) promises to swamp Gastown in its enlightened embrace.

After this crowd is done, will anyone remember that the town's first six businesses were two general stores, one hotel, and three saloons? Will anyone recall that the town's first whorehouse was opened two doors from the parsonage?...

Gastown has become the focus of attention because a whole mess of development schemes suddenly changed the direction of commercial-office building. City hall planners had been trying to lure the big money into the east, but MacMillan Bloedel, Bentalls, and others insisted on building out along Georgia. The planners were losing battles, which is nothing new and in some cases deserved. Then (SHAZAP!) the huge Project 200 was announced, to be built over the next generation by the CPR and Woodward's on the CPR tracks. Next the CPR announced it was going to build housing on False Creek in another major development. And finally the city started acting seriously on proposals for a freeway system that would tie the whole works together with one of the bigger knots situated on Gastown.

The future of Gastown is something like this: All the major developments in the area should skyrocket land values and taxes. Soon Gastown will be too expensive for anyone (hip) to live in. The freeway system, no matter how humanized, will need multilevel garages to handle the traffic daily to be dumped there from all over the Lower Mainland. These garages are the ugliest monument possible to modern society and will continue to eat up space. What historic land and buildings the civic-conscious groups save from the automobile and the CPR developments will probably become nice museums to our past—a place to take the kids on Sunday afternoon. What is to be done?—as the man said (Lenin, I think). There is a spectre haunting Gastown—how do you like your plastic, hard or soft?

Essentially the hip community has to take an inventory of itself and of what it wants its community to be. It has to build a sense of a particular community with a set of values different and worth preserving in the midst of another, larger, homogenizing society.

Sorting It Out from Canada

BY KEN LESTER, MAY 28–JUNE 3, 1969

The Gastown area is strategic and should be claimed by the people for the use of all the people. Overrun it. It should be an area of free energy exchange in a milieu of corporate cannibalism. The streets have character and generate a sense of closeness and solidarity. We must relate to the street consciousness of its inhabitants, picking up on their emotional survival techniques and instant adaptability. We are the new beggars. We will take the revolution out of our heads and into the streets. The streets belong to the people. Use and defend them.... Do what you feel is necessary; enough bullshitting about a New Age and more total involvement participation in creating an alternate society. Community means us, and we must sacrifice labour, money, comfort, time, and not just let meaningless sympathy and indulging platitudes run like diarrhea from our mouths. Put *your* balls on the line, motherfucker.

Occasional Nothings

BY WANIS KOURI (AKA BOB CUMMINGS), JANUARY 28–FEBRUARY 4, 1970

One of this city's better-known early juicers will get ceremoniously erected sometime in February. A seven-foot statue of "Gassy Jack" Deighton, commissioned by the three Town of Granville (Gastown) partners, will be raised on the corner by the wedge-shaped Europe Hotel, where he will face the site of his original saloon ... which is now an intersection. Created by sculptor Verne Simpson, the piece is made of heavy plate-copper over a pipe frame and will be treated with muriatic acid to make it turn green...a hue not unknown to Jack on many a morning.

The work will stand on a four-foot barrel base and has a removable hat lid through which concrete will be poured to make it solid...it's said that Deighton often got stiff from being loaded. The Gastowners paid for the statue out of their own wallets and plan to donate it to the city along with a dozen gas-type metal lamp-standards with eight-day clock mechanisms that they are having restored.

One suggestion: Before erecting "Jack," pass the word around Pigeon Square that he's going to happen. Otherwise, one of the older alcoholics is liable to come weaving around the corner, spot this 11-foot creature hovering over the sidewalk, and disappear forever into the land of the D.T.'s.

Let It Breed

BY ENGLEDINK BIRDHUMPER (AKA BRAD ROBINSON), OCTOBER 7–14, 1970

GASSYBIRDJACK

Someone has ripped off Gassy Jack's head. And it's a drag.

As anyone who has been to the Gastown area knows, Gassy Jack is the statue that stands at the corners of Powell, Water, and Carrall Streets and presides over the corner like a patron saint. And in spite of the commercial bias of the area, Gassy Jack is a happy figure to have around.

But now his head is gone, and nearly everyone in the area is hopping mad about it.

And if you've got it, brother, you'd better give it up peaceably, or otherwise, if you're found out, you're going to be at the receiving end of some pretty heavy action.

That's the word around Gastown.

Start Walking All Over People—Final Solution for Gastown?

BY GEORGE STANLEY, JULY 30–AUGUST 3, 1971

A final solution has been found for Gastown.

North Shore Investigations and Security Systems, a North Vancouver firm, made a proposal this week to various Gastown pubs and restaurants to "rid" Gastown of "the immediate drug problem."

The *Straight* obtained a copy of NSISS's letter, which is reprinted herein. In the letter, R. Murray Dodds, president of NSISS, refers to a "3-Step Program."

The third, and final, step is to "start walking all over people."

Mayor Campbell has apparently given this policy his blessing. Now it will be up to the Gastown Merchants, a somewhat disunited organization, to see if they want to give theirs. Then the heavies can move in....

Why the hard vibes? Is Gastown really a dangerous place? Is it really the soft-drug capital of Canada?

Not according to the people who have businesses here. Two things they're all agreed on:

1) The soft-drug scene is no worse here than it is anywhere else.
2) Campbell's behind all this. Campbell's ego, Campbell's driving need for publicity, Campbell's indifference to the needs of the community, and even to the possibility of violence.

Operation Whirlwind: Who Are the Criminals?

AUGUST 3–6, 1971

SOLIDARITY SMOKE-IN AND STREET JAMBOREE

Maple Tree Square in Gastown 8:30 p.m. Saturday

The Gastown Dopes in conjunction with various disreputable Yippies are calling for solidarity action in Gastown to bring about an end to police drug OPERATION DUSTPAN in a flash of whirling marijuana smoke. The devious plan is this: While OPERATION DUSTPAN is out to lunch searching for heads in Kitsilano, the forces of dope and chaos will be getting it on in Maple Tree Square, Gastown. Hundreds of dope-crazed freeks will set the teeter tottering with a spontaneous Gastown Smoke-in and Street Jamboree; the low-energy forces of the Man will be left helpless.

"Sow the wind, and reap the Whirlwind."

How Not to Get Busted at the Grasstown Smoke-in

AUGUST 6–10, 1971

WHAT IF...

Since the Grasstown Smoke-in was reported in the last issue of the *Straight*, a lot of confusion has been floating around. This confusion basically results from the fact that no one is telling anyone else what to do. It's a spontaneous event.

The Smoke-in is a free stage for all kinds of people to climb up on—and you can be sure there're going to be a lot of acts. Everything in the Smoke-in depends on the people that turn out, how they feel about what they are doing, and whether they know why they are in the street.

People have to break out of their passive spectator roles to create effective high-energy events; they can't keep waiting for others to get it on for them. This is the fundamental principle of successful community action.

What happens at the Smoke-in will be a result of all the trips people bring to it and the collective energy that is generated in solidarity with our imprisoned brothers and sisters. However, people should realize that it is intended to be a peaceful, sharing, and joyous high-energy event aimed at making the marijuana laws irrelevant.

The Gastown riot: 79 detained, 38 charged, over a dozen hospitalized.

Everybody knows what space our heads are in, but we can never predict what insane theatre the police will dig up. This is why the SMOKE-IN is an act of civil disobedience and commitment; it involves a calculated risk, like everything else we do to be free. The alternative is to do nothing, to remain silent and abandon the dozens of brothers and sisters who are still in jail for dealing in dreams, good and bad.

There are several things that we can predict and prepare for regarding police strategy and tactics at the SMOKE-IN. Those discussed here are based upon a study of several police manuals, the U.S. Army Field Manual, FM 19–15, *Civil Disturbances and Disasters*, and the booklet *Confrontations, Riots, Urban Warfare*, by Raymond Momboisse (member of the President's Commission on Law Enforcement). As you can see, the police have a monopoly on how to create violence, so we should be on our guard not to get sucked into their game.

When you get to any people's gathering, you can expect one or a combination of several things:

1) a token uniform presence which will ignore the gathering and plainclothes intelligence personnel which will gather information.
2) a heavy presence of plainclothes infiltrators, with minimal uniformed personnel in the area.
3) a heavy uniformed police presence possibly preventing access to the gathering site.

Depending on the number of people that show up Saturday night, we can expect either 2, 3, or a combination of them. If the SMOKE-IN is less than 200 people, we can expect probability to lean towards 2; if more than 200, it's more likely to be 3. The presence of the police means nothing; they are just freaked out by people getting together. Hopefully, by sensible estimates, their strategy will be one of containment.

Muzzle the Mayor

BY ALDERMAN HARRY RANKIN (COMMITTEE OF PROGRESSIVE ELECTORS), AUGUST 20–23, 1971

It's fortunate that the police incident in Gastown on Saturday night, August 7th, didn't result in even more serious casualties. It easily could have. Those who thought it couldn't happen here have had their illusions shattered. The riot police and the riot sticks were used as Mayor Campbell wanted them used.

The key problem now is to cool it, to make sure that we don't have another and even worse incident. The big party thrown by Gastown merchants Saturday night, August 14th, was a good step to help ease tensions. However, some further action of a long-range nature is needed.

A responsible, impartial judicial probe into the causes as well as the events of August 7, separate and apart from any Police Commission investigation into its own actions, could be useful. Any whitewash job at this stage, however, would only aggravate the situation.

Another necessary step is to muzzle the mayor. His provocative calls for violence by one group against another must be stopped. They were largely responsible for what happened. A mayor who uses the riot police as a personal weapon against the merchants and people of Gastown is a dangerous liability to our city. The mass media also have a responsibility here—that of ceasing to give headline publicity to every inflammatory remark made by the mayor.

Don't we also need a new type of Police Commission, one that will be under public control? At the same time, a Citizens' Review Board, composed of representative citizens, should be established to hear complaints against the police.

Power and the Open Mike

BY MASON DIXON, SEPTEMBER 3–7, 1971

This is the house that Jack built. Jack is the man who aired the report that caused the investigation that led to the crackdown that triggered the riot that launched the investigation. This is the house that Jack built.

We talked to Webster Wednesday afternoon in his Georgia Hotel studio. He began the interview in typical fashion by announcing that he would tape me while I was taping him.

Straight: Gastown. A lot of people held you responsible as the initiator for everything that's happened there.

Webster: No way was I responsible. I've been reporting on hard drugs in this town since 1948. All I did was that when doctors came out with their report that there was an upsurge in the heroin usage among young people in this town I was intrigued by this, because the doctors had been a long time in waking up to this problem.

S: When was this?

W: This was two weeks before the confrontation, if you want to call it that. I immediately thought "this is a good matter for a detailed report." I interviewed the doctors, I interviewed the coroner, I interviewed a number of experts on both sides of the question researching marijuana. I also interviewed two officers of the VPD drug squad. And somewhat to my surprise, they told me live on the program that drugs were out of control in Gastown. Quite out of control. And that acid, hash, whatnot, was being peddled openly in the Gastown beer parlours.

Of course my next step was to get ahold of Tom Terrific. Tom, of course, responded to my hard questioning with his normal hysteria. And that reflected itself in the action of the Police Commission, which became a little bit nervous. Not the police officers themselves. And then your friends, not my friends, created the confrontation by having the Saturday-night YIPPIE! smoke-in. Now that was an obviously contrived affair, to put the police on edge and see if a riot could be created.

S: Now we've overlooked one factor in this history of events...the busts in Gastown that took place and the way those busts were carried out. I think the epitome of it was when a young man had his mouth reamed out with handcuffs.

W: I'm not going to defend police brutality, but it's quite clear that the *Georgia Straight* and the YIPPIES encouraged the climate to create the riot. I say that without any fear of contradiction.

High Fashion

LETTERS, AUGUST 24–31, 1972

I am a traveller and have seen the famed Place Pigalle and the likewise notorious Soho.

Gastown is the match for either in vulgarity.

Vancouverites can well be proud of this sordid promenade. There is nothing like it where I live in Richmond.

Christian Henricksen

THERE GOES THE NEIGHBOURHOOD

Inaugural Column by Milton Acorn

MAY 5–18, 1967

For my first column in *Georgia Straight* I offered my associates a choice. Did they want "Why I Support the National Liberation Front, Not Just Peace" or "The Persecution of the Advance Mattress"? They said, "Vietnam will always be with us, but the Advance Mattress may soon be gone..."

The two Vancouver daily papers, *"illegitimates who go to bed together every night,"* try to give the impression that these attacks on a nonprofit coffeehouse are part of the much-trumpeted anti-LSD campaign. As a matter of fact, the Advance Mattress is a centre of opposition to this sometimes useful, always dangerous drug—especially against the morbid Learyite drug cult. For those who know that this alleged complaint is a vicious lie, it is still possible to believe that the Advance Mattress is being attacked for "Communism."

The truth is that the place runs a Thursday-night "Blab" session in which anyone can get up and say anything he or she likes. In this society free speech is much talked about and little practised. The Advance Mattress practises free speech. No one can help it if the arguments of those who go to the Advance Mattress to try to support the Capitalist Establishment turn out to be pretty puerile. The Advance Mattress is intended as a centre of struggle for human rights, especially student rights. Communists, as well as many others, are interested in this, and help run the place. This is probably part of the reason for the harassment of the Advance Mattress, but I'm convinced it's a small part.

The deliberate, cynical persecution of the Advance Mattress seems to me to be only part of a coordinated attack on the Kitsilano neighbourhood as a whole. Several other shops and places of entertainment have been harassed. The fire department has started enforcing laws which have been ignored for years—though there has not been a single serious fire in Kitsilano.

What Kitsilano has been developing into is a functioning neighbourhood—a place where people live, not just go home to sleep, where people know each other, unite with each other to support common causes, where many of the shops are places of interest and good humour, where people sometimes even smile when they pass each other on the street.

The Advance Mattress (though it's a little bit outside the Kitsilano area proper) is just the kind of coffeehouse such a neighbourhood would need—in fact a place which could help create such a neighbourhood. It's nonprofit...none of the staff and only a few of the entertainers get paid. It's a place where people can come together, be entertained and entertain themselves, talk over their interests—and not be charged a pint of blood, not even half a pint.

This, not its Communist leanings, is the most subversive aspect of the Advance Mattress.

Impo 67 or the Importance of Being Foolish

BY RICK KITAEFF, MAY 19, 1967

What does Vancouver have that no other major city has? Think hard, and you will probably be at a loss to discover any single attribute other than the subject of the following interview—Vancouver's unacknowledged Centennial project, its very own city fool. George Joachim Foikis, Polish-born, ex–social worker, ex-academe, and now self-appointed, full-time fool, has in the past few months become a familiar sight to Vancouverites, with his jester's costume, bauble, and balloon, his nursery rhymes, puns, and philosophical morsels, dispensed from beside the courthouse fountain, in Stanley Park, and virtually everywhere that folly reigns. We at the *Georgia Straight* recognize Joachim as Canada's 35th founding father, emerging from a century of folly, and we urge our readers to join us in our wholehearted support of his bid to obtain a licence to be Vancouver's official city fool (a request which, incidentally, has recently been acknowledged in writing by a city clerk).

Joachim Foikis, town fool.

G.S.: Joachim, how did you first decide to be a fool?

Fool: Oh, I've been reading Shakespeare for many years now. It was only *inside* my head after I'd been in hospital. Then I decided to take on this role, because I think it's time, you know, since we are experiencing a sort of new renaissance, for the fool to come *down* from the stage and confront the people in the street, and this is what I am doing. And this is what is very threatening to many people, because if the fool is on the stage and far away, they laugh *about* him, but they aren't really confronted directly the way I am trying to do it.

My motto, of course, is: "The world is governed by folly." And I thereby identify with the establishment, with the men in power, and I turn upside-down the whole social structure: By putting myself in the very lowest social position of fool and identifying with those people on top, I pull them with me on the very lowest level of the cosmic structure of the universal structure—because the social structure and the universal (or spiritual) structures are in total opposition. Of course, in all religions you have the idea that the world is governed by the fallen prince, or that the prince that governs the world is a fallen prince. This is really the philosophy behind it.

A Fool and His Asses Departed

MAY 14–20, 1969

Town Fool Joachim Foikis brought his donkey caravan to Carrall and Hastings Friday afternoon, and the results were *ass*inine. The comedy began with Foikis clip-clop, clip-clop, clip-clopping his two-ass wagon along Carrall Street at a rate of non-speed conducive to donkeys, children, and Fools too wise to play the ulcer-roulette game of traffic rush.

It became a Comedy of the Absurd when two police officers—befuddled by a situation not taught in the Police Academy—approached the wagon with the command "Just a moment, there!" The donkeys, being true asses, took the police at their word and stopped cold...right in the line of traffic. Finding the position both comfortable and law-abiding, the animals henceforth refused to move.

The two confused cops radioed for a Sergeant, who arrived, moments later, resplendent in his Hell's Angel–SS costume—motorcycle, uniform, boots, badges, helmet, and baggy pants—to take charge of the situation. Leaving his "chopper" to further snarl the traffic screwup, the Sergeant proceeded to berate the Fool in his best Grade 6, neighbourhood-bully style.

Meanwhile, the crowd grew larger, the car-entombed sightseers drove slower, someone began chanting the Hare Krishna, people smiled, drunks laughed, and the donkeys remained totally immobile.

The Ugliest City

BY JOHN MILLS, DECEMBER 15, 1967

At the beginning of this glorious year it seemed that every newspaper I picked up contained a story about people's Centennial projects—a man here was going to paddle a canoe to the St. Lawrence; a man there intended to follow, on foot, Milton and Cheadle's route down the Yellowhead to Kamloops then up to the Cariboo goldfields. A town in the Prairies built a landing pad for flying saucers, and another bailiwick, in the same God-forsaken part of the world, swore to celebrate the Nation's Birthday by administering a sort of Bible-belters audo-da-fé to its outdoor toilets. All this unprecedented activity in places where nothing has happened since the day Louis Riel was returned to Parliament got me wondering how best *I* could serve my country—what could I do as a Centennial project that would be both useful and informative? The answer came to me with the force and immediacy of a voice from a flaming bush:

to discover the answer to a problem that has puzzled generations of my countrymen and to settle it once and for all. And the question, of course, is this: which, finally, is the ugliest city in Canada?

I therefore convened a panel of experts from different provinces and chaired its meetings in accordance with Robert's Rules of Order....

Mr. Chairman, said the representative from Vancouver, I have listened with interest and amusement to my fellow delegates. Not one has provided me with what I would call evidence. We are asked to decide on Halifax on the grounds that its hinterland is miserable, Winnipeg because its citizens are dolts, Sudbury on account of its yellow and treeless surroundings. Next thing we'll know will be this gentleman from Calgary, who is so obviously itching to speak, asking for our support on the grounds that Alberta is run by a crypto-fascist junta composed of Fundamentalists.

(At this point, the Albertan, his thunder stolen, sagged back in his chair.)

The setting of Vancouver, the man continued, is delightful but only negatively relevant. It merely serves to accentuate the odiousness of the actual city. Our people are as dull as those elsewhere and our political bosses are just as crooked and peculative as those that any of these gentlemen could show me. In fact, I admire our city councillors—their real-estate manipulations are responsible not only for their own wealth but also, in large part, for Vancouver's spectacular ugliness. It is due to their efforts that we can claim the most modern 20-storey slums in the nation.

We in Vancouver, he continued, warming to his theme, find it hard to believe that the human race, which includes Beethoven, Leonardo da Vinci, and our own Mayor Tom Campbell, could also include those responsible for Dingsway [*sic*], the Simpson-Sears complex, Bowell-Maclean's, North Vancouver's Marine Drive, and that section of Hastings Street between Boundary Road and Willingdon. They seem to have been perpetrated by a race of gnomes bent on rendering life for human beings as wretched, mean, oppressive, and ill-favoured as possible. Similarly, no one who has not driven along the concrete, treeless, desert-strips of Broadway and Fourth Avenue is qualified to speak of ugliness. No one who has not seen the networks of trolley wires and power lines, and the parade of signs and billboards of Vancouver's so-called downtown section can know the Grotesque at its most intense. Neither is a man unacquainted with the Alphavilles of the city's West End entitled to broach the subject of glass-and-concrete sterility. Gentlemen, have you visited False Creek? Granville Island? Lonsdale? Have you seen the dank, rotting mansions of Shaughnessy? Have you driven through the exclusive areas of West Vancouver and the British Properties, whose inhabitants make up for their brashness by their lack of taste?

It would take the pen of a Swift, the excremental vision of a Céline, to do justice to the true hideousness of the streets and buildings of Vancouver. There are, in the entire Lower Mainland, perhaps a handful of buildings worth looking at, and one of these is in Burnaby, another is tucked in a remote corner of UBC, and the third lurks, shamefaced and almost invisible, along Point Grey Road. The rest of it is a nightmarish collage of used-car lots, rusted piles of junked automobiles, dreadful, truncated skyscrapers with iron fire escapes ricketing down the outside, sad and decrepit wooden houses converted into sleeping rooms, vast parking lots, littered sidewalks rolled up, in most places, by 9:30, semi-bankrupt dry-cleaning and coin-laundry establishments equipped with huge and graceless signs, car dealerships strung with tiny, fluttering plastic flags, fly-blown little Pay 'n Save marts sinking into indigence, tens of thousands of secondhand shops eking out a living by taking in empty beer bottles, "modern" thin-walled apartment blocks owned by extortionists and janitored by surly morons, acre upon acre of fetid slums and fifth-rate housing. Gentlemen, I pause for a reply.

We could give him none. Persuaded by his eloquence and examples, we gave him our vote and, one by one, drifted home to our respective substandard homes.

'UNDERGROUND' EDITORS HELD AT GUNPOINT

See inside

GEORGIA STRAIGHT

VANCOUVER FREE PRESS

15¢

New Psyche Shops

BY MOUSE (AKA NANCY TAYLOR), JULY 12–25, 1968

Two new psychedelic shops have opened up on Fourth Avenue: the Sound of Om at 1833 W. 4th and the Polevault at 2645 W. Fourth. The front of the Sound of Om is brightly coloured with fashions and coloured wool and wire hangings in the windows. They carry beads, incense, leatherwork (the usual), and a few posters, and feature men's fashions by Hildie and women's fashions by Anne. In one corner an artist does pastel portraits.

The Polevault is quite different. Its windows are patterned in bright transparent colours, and coloured lights filter through parachutes hung from the ceiling. In a curtained-off section of the shop a black light illumines fluorescent posters of all sorts. The ones that interest me the most are the zodiac posters. You could sit and groove on them for hours; and what's more you can do just that at the Polevault. There are lots of chairs, cushions, and ashtrays, and the owners encourage customers to come in, sit down, and enjoy themselves. I walked in there and immediately felt right at home. It seemed more like a friend's living room than a shop, and all the people there quickly became friends. They carry hookahs, beads, sculpture, books, incense, posters, art, clothes, you name it, and if you've made something you'd like to sell, take it down to the Polevault, they'll probably be able to help you.

Occasional Nothings

BY WANIS KOURI (AKA BOB CUMMINGS), OCTOBER 15–22, 1969

Robson Street (the title Robsonstrasse has become too "cute" for words) is in danger of disappearing. The profit-mongers are buying up the south side of the 1000 block and hiking the rents so high that most of the small European shops may have to move. City council, true to its image as the patron saint of landlords, voted last week to ask planning director Bill Graham to report on the prospects of rezoning the block from commercial use to comprehensive development. This would open the door to high-rise apartments, underground parking, and those commercialized subterranean crypts called shopping malls.

Ecology Happening

BY J. ARTHUR, JANUARY 28–FEBRUARY 4, 1970

The ecology problem took to the streets last Saturday afternoon.

Bells, drums, flutes, and bicycles took the message to the people on Granville between Robson and Georgia.

While about a dozen young people—many wearing bright costumes and long flowing robes—played music and rapped to the people passing by about ecology and air pollution, bicycles were parked in parking spots usually reserved for cars. In a little over an hour three or four parking meters were "liberated." A bicycle doesn't pollute your air. Signs placed on the bikes asked for a rapid transit system to replace the obsolete auto, and warned "Your Car Kills."

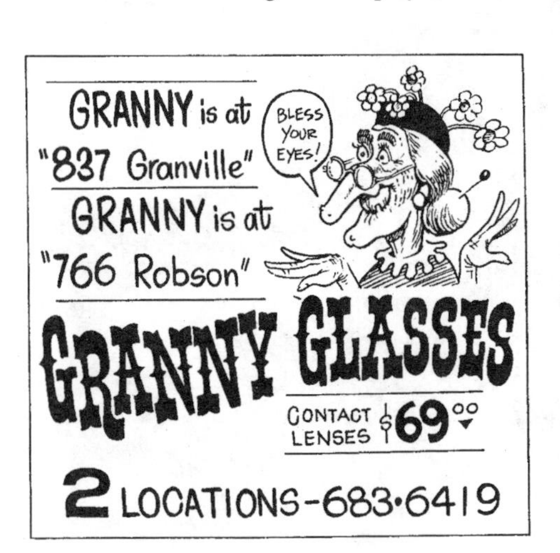

Greenpeace

FEBRUARY 18–25, 1970

The symbol...designed by Paul Nonnast, is of a group called the Don't Make a Wave Committee, whose aim is to prevent the aforementioned explosions and the earthquakes, tidal waves, and radiation pollution that could result [from nuclear testing on Amchitka Island]. It has green (growing things) figures on a yellow (sunlight) background and combines the goals of peace and ecology.

Last Saturday the group formalized plans to send a ship they'll rename the *Greenpeace* into the Amchitka area before the next test. The idea was inspired by the voyage of a number of Quakers on a ship called the *Golden Rule* near Bikini Atoll during the early A-bomb tests. That voyage created widespread interest in atomic testing and the need for a halt to nuclear insanity.

GREENPEACE is an ambitious and maybe an impossible project, but so is anything that tries to promote a sane approach to the world we live in.

Greenpeace Is Beautiful

BY IRVING STOWE, SEPTEMBER 23–30, 1970

CAN AN ENEMY OF THE WHALES BE A FRIEND OF THE PEOPLE?

When Dr. Pat McGeer was queried about the DEATH of three captured narwhals, he was quoted as saying: "It's really a much better life for a narwhal in captivity because of the dangers to them in the Arctic."

Did you dig this DOUBLETHINK? Do you feel godlike enough to decide that death-trip captivity is a "better life" for a whale than its normal environment? Could you believe a politician OUT of office giving out with such a witless and REVEALING utterance? (At least Bennett's pontificating that he was "plugged into God" occurred AFTER he spent and conned his way back into office.)

Shitpower Gives Birth to Shitcar!

BY JEANNINE MITCHELL, NOVEMBER 18–25, 1970

Remember Shitpower—that magical process by which you can hook up an outhouse or two to a tank, throw in spare apple cores and carrot tops, and use the gas that results from decomposition to supply your home with heat and electrical power at minimal cost and pollution?

Well, now you can run your car or truck with that very same gas: CH_4, or methane. Harold Bate, an engineer-farmer in England, is now selling devices that will allow you to convert any car over to methane, propane, or any other type of gas. The cost is $25.

Methane is part of natural gas and appears to be far superior to gasoline as a fuel, being far cleaner and easier on car parts. That, of course, is just why Detroit is so het up on gasoline—it may kill us all, but that's where the money is. And so many oblige, feeding the hand that bites them...

BUM OUT THE OIL COMPANIES

Mr. Bate appears to be a sincere man, and in the 15 years he has worked with methane, has had many articles written on him and his Incredible Invention: the chickenshit car. He has demonstrated his device on CBS and BBC, and the British Ministry of Transport has announced their approval of it.

Bate writes that you can use "all kinds of manure: Chicken—Pig—Cow—Sheep—Horse and Human" for methane production. I assume this would include Goats—Dogs—Cats and Rabbits too. If this is the case, the average communal house has quite a vast potential gas supply. (Freeks—earn $$$$ in the comfort of your own home—produce and sell methane for fastidious straight people: it's the ideal cottage industry!)

Or course, those of you who don't feel ready for shitpower just yet can always get the device and run your car on propane, which is available at a growing number of gas stations.

Everywhere We Went We Spread the Plague

NOVEMBER 4–11 AND 11–18, 1971

Excerpts from a two-part interview with Bob Hunter, a Greenpeace One *crew member, upon his return from the Amchitka expedition.*

Hunter: We had a hell of an argument over turning around because we were trying to operate on a consensus thing. We didn't want to do an authoritarian thing or a voting trip or any of that. And it turned out that the consensus is about the hardest way to do it. Some pretty rational arguments came out. It got down to the fact that some of us were pretty bombed out and we weren't going to move much, so the thing just kind of petered out. So we might as well shape up and head home. Then there was the other view that we should sneak out at night and pull the chain up. That was pretty bad news, because the weather was unbelievable at that point. The skipper, Cormack, had this mystical notion about the power of the boat and I tended to agree with him. It was the *Good Ship Lollipop*—it seemed charmed. But we were going to have to go up the north side of the Bering Sea, and if we had had any engine trouble at all we would have been wiped out on the rocks, and that seemed kind of a drag. It became unrealistic to do it. Also that radio of ours—you know the McLuhan age and all that shit—it's a lie. A couple of times we tried the SOS MAYDAY frequency—nothing. We couldn't even raise the Coast Guard and they were trying to find us....

They're just scared shitless in the States. Most of the places we visited in Alaska had never heard of the thing and they weren't about to do anything because they're so used to living with this 10,000-mile-high wall around them. It's like a concentration camp. But ego has a function. They'd look at us and their egos would get hurt because a bunch of 33-pounders and mattress-lovers like us who come from Canada of all places are doing what they should have been doing all along. Then you'd get the fishermen trying to do their balls-on trip and saying, "Well, I guess I'd better get out and do it," but they didn't, I noticed. But now it's a different situation: there's a Greenpeace thing in Kodiak and one in Juneau and one in Ketchikan and one in Sand Point. Everywhere we went we kind of spread the plague. They're now at the stage we were at about three years ago.

G.S.: What do you think of the *Straight*? What criticism would you make?

Hunter: I saw Harold Hedd's gay-lib trip and I've been calling [Bob] Cummings a representative of the queer press ever since. If it weren't for the *Straight*, I wouldn't be allowed to move in some of the directions I'm allowed to. The underground press has forced the straight press to move and do things they wouldn't have done otherwise, but now I think things are beginning to move the other way and the alternative press is going to be forced by the straight press to become more consistent. I think the *Straight* indulges in too much left rhetoric, left posturing, where it shouldn't. I think the ideal newspaper would be one which could one day say Tom Campbell is a king because of something good he did and the next day say he is a shit because of something bad he did.

The skipper of the *Phyllis Cormack* was adjusting to the point where he was really enjoying sipping a sherry and eating fancy food. But he still had little trips from out of his culture (he is much older than us). Like he would get very uptight about us swearing in front of women, but he could outswear us any day among men. He was a marvellously adaptable cat. I just turned 30 and I have a feeling of impending obsolescence.

Originally, there were about three women supposed to be on the crew. One of them was the girlfriend of one guy. We decided that we would get very uptight because the rest of us would be being deprived. Then Jim Bohlen's wife was going to come, and I don't know what her reasons were for deciding not to. It should have been half men and half women. In fact, if it had been anything, I think it should have been all women. That would have been beautiful for the skipper's mind. We just weren't ready to handle that whole problem because there were just too many old-fashioned sexual hang-ups going on and needs that couldn't be dealt with in that kind of pressure-cooker situation. A few of us had curtains which we thought we were very discreet about, and the skipper came down and said, "Oh—jerk-off curtains, eh?"

Dan McLeod selling issue number 20 in June 1968.

Rapid Transit System

BY ESTEVAN PARDO, JANUARY 6–13, 1972

Rapid transit is a put-on.

It's a snake-oil concoction being peddled as a cure-all for the plague of freeways that threatens our city.

It's a hoax being foisted on an ecology-minded but unsuspecting public by a swarm of profit-minded but myopic bureaucrats, technocrats, and plutocrats.

It's a sham and a charade that will play to its climax in a noose of concrete, choke to death in its own noxious pall, suffocate for lack of breathing space, and plunge off the deep end in an obsessive frenzy of money mania.

A bit overstated? Not by much, and anyway it's about time that the sacred cow called rapid transit was brought to heel a bit. For, despite all the current schmaltz being put out about it, rapid transit isn't a cure for what ails this city. In fact, it merely treats the symptoms in the same way that a military medic does: patch up the patient, so he can go out and continue his errant ways.

After all, what is rapid transit really meant to do?

Rapid transit (at least, as envisioned by most North American so-called planners, including Vancouver's) is designed to rush you downtown to work each morning in huge numbers and then (hope against hope) back home again in fairly short order.

Rapid transit is designed to protect and enhance the investments of those individuals and corporations who control the downtown real estate, and who fear that the uncontrolled proliferation of the automobile will render their holdings a congested—and unprofitable—mess.

Rapid transit is designed to promote the concept of the city as a temple of commerce, where the main activity is the making of money and where the population consists of drones who are ferried back and forth in furtherance of this end.

In short, rapid transit is designed to serve the very same anti-human, anti-life ends as are freeways and other symptoms of money mania—only to do it in a more efficient and cheaper manner.

Viaduct Opens

BY SYLVIA HAWRELIAK, JANUARY 13–20, 1972

Some of ecology's militants turned out for the Georgia Viaduct opening, Sunday, at Beatty and Dunsmuir, to show their opposition to the first phase of a freeway for Vancouver.

Almost 500 people were on hand for the ceremony. About 300 of them demonstrated against the viaduct, carrying placards reading "Today the Viaduct—Tomorrow 3rd Crossing," "Don't Pollute to Commute," "Another Piece of the Freeway Puzzle," and "Save Our City for People."

Before the ceremony, the demonstrators marched peacefully in a circle in front of the speakers' platform. Members of the Chinese community of Strathcona, who feel a freeway will wipe out their district or make it unlivable, attended. They have recently built an old-people's home on Keefer Street.

Mayor Tom Campbell officiated, visibly shaken by the shouts and noise of the crowd during speeches. Catholic Archbishop Carney read a prayer to shouts of derision, while the speaker from the firm of consultant engineers was inaudible above the drums and tambourines of the Vancouver Street Theatre.

Just Another Polluter

LETTERS, JANUARY 27–FEBRUARY 3, 1972

What a bunch of fucking HIPPY-CRYTES! You devote all those articles to denounce polluters—and you yourself are a fucking POLLUTER!

The ink in your newsprint contains mercury, which inevitably ends up polluting the biosphere—polluting the air when burned, polluting the land and water when buried or recycled—INEVITABLY. Use vegetable-dye ink and get it ON!

If you print a response to this, consider yourselves cool.

The eyes that see all

Kitsilano: Oceanside Sketches of a Doomed Village

BY MICHAEL WALLIS, MARCH 24–30, 1972

Kitsilano. The landlord has just collected the rent. The house seems quieter, emptier. Last year, Old Joe, who drives a 1959 clunker with permanent shock damage on one side, made $80,000. "I make $80,000 last year," he wheezes, supporting his great bulk against my doorway. "And that was clear," he adds. He tells me this each time he collects my rent.

But money can't give him everything. Not even the girl who lives in the basement. In a small room. A little hippie girl. No brassiere. So cute. Always jiggy-jiggy.

"He was showing me how the heater worked. He kept getting closer and I could smell the beer on his breath. Then he put his hand on my thigh and tried to feel me. You should have seen his face, all red and puffy like he was in pain. 'Don't you have a wife?' I asked. 'Yes,' he said, 'but it's not the same.' I just couldn't do it though. I felt sorry for him, but I just couldn't do it. So I told him, 'Excuse me, I'm not that kind of girl.'"

Good old Joe. Instead, he makes more and more money. The house, minus the cat shit, would rent anywhere else for less than $300. In Kitsilano, Old Joe gets over $800 a month.

$30,000 for This?

BY DANIEL WOOD, JULY 13–20, 1972

A walk along the seawall near Lumberman's Arch will take you past Vancouver's newest piece of sculpture: *The Girl in the Wetsuit.* She sits about 30 yards offshore, on a rock, her knee already stained with birdshit, staring toward the Lions Gate Bridge. She's uncomfortably angular and stiff-backed, a grey-black steel colour, totally inappropriate; altogether a weak piece of art. What's more, she cost the city $30,000! A tidy sum for such an ugly gift to posterity....

Why couldn't it have been *W.A.C. Bennett in a Wetsuit*? Imagine! He might have dieted off 20 more pounds to pose for it. Or Phil "I'll Die Dangerously" Gaglardi with an aqualung. Or two. Maybe a statue of Tom Campbell, electrified by Walt Disney Studios so that every 30 seconds his hand rises (a bit unsteadily) and stuffs a two-foot-wide hamburger into his perpetually smiling mouth. At this moment an orange

neon sign on the statue's stomach would flash: Terrific! Terrific! Terrific!

I can imagine a bronze log to commemorate the 2,739,471,365 ¼ logs that clutter B.C.'s shorelines. Or a 12-foot-high plastic girl in a bikini, painted with Day-Glo, so that she gleams all night. Or a model oil tanker, cast in steel, obviously wrecked on that same rock where the *Girl* now sits.

Honestly, wouldn't they remember Vancouver back in Red Deer and Cincinnati if only our City Fathers had had the humour to commission an 18-carat gold seagull turd for that rock? Wouldn't they?!?

"Harry, you wouldn't believe it. They've got this sorta sculpture in Vancouver an' it's...it's...gold. Real gold. An' it's a pigeon dropping or something. Made of real gold! Can you believe that? A gold pooh-pooh!"

"Oh, Eleanor! That's ridiculous!"

"But it's true! I SAW it. A golden pooh-pooh!"

"Pass the sugar."

Patching Up the World

BY GARY GALLON (SPEC), SEPTEMBER 7–14, 1972

Two ships have made love in the Strait of Juan de Fuca without spilling any oil. The American *C.E. Dant* inserted its bow into the Liberian *Aegean Sea* and copulated to the undulant motion of the Pacific Ocean. The matchmaker, Juan de Fuca, has been throwing quite a few ships together for S/M romances. Juan de Fuca, the cupid, is sharpening her arrows for the big climax, when she slams two oil tankers together in a Mazola-party grand finale. Slurp.

Free Mattress

BY BUTCH, JUNE 29–JULY 6, 1972

Saturday evening the revolution reached Kitsilano as the community turned out to protest the New Advance Mattress eviction. About 150 old folks, freaks, and kids met at the coffeehouse and discussed a future.

Speakers expressed the need for a community gathering place and pressed people to "show what they can do."

Later in the evening the children led a march along Broadway. People sang "We Shall Overcome" and chanted: "Free the coffeehouse now—a place for the people, people for the place."

FACING PAGE: Acidman cartoonist Peter "Zipp" Almasy (centre) and friends on the courthouse steps.

COMMUNICATION BREAKDOWNS

Letters

AUGUST 11, 1967

I think you, your paper, and every hippie in Vancouver are completely insane.

It's a crime to society you can't all exchange places with the poor legitimately sick people at Riverview Mental Hospital, but then that's an insult to them, as well as if I signed my name I'd insult myself.

Signed,
Read your paper out of curiosity only.

I had been hopeful that *GS* was going to facilitate true communication in Vancouver. The June 28 edition deflated that hope severely.

Its layout was confused. The letters to the editor were a collection of trite panegyrics. The Fool sacrificed sense for time. "Violence/Love Street" approached paranoia. Both of your star gurus, Edward English, who seems to be a crummy poet, and the deluded and incoherent Sun Ra, cast doubt on any pretensions to wisdom, tossing about the word *God*—there ain't no such thing. "I Live" by communications company failed to communicate (what's wrong with grammar?). The final piece of crap was "Anne Panders," an unbelievably juvenile ejaculation.

It seems *GS* has consistently fallen for sensationalism and faddism. If it is ever going to rise above this, the editors will have to pot their grass and THINK while they work.

Unsigned
N. Vancouver

Congratulations for your profound and courageous appraisal of the true meaning of our work. Eds.

What Makes a Hippie?

BY ALDERMAN HARRY RANKIN, SEPTEMBER 8, 1967

City Council has set up a committee to investigate the "hippies" of Vancouver. I opposed the motion in council. Investigating people just because they are different smacks of a political inquisition.

When City Council decided to go ahead and investigate the "hippies," I agreed to go on the committee, mainly to make sure they received a fair hearing.

What makes a "hippie"? What are they after?

"Hippies" are rebels, even if rather unconventional ones. They're rebelling against the widespread violence and wars of our society. They're disillusioned with false middle-class values and standards, with status seekers, with people living beyond their means, with the vulgar materialism and the bitter competition so prevalent today. They're suspicious that automation will make man into a workhorse, a cog in an immense machine.

"Hippies" want a more rational world, with the emphasis on the freedom of each individual to develop his own personality. Their disillusionment with unhealthy aspects of our social order and their opposition to the hypocrisy of the Establishment is understandable. I don't like these things myself.

What is more difficult to understand, of course, is their form of protest.

The outlandish appearance of many "hippies" is not only a source of despair to barbers and shoe salesmen, it's a source of wonder to many of us.

Apparently they don't believe in action to abolish the evils against which they protest. Their philosophy is to withdraw from society, to turn their backs on the world, to do no more work than is necessary, to follow their own interests, and to help each other.

This "opting-out" doesn't make sense to me. I believe we can only make society better by chipping in and doing our share.

However, you can't wish "hippies" away just because you may disagree with some of the things they do or don't do. They're here; they're one of the facts of life. Personally I don't think they can stay forever in this in-between make-believe world of turning their backs on a society that they must live in whether they like it or not.

What we should avoid at this stage is being stampeded into taking police or legal action against them. Ideas can't be suppressed by force, but we can act to correct the conditions that give rise to those ideas.

Turn On, Tune In, Take Over!!!

SEPTEMBER 8, 1967

If you drop out of school, you'll probably have to get a job. You'll hate *that*, too. The pay will be low, and it'll be even more boring than school was.

If you don't get a job, your parents will do all they can to make life rough for you.

You could leave home, but what happens then? It's getting too cold for sleeping outside or hitchhiking around the country. Staying with friends can be fun—for a little while. But you'll find it impossible to *do* anything. You'll soon grow tired of "making the scene" and living on somebody else's terms.

ACTION is the answer. When you close yourself up in your own little world, you're just avoiding questions that will have to be answered, sooner or later. If school is a drag, it's up to you to make it better. If you're thinking of leaving school anyway, what's wrong with getting KICKED OUT?

Nobody has the right to tell you how to run your life. You know more than the "elders" do about the things that are really important today. *Make* school interesting, by taking it over. How can you begin? Here are some ideas:

- Organize a union, to put pressure on the teachers and principals, so they'll give you what you want.
- Petitions can be circulated, to get rid of bad teachers and principals.
- A delegation can be sent to every PTA meeting, to present student demands. Don't ask for permission; tell them what you intend to do.
- Fight against all age restrictions. If you want to do something, go ahead. If you get caught, call the *Georgia Straight* Defence Fund. The "laws" are so bad that, nowadays, it is dishonourable *not* to have a criminal record. Just forget about building a future in *their* society. *You* can do better.
- Organize love-ins in schoolyards, perhaps for every noon hour.
- During fire drills, act as if there were a real fire. Once you get outside, keep going.
- If you don't like a textbook, lose it.

TAKE OVER!

- Stamp out corporal punishment. If any teacher or principal hits you, charge him with assault. One student actually hit back when a teacher attacked him. This is not recommended, however, except in extreme emergencies.
- Insist that schools be left open at night, so you can have a place to sleep in case home conditions become unbearable.
- Plan out your own courses, and teach them yourselves. Ask sympathetic teachers to help you.
- Start up school newspapers. *Georgia Straight* will help in any way possible. If you are interested, come and watch us in action (?). Also, send us anything you think we can use.
- Let your imagination run wild. Each day should bring new ideas Once you get started, nothing can stop you.

All ideas and questions will be gladly received and personally dealt with. Write to: Project X, GEORGIA STRAIGHT.

Book Review

BY IAN WALLACE, NOVEMBER 24–DECEMBER 8, 1967

Dunhill, Alfred. *By Appointment...Smoker's Requisites.* Alfred Dunhill Ltd., London. Farms, Jersey. *One Half Gallon Homogenized Milk.* National Paper Box Co., Vancouver, Canada.

These two books are interesting from a certain point of view, but they have nothing to say. The Dunhill book is much smaller and flashes much better in the light. It also can be transported in the pocket. The interior is very interesting and can be inspected easily. Very elegant, the detail is amazing, and the variety and complexity of the relationships can keep one absorbed for hours.

Comparison of the back cover of the Dunhill book with the palm of my hand left me with some strange questions in my mind. Mail your reactions c/o the *Georgia Straight.*

The Farms book is bulkier, less fancy (more homey), and is harder to get into, but once one has discovered an essential catch, he is well on his way to some very revealing in-depth involvements. The problem is that of penetrating the interior, for the principal motive in this book is the concept of containment. The opening is well ordered and forms an exciting beginning for a journey into a strange universe of impalpable forms.

I would suggest that the reader pursue these two very contemporary works beneath strong lighting, especially in the latter work, where an intense backlighting will illuminate some hidden meaning.

Fellatio Rock #1

BY GEORGE BOWERING,

JULY 26–AUGUST 8, 1968

All those parents & slipped-disc jockeys who are worried about the super-communist plot to put obscene records on the slop 40 charts must feel a little more secure after reading *Time* magazine's piece on pop music last week.

Time says "Yummy Yummy Yummy" is an example of a new subteen fare they call "bubble-gum music." Heh heh. I mean, dig this tableau in the pleasant North Van bungalow.

"Hey, you kids, stop that. It sounds like you're French-kissing in there."

(Voice from parlour) "Not so, Mommy. I just got love in my tummy."

That's right. We just entered the era of Fellatio-Rock. Gobble-Raga, Ed Sanders would call it. For those collectors who want a taste in their own homes, the disc is a 45 on the Buddha label, by the Ohio Express.

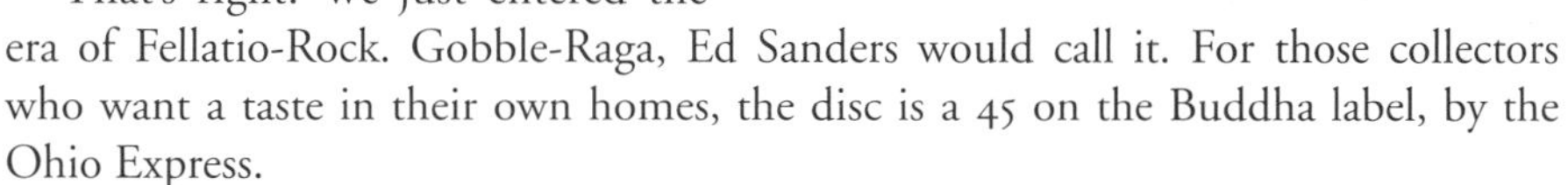

All you other freaks listening to FM to hear the real frank lyrics, forget it. Dig the Ohio Express: "Love, you're such a sweet thing, good enough to eat thing/And that's just a-what I'm gonna dooooo."

Slurp music is nothing new. It's been around a long time, especially in Soul poetry. Dig the Supremes a couple years ago, singing "Going down for the third time."

But Soul is grown-up music. Buddha records is after the Tillies. Their biggest hit was "Simon Says," a good example of Indoctrination-sexual freedom that's been done with Love and Peace and Nehru. Sell it. Get the money. Then get on to the next thing: bestiality-rock.

I give them one year or less till the first ditty about schtupping a sheep.

Meanwhile those parents who grew up in the petting era can ask their nine-year-old kids what today's experience tastes like.

"Kinda like sugar, kinda like honey..."

Kinda like Borax bleach.

Lennon Lie-in

EXCERPTS FROM A TELEPHONE INTERVIEW WITH JOHN LENNON BY FRED LATREMOUILLE AND DAN MCLEOD, APRIL 4–10, 1969

Fred: John, what are you doing over in Amsterdam in bed?
John: I'm holding a protest.
Fred: For what?
John: A protest against violence. We're saying that anyone interested in protesting, instead of protesting violently—protest peacefully, and this is one way of doing it. We've donated one week of our holidays doing it; anybody can do that if they're interested. Housewives can do it; anybody can do it at all and grow their hair for peace.
Fred: Or shave their hair off.
John: Well, if they like. If someone wants to shave their hair off for peace, that's good too. Anything they do for peace....

I think Mahatma Ghandi and Martin Luther King were good examples, they were peaceful...

Fred: But they both got shot.
John: Yes, I know, but I think the difference between us and them is that we're doing it with a sense of humour, and the worst that we could do is give people a laugh.

Sun Writers Smoke Pot: 33 Fail to Turn on Publisher

BY VERITAS (AKA STEPHEN BROWN), JUNE 4–10, 1969

Sun reporter Peter Ladner was fired recently for being honest.

He was dismissed within 36 hours after he had told a PTA meeting on drugs that he knew of about 20 writers or editors at the *Sun* who smoke marijuana regularly.

The official reason the *Sun* gave Ladner for his dismissal was incompetence. But Ladner said he was told by a senior editor who handled the firing: "I'm not going to pretend that your statement on drugs has nothing to do with your dismissal."

He made the remark, which brought down the wrath of the *Sun*, at a recent meeting of the Hillcrest Elementary School PTA in Coquitlam.

He had been invited to be a panelist representing university students. This is an important point, since he was not representing the *Sun* in any way.

During the question period, a woman asked Ladner if it was not true that pot users become irresponsible, their marks fall, and they cannot hold jobs.

Ladner replied: "Not so. It is quite possible to smoke pot and function in society.

"I know of 20 people...who are quite responsible—some support a wife and family very well—who take pot regularly, like every weekend."

Unfortunately for Ladner, another *Sun* reporter, Richard Blair, was covering the meeting and put Ladner's name and remark in the story he wrote on the meeting.

Blair wrote, in part: "UBC student Peter Ladner, in response to a question on drugs, said: 'In the organization I work for I know of 20 people who smoke pot regularly.'"

The ironic part of the whole thing is that Ladner's estimate of 20 heads on the *Sun* editorial staff is a very conservative one, according to several informed sources.

The actual figure, according to one *Sun* staffer who did a head count of heads, is about 33—about one-third of the total editorial staff and an overwhelming majority of the staff writers under 25.

Dr. Spong Wails

EXCERPTS FROM AN INTERVIEW WITH PAUL SPONG BY LANNY BECKMAN AND STAN PERSKY, JUNE 26–JULY 2, 1969

WAIL AWAY

The whale is number one on this planet. The whale's the highest creature. Believe you me, baby, and I'll prove it to you one of these days, see? I won't prove it, excuse me Skana, I won't prove it, the whale will prove it. Let me tell you, as soon as I can get some liquid crystals in my hand, the whale will start talking to us, talking to us in English. In words that we can see, like the *I Ching*.

I have climbed on her belly, on her back, I have put my arms around her, and put my head in her mouth, I have put my feet in her mouth, and she has gone across my feet—pshhhhhhew!—so the top of her teeth went across here, and the bottom of her teeth across here, just enough to let me know that

Yin is yin and
Yang is yang
And let it all hang out, baby
Let it all hang out
The killer whale is king of the ocean
The killer whale is king of the sea
The killer whale is for me, baby

The killer whale is number one on this planet. That's my opinion. That's just my thought, man. But then I'm crazy, you see.

I said, LET THE WHALE GO!!

I take droogs and they said, Why do you take droogs, Dr. Spong? And I said, It helps me work. Helps me tune in to the killer whale space. 'Cause when I take droogs, the killer whale warms up her nose, and steam comes off her nose, and who knows.

They didn't understand, man, but that's OK, they'll come round, y'see, cause the *I Ching* says so.

I was thinking of destroying the Vancouver Public Aquarium, and letting the whale go. I was just beginning to get into Skana's space, just beginning to feel what the whale needed, what the whale wanted, WHAT THE WHALE WAS, just beginning to feel it, man. And they fired me. And I thought, Oh well, cool it, kid, just sit down and cool it and you'll figure it out, and if you can't figure it out, check out the *I Ching*, so I checked out the *I Ching* and the *I Ching* said, Everything's cool, baby, everything is cool.

The night before, I dropped the mescaline, matter of fact, I dropped two and I went wailin' away down to the whale. And the cleaning lady said, Hey, man,

Who's that shoutin'? who's that singin'?
Who's that makin' those crazy noises out there?
Why it must be that crazy flippie hippie
Crazy flippie hippie yippie
Crazy flippie
Why that flippie must be flippie
I mean why that hippie must be flippie.

Letters

JULY 2–9, 1969

Dear Peace sheep:

I dropped green a few days ago and I realized the power of Peace. Peace was an acid out a while ago and I just came down. To people who dropped Peace, from Easter until now has been fantastically strange, and I think it was Peace that did it. So to fellow Peace sheep I say hello and try green. Peace has two sides but peace is confusing. Peace will make you fail or will make you pass all according to plan because Peace is a plan and I would like to see the plot.

from a fellow searcher

Street Communication: Turn Over a New Leaf

BY MUZ MURRAY,

SEPTEMBER 10–17, 1969

Why not use a LEAF as our SYMBOL of COMMUNICATION? Supposing you see someone you like the look of, male or female, go over and hand them a leaf. Just an ordinary fallen leaf from a tree. There is no need to denude the parks and gardens by giving a flower and getting the growers uptight. Besides, spiritually a flower is a sign of parting and not meeting. An Indian guru will hand a flower to a devotee when he feels it is time for him or her to leave and puts his parting blessing into it, that they may carry his love with them. But a simple tree leaf will not be missed by anyone and may mean the first human contact in a long grey day, week, or month even, to the one who receives it.

So if you see anyone you would like to talk to, walk over and silently hand them a leaf. Then wait expectantly.

Letters

SEPTEMBER 10–17, 1969

I am taking the time to drop you this short note so that you may, through your paper, clear up some points regarding the relationship of the so-called hippie community and the homosexual community; I will list a few of the sore points below. You may or may not think this letter is worth answering in your paper; however, I would like to assure you that these points I am about to make are much a topic of conversation with the local gay crowd. To quote Allen Ginsberg, "If there is one thing the beat generation has taught these kids, it's not to discriminate against homosexuals."

1. When the Big Mother was open, a couple of queens parked their cars on Beatty St. and went to the bus station for reasons of their own. On the way by the Big Mother they were spotted by some of the crowd that used to stand around there. When they returned to their cars, they found windows broken, etc. and the same old shitty words written on their cars. Another time three queens were walking by the Big Mother and they were chased by about eight hippies.

2. An old queen met a young hippie couple on Granville St. (a boy and a real girl). The girl was real sick...really sick like ill, they had no place to go, etc., etc. The queen took them in; they stayed a week. One day the queen came home from work and they were gone. So was the radio, a tape recorder, etc.

3. Two queens went into one of the new coffeehouses in Gastown and were greeted with the remarks, "They're not going to start coming in here, are they?"

So much for the flower children and their love-everybody bullshit. By the way, I should like to point out that in all the incidents above, the queens had no relationships with the hippies at all. I could list many more things of this nature, but I think these will do. I'll be watching your paper for your comments on this letter; that is, if you have anything to say on the matter.

A Hippie-Hating Faggot

Implosion

BY LANNY BECKMAN, DECEMBER 17–24, 1969

I can think of only one reason why anyone would want to see *Explosion*, and that is if you happen to be in it. Because it was shot in Vancouver, most of the extras are locals, which would account for about half the audience, including me. People all over the theatre were poking their neighbours, whispering, "There, did you see me? That was my arm. I recognized the hole in the sleeve." "Hey, isn't that your nipple?"

There's only one reason anyone would want to make *Explosion*—money. The plot elements are added like ingredients in a recipe, Osterized for maximum slickness, and served up lukewarm. It's all there: violence, protest demonstrations, draft-dodging, communes, drugstore psychology, and, of course, nudity—which, contrary to Mr. McDonald, is not excessive. The only thing excessive about the movie is its commercialism.

Why it was shot in Canada is pretty obvious. It's cheaper here. Hollywood imperialism opens up another foreign market swelling with cheap labour. Someone ought to write a book on the subject called *Marx Looks at the Movies.* If the present trend continues, it will be possible for Vancouverites to earn starvation incomes solely by acting as extras in American films. Someday bookstands will carry great autobiographies with titles like *My Life in Film: Memoirs of a Canadian Extra....*

Go see *Explosion* if you're in it and narcissistic enough to suffer thru 90 minutes, possibly to catch a two-second glimpse of yourself. Otherwise, save the buck fifty.

Occasional Nothings

BY WANIS KOURI (AKA BOB CUMMINGS), DECEMBER 31, 1969–JANUARY 7, 1970

Incredibility-gap: Eaton's has a "Teen Hang-Up" shop in its downer-town store. Obviously a brainstorm from the wrong side of the generation chasm, the name conjures up visions of a horror-house filled with adolescent anxieties and plastic paranoids but is, in reality, just another absurd misuse of today-talk as a clothes-peddling gimmick. The mother-aged clerk said that sales were poor and blamed changing styles. Because it was Christmas, I didn't tell her that the place-name had the same turnoff effect as a flatulence at the perfume counter.

We may not know where it's at, but we know where it isn't...Eaton's!

Let It Breed

BY ENGLEDINK BIRDHUMPER (AKA BRAD ROBINSON), MAY 27–JUNE 3, 1970

ENGLESCOOP

Well-known desperado and former *GS* editor Paul Tarasoff popped into the office last week shortly before he left for Montevideo, Uruguay. As we sat over a couple of beers talking through old times, he told me an amusing situation that occurred at the most recent Cannes Film Festival.

One evening as he was leaving his hotel, Paul told me, he stepped out onto the street to be confronted with the spectacle of a large group of students chanting "Give Peace a Chance." They were marching in the direction of the theatre where the festival was being held and, as that was where Paul was headed, he straggled along behind. The band of students soon broke into "We Shall Overcome" and suddenly a phalanx of police began to advance on the demonstration, clubs ready to strike out.

The crowd stopped faster than a mosquito hitting the door of a bank safe. Then one of the demonstrators ran out in the direction of the police hollering: "No! No! We're a promotion stunt for *Woodstock*!"

Unknown vendors selling the *Straight*.

Face the Moussaka

LETTERS, JUNE 24–JULY 1, 1970

I liked your recipes for Moussaka and Keskul—they were quite a tongue trip. But—

Poached Stuffed Oranges was just too heavy. You want me to get 12 dates!! I did it, and I even got them all stoned at once, as you suggest. Though we were all pretty out of it, there was NO WAY I was going to con the chicks into a little spin in the blender—to get shredded.

Furthermore, should I insist they shave their hair?

Many oinks,
The Edmonton Foodfreak

Sex Ads Found Wanting

BY LANI, JULY 15–22, 1970

Over the years the *Georgia Straight* has been publishing, the most controversial part of the paper has always been the classified/unclassified ads, the sex ads of course. Reaction to this small segment of the paper has ranged from pure horror to great amusement.

This hassle has by no means belonged just to the people who read this paper—staff are now divided on the issue of whether we will continue to run the sexist, exploitative ads.

How to end these sex ads is another problem. A few say we should just refuse to take them; others, myself included, feel that perhaps it would be better to do an exposé on the classified/unclassifieds. We feel we should let all you "slithery old men" (that's my term) know just what a suck the ads are.

Let the truth be known! The ads that are never! I repeat, never! answered are the "Horny guy looking for horny chick" type. The only ads answered with any kind of regularity are the gay ads, especially the "Young gay, hip, wishes to meet the same for friendship and" type. I hope we continue to run these latter ads. They are neither exploitative nor sexist and they do serve the gay community.

Many of our readers think the ads are a joke. No, I assure you every week a number of men come in here thinking we will save them from the need of jerking off every day and will also provide them with free maid service to boot.

This male attitude shows up in the ads and actually scares women away rather than attracts them. Women do not use this ad service (if you can call it that), because they realize they would be deluged by a horde of horny men who have nothing to give but some sperm. Then again, it could be that society has caused women to suppress their sexual fantasies and desires. In any case, there have been two, perhaps three, ads from women in the last year. While they were flooded with mail, I was flooded with phone calls offering me money if I would just give this guy, this great lover, her phone no., address, vital statistics, etc., or if I would only phone her and plead his case. These guys are the same type as the male ad-writers who slither into the office in the hopes that no one will see them deposit their ads or who demand their mail be sent to their homes or offices in plain envelopes so no one will associate them with the *Georgia Straight.* Mister, if you have no pride in your desire—if you think sex is dirty and a woman is to be used—we can't help you....

Our society has to change. No longer can we expect others to be our slaves. MEN, YOU WILL NEVER BE FREE UNLESS WOMEN ARE FREE!

Peace and a better way of relating to others.

Listen, Hippies

LETTERS, AUGUST 5–12, 1970

The trouble with hippies is they take on such a pretentious air when they are writing reviews of books & things, an air that wouldn't be so bad if they weren't so ignorant. The combination of the two is something that pisses me off.
George Bowering

Holy Shrist!

LETTERS, OCTOBER 28–NOVEMBER 4, 1970

Genitalmen: I have just finished reading the latest issue of your paper.

What's happening?

I don't seem to be able to understand the purpose of your paper.

I get the distinct impression you're painting a very black picture and not even putting a frame around it.

I realize there isn't too much happening that isn't fucked up, but Holy Chit, there's gotta be something good that happens that's worth printing. Your paper continually prints stories of Pigs vs. People; People vs. Pigs; People vs. People. Christ, there's gotta be more to what's going on that just what you seem to print.

I am not saying you print only chit; however, I am saying you seem to print a helluva lot.

I realize that the money is where the news is and the news today is pretty fucked up, but why don't you do something constructive? Again, I'm not saying you haven't done anything, but I think I could say that there's room for a helluva lot of improvement. What say?

Finally, genitalmen, a newspaper like yours, with a fairly wide circulation, is a very powerful instrument. Used properly, it could do a lot of good and a lot of bad. Ship *GS* is operating at 75% power loss. Get it on.
Love & Lumps,
HOT RATS

Women's Occupation Issue Introduction

APRIL 8–13, 1971

Today a group of angry women have taken over the *Georgia Straight.* This action stems from the outrage we felt at the cover of Wednesday's issue, which used a gross cartoon of a woman's body to sell a paper devoted largely to the visit of the beautiful women freedom fighters of Vietnam and Laos.

This rip-off of women to sell *Georgia Straights* has been going on a long time. Papers with naked women on the cover sell more copies. The *Straight* staff prefer to exploit women rather than change the paper to reflect the needs of the people of the community.

The women of this community will put out a women's issue. We have been exploited and degraded. We have been denied editorial control. Articles women have written have been denied due to lack of space. Women belong on the *Straight* staff only as naked bodies, pretty faces.

We are tired of being sex objects and slaves. We have occupied this office not to destroy it but to use it. We will produce a *Georgia Straight* which reflects women's power, revolutionary outlook, and joy-of-living. SISTERS JOIN US. Together we will produce the first issue of the *People's Straight.*

The Failure of the *Georgia Straight*

OCCUPATION ISSUE LETTERS, APRIL 8–13, 1971

The *Georgia Straight* has carried good articles on the community, on politics and culture, and on revolutionary struggle. But its main content is anarchy: self-indulgence, defeatism, irrationality, speculation, sexism, and rip-off culture. The paper's line seems to be that in order to sell, you must appeal to the worst in people; that is, to everything that has been conditioned into them by capitalist society. This is an insult to the readers and no doubt explains why the paper is $3,000 in debt. There is nothing uplifting in a story about the narcotics squad wrecking a dope dealer's house; nothing revolutionary in treating Tim Leary and Eldridge Cleaver like entrants in a personality contest; nothing informative in the inanities of Engledink and Wanis Kouri; not a trace of "new culture" in Agrodome rock concerts (promoters' benefits) or crackpot religions; and no respect for anyone in sexist personal ads. The underground press is supposed to be an alternative to the lies of government mass media and trashy magazines, not an addition.

No doubt the *Straight*—just like the capitalist government—blames the stupidity of the people for its inevitable collapse. But the people aren't stupid; only the paper is. If the *Straight* printed factual, reliable, relevant information, it would be well supported. But the *Straight* cannot do that, because it has no idea what the people (and I don't mean just the so-called hip community) need to know, makes no attempt to find out, and couldn't care less anyway. The paper, just like the *Sun* or *Province*, prints what its owners think will result in a profit for themselves. In the final analysis, that is the basis of its policy. And, like any other institution that refuses to serve the people, it will either go out of existence completely or be taken over by the people. Either way its fate is inevitable.
D. MacDonald

Occasional Nothings

BY WANIS KOURI (AKA BOB CUMMINGS), JUNE 25–29, 1971

While scrounging through the White Lunch garbage pails for his dinner, editor Dan McLeod came across a copy of Al Fotheringham's column claiming that the $15,000 fed-grant we almost got was "small potatoes" to us. Pooling our collective weekly salary, the staff purchased a *Sun* to read that part of the item eaten by Tony Tugwell because of its fishy aroma. In it we learned that we have had our "eyes on a $200,000 press" and "turned down" an offer to buy College Printers…to which Peter, Lani, and Dara banged their begging bowls in mirth. While it is true that we have "joked" about buying College Printers and "dreamed" about owning our own press, we have also "decided" to make Korky Day Minister of Masturbation when we take over the government, which, at present, has an equal likelihood of happening.

Strange? We smoke the pipe and Fotheringham has the dreams!

From the Harold Hedd comic strip.

No (FLASH in the PAN)

EXCERPT FROM AN INTERVIEW WITH THE LOCAL BAND FLASHPAN, OCTOBER 29–NOVEMBER 4, 1971

Flashpan: I'd like to ask you a question—I'm just wondering why the *Straight* doesn't have a column or at least devote some newsprint to local bands. All they devote most of their time to is reviewing albums. Well, Jesus Christ, if we want to read an album review we can go buy a *Rolling Stone*, 'cause they do their reviews there in a lot more detail…. The *Georgia Straight* is so fucking apathetic about anything to do with Vancouver rock and roll it's ridiculous. It's the only community outlet for a printed music media and they're not doing anything about it. All they're doing is these record reviews and Led Zeppelin concerts.

The Continuing Saga…

DECEMBER 2–9, 1971

At the *Georgia Straight* general staff meeting on Monday, November 29, Dan McLeod declined to relinquish his legal ownership of the paper and join as an equal member with the rest of the staff. His refusal came in response to a resolution passed by a 21 to 8 majority at the previous staff meeting.

Monday's staff meeting was attended by 23 of the *Straight*'s 31-odd staff members, with an additional four being represented by proxy votes.

In light of Dan's refusal and after considerable discussion, the meeting voted on a resolution which stated "that the staff of the *Georgia Straight* reaffirms its desire to become a legal cooperative." This vote was passed by a 19 to 8 majority.

This resolution was followed by more discussion, during which several people left the meeting to attend prior commitments. The people who left delegated their votes to others who remained.

The discussion resulted in the following resolution: "That the staff of the *Georgia Straight* in general meeting cannot accept Dan McLeod's decision not to make the *Georgia Straight* a legal cooperative, or his reasons, and that we decide on what actions to take."

Before voting, several people objected to the inclusion of proxy votes because they would be given without the benefit of subsequent discussion. It was agreed to disallow the proxy votes.

The resolution passed by a 13 to 5 majority.

The general meeting then elected three people—Sylvia Hawreliak, Korky Day, and Peter Burton—to form a negotiating committee and to begin discussions with Dan in the hope of resolving the conflict.

Dan and those at the general meeting then agreed to maintain the status quo (i.e., business as usual) until such time as negotiations reached a solution or were broken off.

The first meeting between the negotiators and Dan took place on Wednesday afternoon, with the negotiations to be resumed sometime in the next few days.

The staff members agreed that no media statements would be made, as they might tend to interfere with the negotiations.

Watch next Thursday's paper for further developments.

So, What's New?

OCCASIONAL NOTHINGS BY WANIS KOURI (AKA BOB CUMMINGS), DECEMBER 9–16, 1971

Complicating the current constipation between the staff and Dan McLeod over legal ownership of this paper is the feeling on the part of staffers that the *Georgia Straight*'s political slant is both too political and too slanted. The fear—well-founded or otherwise—is that a collective might be dominated by a few highly motivated and articulate people who could lead the paper deeper into the Red. At the same time, many of the self-same dissenters are opposed in principle to single ownership of the paper.

While this bit will no doubt be termed "washing our dirty undies in print," you are the ones who buy our shit and thus, in my opinion, have a right to know some of the whys behind the wherefores.

All in a Day's Work

BY WANIS KOURI (AKA BOB CUMMINGS), JANUARY 20–27, 1972

Normally—if such a word can be applied to the underground press—it takes about four days to put together an edition of the *Georgia Straight*. Reporters and columnists like this much time to gather and write their material, the coordinators (editors) like three days to read and select copy, and layout likes two days to put everything in printable order. That is what we like.

What we got was a telephone call from the "Collective" less than 24 hours before the paper was to be at the printers, telling us that the office, the typesetting equipment, the layout desks and materials, the typewriters, and all LNS, UPS, and exchange copy had been seized....

Which is all to explain why the *Straight* is smaller than usual and how we managed to get a paper out at all. Please accept our apologies until next week, when the *Straight* will be back to what we loosely term "normal."

Benevolent Dictator Talks

EXCERPTS FROM AN INTERVIEW WITH DAN McLEOD, JANUARY 20–27, 1972

Why did you decide not to give the publishing company to the majority of the staff?

I claim that the paper and the community it serves are more important than the staff, and that if the paper folds, it is the community which will suffer most. I believe it is quite possible the paper will fail under collective ownership, and this must not happen.

Aside from the issue of who should own the Straight, *the group said that they didn't like the way the financial end of the paper was being run...*

The books are and always have been open to every member of the staff. I have invited them many times to look, or appoint someone to look at them, but they haven't shown the slightest interest in actually doing so; they just criticize instead.

...and they also disagreed with having one person as editor, having the final say on everything.

If the collective wants to put out their own newspaper, they can do so, but it can't be the *Georgia Straight.* There can only be one *Georgia Straight.* We offered to help them to do this in any way we could; we offered the use of our typesetting, addressograph, and distribution system to help them to start up their own paper. The *Straight* started with NO money. We busted our asses begging for the $150 needed to print the first issue. Which came out ON SCHEDULE. They have the *Straight* office and equipment and the use of the *Ubyssey* office and phones, and still they're complaining.

I think there is a need for the type of paper the collective wants to put out, but I don't think it is up to either of us to decide which papers survive; if a community decides to support a paper, it will succeed....

Why are you the sole owner of the Georgia Straight*?*

I never wanted to own the *Straight,* but I've always felt very strongly that the *Straight,* or a paper like it, MUST survive. I have never found, though I wish I could find one, an alternative to single ownership which would ensure the survival of some kind of free press in Vancouver.

Is the Georgia Straight *making a lot of money, being the only underground paper in Vancouver?*

It is very difficult for any kind of underground paper to survive; the history of the underground press shows this. If you REALLY understood what is happening and everything that has happened at the *Straight,* you would have to admit that it is a miracle we have lasted this long.

A Short Vocabulary Lesson

BY GEORGE PEABODY, FEBRUARY 24–MARCH 2, 1972

By learning and properly using a few of the following simple expressions, you too can become a radical, impress your friends, shock your parents, and strike terror into the heart of the establishment.

POWER TO THE PEOPLE: A good slogan to close with should you unexpectedly find yourself addressing a rally. Also used by B.C. Hydro as a motto (in a slightly different sense from the original).

RIGHT ON: Formal response to the preceding. Except for that, should be reserved for important occasions, such as replying to the query "Le's have another beer." Has fallen into slight disrepute since the Bay began using it as an advertising slogan.

NOUS VAINCORNS: A handy phrase for ending speeches about Quebec. Should not be used if the speaker is unilingual English and there are Québécois in the crowd.

GROOVY: Should be used ironically, unless you are John B. Sebastian, Donovan, or have your head in 1968.

RIP-OFF: What stores, record companies, corporations, etc. do to us.

LIBERATE: What we do to the products of the stores, record companies, corporations, etc.

CAPITALIST: Anyone who seems to have more money than you do.

DEVIATIONIST: Anyone who disagrees with your opinion.

FASCIST: Anyone who owns a car, particularly if they don't pick you up when you're hitchhiking.

CHAUVINIST: Any male.

Note—should you wish to add force to the preceding four expressions, simply tack the word *pig* onto them.

RUNNING DOG: Handy epithet to be tossed into the conversation while you're thinking of something nastier.

LACKEY: To be added to the preceding if you still can't think of anything nastier.

IMPERIALIST MOTHERFUCKER: The something nastier that you should have thought of.

Be-in a Love-in

LETTERS, MARCH 24–30, 1972

Open Letter to the Be-in Committee

Now hold it steady brothers and sisters...just what is the Easter Be-in all about, anyway: love, peace, music...STONED. So what in Ginsberg's name is all this rap about committees, freak-out services, hippie police with armbands, children's energy centres, two or three stages so the acoustics won't beat on the electrics, shutting off the "electric stage" for three hours to ALLOW people to "be" and communicate?

Just WHAT is our Easter Be-in ALL about anyway??? We wait the full cycle of a year playing roles, being organized and divided, looking forward to our stoned day of rest, our annual get-together, community bury-the-hatchet party, where we get so loaded (high, remember?) we couldn't possibly hold a grudge because it would be too much like having an ego. Surely we can get together and be able to cope with the difficulties created by large crowds. And do the children really need their own energy centres? Are they not a part of our community? Are we cutting them out from the action? To protect them? Do we want to split up entertainment, the music we are, a little of everything? A love-in is a celebration. With one centre for everybody there. Rock, country, or whatever, just the favourite entertainment, not mine, not yours...ours...to secure us when we want security. Surely that will be arranged by our word-of-mouth communication, which far exceeds in speed and accuracy any other form of communication, and then we can look ahead to the beauty of surprise, the spontaneity of our own trips we all plan for each other.

Bring your LOVE and I'll see you there.

Amazing

P.S. LOVE is what you want it to be. Bring it anyway.

And Now for Something Completely Different

BY DANIEL WOOD, MAY 11–18, 1972

Tonight I decided to go to the pornos. I'd never been. I've tired of being conventionally hip, of going to those places and doing those things that are stamped with the subtle approval of the subculture. Perhaps I've been straight all along. I don't think so. What I think is that for too long I've turned myself off to new trips, to those frighteningly unfamiliar situations we call adventures. (When, I ask you, did you have a real adventure?)

I decided to visit the Golden Kitten Video Lounge to see a stag film called *Sandra.*

I never got to see the film, I'll say from the start, but I did glimpse one of the less tangible fears I have. This fear concerns acceptance; in this case my fear of being seen at or having friends know that I had gone to a place that was on the unwritten Underground Index. Disapproved! The Golden Kitten? Sexist! Cheap porno! What for? friends might ask with a hint of condescension in their voice.

Yeh, I asked myself: What for? Not getting it at home? Cheap thrills? These were both partly true, but there was more. Much more. And it is this aspect that bothers me tonight and has, for that matter, for quite some time. In a word, I'm concerned with Conformity, the dulling and dying of visions and the subsequent stagnation of reactions, values, and plans.

You see, last Christmas Eve myself and a group of friends got stoned in preparation for High Mass at a local Catholic church. Shortly before midnight we squeaked across the cold snow and clambered into my VW van, huddling together for our ride to

FACING PAGE: A Be-in c. 1968 in Stanley Park.

Church. It had been years since most of us had been inside one. Decent thing to do on Christmas Eve! A real trip! Six furry, ebullient, magnificently motley freaks recalling Sunday-school trips of a decade before.

BUT, when we saw the priest standing on the top step of the church greeting his well-dressed, shiny-shoed parishioners, all the huddling we tried couldn't subdue the tremors.

"We don't really want to do this, do we?"

"What a bummer it'd be."

"I dunno about this..."

We were, in short, chickenshit.

Reluctantly I turned the van around and we headed home, feeling perhaps a little like a Joseph without a manger. Perhaps, too, feeling relieved by avoiding the prospects of showing our shagginess in such a public place. Church! Christ! A High Mass with Communion and those dry wafers and wine, no less! (Would it have been REAL wine?)

I was pissed! We were afraid, yes, AFRAID to go in there. We had successfully made ourselves victims of our own paranoia. And in order to justify our fear we'd soon devise all sorts of mind-tricks: a little somersault here in order to blame the parishioners for their spiffiness; a dextrous sleight of hand there to blame the service for being challengingly long....WHOOSH! We had seemingly solid reasons for NOT going anyhow. In fact, we had rationalizations to excuse ourselves of our fear.

Now, what has this to do with my going down to the Golden Kitten to see a stag movie? Since that initial revelation on Christmas Eve, I've watched myself and friends mind-fuck ourselves many times, let our insecurity and conformity tie us to a value system that, however different from our parents', contains as rigorous standards, as subtle prejudices, as any generation lives with.

Our parents frequently got hung up on alcohol, dark-coloured suits, and light-coloured skins, on possessions like electric can-openers and Jolly Jumpers, on how they look and how others think they look, on money. Yes, they really got hooked on money!

And we? Ah! We have jeans! Enough jean material in Vancouver to sew into one gigantic sail to hoist above Mt. Arrowsmith and let the west wind blow Vancouver Island ashore! We have attitudes toward old people and police. We have prejudices about hair, food, dress, music, entertainment, education that separate ourselves from the older generation only by their difference, not by an overwhelming openness or feeling of security.

I know I'd feel uptight going to the Upstares ("It's a funken good gay club"). I'd worry about going to church, any church! I've seen acquaintances apologize for eating at the A&W. For not having anything but white sugar. For liking Baroque music. For having NEW bell-bottoms. And here am I apologizing for trying to see *Sandra* at the Golden Kitten! My mind trips out on all the places I'm afraid to go to and things I wouldn't do because I'd be embarrassed.

Not only did we never see the High Mass, we never got to see *Sandra.* A SIGN IN THE WINDOW READ: CLOSED. I was disappointed again. I really wanted to begin making adventures out to those places that most frightened me.

After all, the only way to assure oneself that no demons live under the basement stairs waiting to grab one's ankle is to turn around and look there.

I want to go back to the Golden Kitten, my fears overcome, just as I want to go to a High Mass because I want to try—in the words of Monty Python—"Something completely different!"

I've never been to a Scientology session, a home for the elderly, prison, a Women's Liberation Alliance meeting, the Sunday feast of the Hare Krishna Temple, sailing from Jericho, a city council meeting, a massage parlour on Hastings, a Synergy movement class, the top of the Blue Horizon on Robson, the Sally Ann feed-in, a GATE meeting, the top of Grouse Mountain on a clear night or a horror double-feature on a dismal one.

In my mind I envision the huge Monty Python foot appearing out of the sky to squish me should I try something completely different. Still, it's worth the risk.

News Item: The *Grape*

SEPTEMBER 7–14, 1972

The *Grape*, that other paper in town, has suspended publication for this week. The paper was formed last winter when the more radical members of this paper decided that they could no longer work on a paper owned wholly by an individual and split to start their own paper. Though they published what was perhaps one of Canada's better political papers, they never got the community support that they needed, the community proving a little too apathetic for the type of material presented in the *Grape.*

The suspension is due to financial reasons which they hope to eliminate shortly. Perhaps Vancouver isn't large enough to support two papers catering to basically the same readership. One hopes that if the *Grape* does reappear they will have changed their format sufficiently to capture a large enough readership to prove otherwise.

A Mother's Lament

LETTERS, DECEMBER 21–28, 1972

I hear your paper is read by young and old alike. Could you please print this?

Where's my wandering boy tonight
The boy of my tender care
The one who was my pride and joy
Go search for him everywhere

How many parents are worried about their teenage children who have hitchhiked across the Prairies to reach that beautiful city of yours? How many have ended up hungry, lonely, half sick and still not found what they are searching for? My heart aches for them—my son is included.

Well, Son Charles, if you read this letter please get in touch with your Aunt Pauline again, as she has a message for you from home.

I pray all the young people who are away from home think of their parents once in a while and drop them a line or a card.

"We care."

Your loving Mom
Mrs. Faith Rogerson

FACING PAGE:
Dan McLeod (right) backstage with Janis Joplin.

CHRONOLOGY 1967–1972

1967

FEBRUARY It is a winter of disaffection before the Summer of Love. Among the disaffected is Dan McLeod, a young Vancouver poet and former UBC math student. At a party at a Point Grey home following a reading by Leonard Cohen, the idea of creating a newspaper to represent the growing local counterculture and provide an alternative to the mainstream media is discussed. McLeod is inspired by a paper in Detroit, *Guerilla*, which features jazz coverage, politics, poetry, and stories.

MARCH Vancouver's first Easter Be-in is held in Stanley Park on March 23.

APRIL The proposed paper is christened the *Georgia Straight* over beer at the Cecil Hotel. The name aims to play on the fact that the weather forecasts will offer free publicity: they're always issuing gale warnings for the Georgia Strait.

MAY *Georgia Straight*'s first issue appears May 5. It costs a dime. Stories include a local art censorship bust at the Douglas Gallery, a report on the youth movement in Amsterdam, and an article from San Francisco claiming that hard drugs, capitalist head merchants, and corruption of young runaways are serious problems in Haight-Ashbury. The 12-page paper is produced out of Dan McLeod's $30-per-month apartment at 1666 West 6th and a warehouse studio on Prior Street. On May 12, it moves into its first office at 432 Homer; later that day, Dan McLeod is taken away in a paddy wagon and jailed three hours for "investigation of vagrancy." College Printers refuses to print the second issue. Martin Luther King leads a New York anti-war march. Jefferson Airplane, the Collectors, Painted Ship, and Magic Fern play the Richmond arena.

JUNE The Beatles release *Sgt. Pepper's Lonely Hearts Club Band*. All local web presses refuse to print the *Straight*, even

though the content has been cleared by a lawyer. With some difficulty, 5,000-plus copies of issues two and three are printed on a small flatbed press. The nightclub Dante's Inferno reopens as the Retinal Circus (now Celebrities) on Davie.
JULY Canada turns 100. A crowd of 32,000 listens silently at Empire Stadium as Chief Dan George recites "A Lament for Confederation." Three weeks later in Montreal, French President Charles de Gaulle calls for a free Quebec. Abe Snidanko, the RCMP drug officer immortalized as Sergeant Stedenko by Cheech and Chong in *Up in Smoke*, has his home address printed in the July 7 issue.
AUGUST The *Straight* finds a printer with a web press in Victoria. On August 20, the Easter Be-in is reprised with a *Straight*-sponsored Super-Human Be-in.
SEPTEMBER Peter Almasy's Acidman comic strip appears, chronicling the "head of steel" and his battles with Egocop. From a VD clinic ad: "If you like 'em enough to ball them, you like 'em enough not to give 'em the clap."
OCTOBER A parade is held on Pender Street to protest a proposed freeway through Chinatown. The *Straight* advertises for a co-ordinator to handle "love-ins, freak-outs and schoolyard invasions." Circulation is 60,000 every two weeks. The *Straight*'s business licence is suspended, and McLeod serves Mayor Tom Campbell with a writ. The licence is reinstated.
NOVEMBER Four *Straight* editors, including Peter Hlookoff and Milton Acorn, resign to start their own paper; Fred Latremouille becomes co-editor. *Rolling Stone* magazine is launched in San Francisco. Classified ad: "Turning on for the first time? Feeling suicidal? Dissatisfied with your present analyst? Suffering from a bad case of RCMP? Consult Good Trips Incorporated."
DECEMBER The Powell Street Dugout opens to shelter Skid Row homeless. On December 11, the *Straight* puts out one "daily" issue that includes TV listings and a stock-market report during a brief Pacific Press strike.

1968

JANUARY January 12 *Straight* headline: "We Are All God, You Are All God." Story asks: "Do you know that you are God? You are God—but do you know it?" R. Crumb's Mr. Natural comic character makes its *Straight* debut. On January 29, the Viet Cong launch the surprise Tet Offensive.
MARCH Laurier LaPierre, former host of *This Hour Has Seven Days*, contributes his first *Straight* column. The second Easter Be-in is announced with an ecological focus: "To help repair any damage that may be done to the meadow everyone is urged to bring along plenty of grass." The *Straight* is turned down for a business licence by the New Westminster city council in an effort to ban street-vending. A reported 400 people attend the first public meeting of the hippies' own City Government; acting Mayor is Stan Persky. Police raid a benefit for Cool-Aid, an independent youth-services organization founded in the *Straight*'s office by Ray Chouinard and the late Elmore Smalley. Cool-Aid will eventually launch a young bald lawyer in plaid shorts and sandals into political orbit. Yes, we're talking about Mike Harcourt.
APRIL On April 1, Joachim Foikis is declared Vancouver's official Town Fool, thanks to a $3,500 Canada Council grant. The *Straight* runs a piece by Stokely Carmichael on the murder of

Dr. Martin Luther King. Timothy Leary's writing is featured in a two-page spread, Eric Burdon and Jimi Hendrix are interviewed, Stan Persky is arrested for loitering, and the first steps are taken in acquiring land for an underground shopping mall off Granville Street.
JUNE The *Straight* offers a lifetime subscription (valued at $150) for the donation of a TV and/or a "priceless eternal subscription (includes afterlife)" for a colour set. *Straight* vendors challenge the ban on selling the paper in New West by openly selling issues in attempts to get arrested. Robert Kennedy is assassinated. Dr. Spock the baby doc is found guilty of encouraging draft resistance. Pierre Trudeau is elected prime minister. The *Straight* runs its first ad for A&B Sound.
JULY Classified ad: "The *Georgia Straight* needs typists. Why not just drop in to our office one day and type?" The *Straight* offers a new subscription incentive—a free album. Choices include Ornette Coleman, Holy Modal Rounders, and *Let's Sing in Esperanto.* The Doors play Pacific Coliseum.
AUGUST The *Straight* begins a (mostly) weekly publication schedule. The *Straight*, Dan McLeod, and Bob Cummings are charged with criminal libel for awarding Magistrate Lawrence Eckhardt the Pontius Pilate Certificate of Justice. Soviet troops invade Czechoslovakia, ending the reforms of the Prague Spring. Chicago police attack demonstrators outside the Democratic National Convention.
OCTOBER René Levesque is declared first leader of the newly formed Parti Québécois. The *Straight* runs interviews with Johnny Cash and Jerry Rubin, plus features on Buckminster Fuller and "High Priest of LSD" Timothy Leary. Yippie leader Jerry Rubin and Students for a Democratic Society occupy the Faculty Club at UBC for two days, resulting in $6,000 damage and, probably, some really lousy grades from parched professors. The first of Gilbert Shelton's Fabulous Furry Freak Brothers comics runs in the *Straight.* At a Hallowe'en party at the Retinal Circus, Terry David Mulligan's old RCMP uniform is displayed, to much amusement.

Classified ad: "*Georgia Straight* bookkeeper wanted. Must be willing to work for free, to work long hours, and to put up with the rest of us."

NOVEMBER Al Sorenson begins Poppin, the *Straight*'s first regular local music column. Classified ad: "OPERATION FREEDOM. Destroy Plan A, use Plan B." The *Straight* runs an article praising Scientology written by William S. Burroughs. Richard Nixon and Spiro Agnew are elected. Students occupy the SFU administration building for three days; 114 are arrested.
DECEMBER An article by Ralph J. Gleason observes that the capitalist system "may be so open, in a curious way, that it will be just as possible to make millions out of it by espousing revolution as it is by manufacturing mace."

1969

JANUARY *Straight* newsman Eric Sommer reports on the abortion underground. The Heads Captured column begins, reporting on drug arrests, convictions, and sentencing.

A sports column appears; first one is bylined Dummy Boydshit. The Strathcona Property Owners and Ratepayers Association is formed to oppose an urban-renewal project that includes a $41-million freeway. The *Straight* is fined $1,500 for defamatory libel of Magistrate Eckhardt; later the decision is overturned as the result of a landmark appeal.

FEBRUARY A *Straight* feature details the undesirable effects of blasting an eight-lane roadway through downtown. Classified ad: "*Georgia Straight* bookkeeper wanted. Must be willing to work for free, to work long hours, and to put up with the rest of us."

"He's got a real big rig. He was very cooperative—most cooperative. His hair got stuck in the mould and he didn't get worried or upset or anything."

MARCH The *Straight* advises: "Don't sell your drugs to the RCMP! They don't smoke them!" Bert Hill analyses Pacific Press: is it an illegal monopoly? A benefit with Allen Ginsberg and Phil Ochs is held at the Gardens to raise money for the *Straight*'s legal defence fund.

APRIL The *Straight* reports attendance of 5,000 at the Easter Be-in. An interview with Cynthia Plastercaster reveals her techniques for immortalizing rock stars' penises in plaster, along with an account of Jimi Hendrix's session: "He's got a real big rig. He was very cooperative—most cooperative. His hair got stuck in the mould and he didn't get worried or upset or anything."

MAY Nine obscenity charges are laid against the paper and its principals. At issue are the Cynthia Plastercaster interview, a cartoon depicting Acidman's genitals, a cartoon of a dog urinating on a fire hydrant, and a classified ad placed by a man seeking women for the stated purpose of "muffdiving, etc." Three charges of "inciting to commit an indictable offence" are also laid for an article on how to grow marijuana. The May 21 issue features advice from Dr. HIPpocrates on avoiding pain during intercourse and a new masthead featuring Crown Prosecutor Stewart McMorran as Editor, W.A.C. Bennett as Reporter, Mayor Tom Campbell as Advertising Manager, and Ernest Muffdiver in charge of subscriptions; 2,000 copies of the issue are seized and four more obscenity charges are laid for the HIPpocrates column.

JUNE A policeman's threat to the *Straight*'s editor is reported: "I'm number 363. Remember that number...I'm going to nail you one of these days, McLeod."

JULY The July 9 cover features photo of future *Straight* editor Bob Mercer and playwright Leonard Angel being arrested for disturbing the peace while holding a licensed performance of their Vancouver Street Theatre group. Convictions are later quashed by B.C. Court of Appeal. Neil Armstrong becomes the first man to walk on the moon. Arthur Clarke becomes Vancouver's first black police officer.

AUGUST Prime Minister Trudeau abandons an attempt to address Vietnam War protesters at the Seaforth Armouries when their shouts drown him out. The August 6 issue includes the first chapter of Fugs member Ed Sanders's novel, which results in another

obscenity rap. McLeod foils an attempt to hold him in custody over the Labour Day weekend by raising the $200 bail. Sharon Tate and four others are murdered by the Manson Family. A week later, Woodstock begins.
SEPTEMBER The September 3 issue has a new cover price of 25 cents. A reprinted article on the diminishing Amazon rain forest appears. The nine obscenity charges are dismissed by Judge Bernard Isman, who asserts that the prosecution failed to provide an adequate definition of the word *muffdiving*.
OCTOBER The success of a Peace Arch border-crossing blockade to protest Amchitka nuclear tests is followed by the formation on October 1 of the Don't Make a Wave Committee, which member Bob Darnell hopes will lead to a "green peace." A firebomb is thrown at the U.S. consulate. The paper moves to 56A Powell Street. The *Straight* reports on a controversy over *Province* theatre critic James Barber appearing at the opening of *Salome* wearing "sandals and an embroidered sunburst jacket (showing his chest to the navel)." Obscenity charges for the Sanders novel excerpt are adjourned. The *Straight* publishes its first literary supplement. Jack Kerouac dies.
NOVEMBER *Billboard* magazine acclaims Vancouver as a future boomtown of pop music.
DECEMBER Chicago police shoot two Black Panthers while attempting to arrest them. The *Straight* reports on a death at the Rolling Stones' Altamont festival concert, after Hell's Angels "security" personnel get out of hand.

1970

JANUARY B.C. Hydro chairman Gordon Shrum tells the *Straight*'s Stephen Brown that nuclear generating plants are the answer to B.C.'s growing power needs. The Tribes column—by Alice Too (Ken Lester) and later Mason Dixon—debuts, covering rural communes.
FEBRUARY Three bombings in a month at UBC damage Brock House, a wall of the mathematics building, and an office in the geology building. Due to a Pacific Press strike, the *Straight* briefly tries out a broadsheet format and stronger news focus. Timothy Leary is sentenced to 10 years for possession of two joints.
MARCH Christian organizations begin placing classified ads in the paper to save hippies from eternal damnation. Bob Cummings sets off to sea with Greenpeace. Dan McLeod and legal counsel John Laxton present a brief to the Senate Committee on Mass Media on behalf of the *Georgia Straight*, including a chronology of harassment and criminal charges. The paper details the dangers of oil supertankers off the B.C. coast.
APRIL A strawberry-flavoured *Straight* appears, printed on pink paper with essence of strawberry added to the ink. Paul McCartney issues a High Court writ calling for the dissolution of the Beatles.
MAY The paper's news-oriented redesign prompts the *Globe and Mail* headline: "The *Straight* Going Straight?" National Guardsmen open fire on demonstrators at Kent State University, killing four students.
JUNE Vancouver's first gay-issues column, by Kevin Dale McKeown, debuts in the *Straight*. A riot at English Bay precipitates a week of clashes between youth and police. American guards along the Canadian border are given guns for the first time since the

War of 1812, when, incidentally, we kicked their butts and burned down the White House. The Party is held at Stanley Park, featuring free music, free food, and free dope. Bands include Phil Ochs, the Seeds of Time, and the United Empire Loyalists.
JULY A column by Irving Stowe, co-founder of Greenpeace, debuts in the *Straight.*
AUGUST Wreck Beach busts result in 13 convictions; a Nude-in is scheduled to protest. A recycling guide appears.
SEPTEMBER Jimi Hendrix dies. Letter to the *Straight:* "When the revolution comes, you will be the first ones stood up to the wall and shot by the commies as drudges, useless scum of humanity."
OCTOBER The Vancouver Canucks lose to Los Angeles in their first game at Pacific Coliseum. Janis Joplin dies. The Front de libération du Québec kidnaps British Trade Commissioner James Cross, then provincial Labour Minister Pierre LaPorte. The War Measures Act is invoked. Seven people are taken into custody in Vancouver for distributing FLQ literature. The *Straight* reveals that representatives of several major advertisers in Vancouver's dailies sit on the board of Pacific Press, which prints the papers.
DECEMBER *Straight* headline reads "Crown Loses Sex Appeal" as the paper beats the appeal of an obscenity charge dismissal. The *Straight* features an interview with James Cross's kidnappers.

1971

FEBRUARY Spiro Agnew, playing in the Bob Hope Desert Classic, hits three spectators with his first two shots. The male electorate of Liechtenstein refuses to grant the vote to women.
MARCH Haida artist Robert Davidson opens his first one-man show at the Centennial Museum. The U.S. detonates a hydrogen bomb beneath Amchitka Island, Alaska. Prime Minister Pierre Elliott Trudeau, 57, weds Margaret Sinclair, 22, in West Vancouver. A $10,000 statue by Rodin goes missing from the Vancouver Art Gallery; it is mysteriously returned by mail three days later in an old brown satchel bearing a six-cent stamp.
APRIL Women outraged by the *Straight*'s Easter cover of Christ crucified on a female body seize the office the next day, bar all men, and put out a special feminist edition. Publisher Dan McLeod is not allowed in, but he and the staff decide to pay the women $800 for the week. On April 16, the *Straight* becomes a twice-weekly paper.
MAY Youths tear down a fence to occupy the site of the proposed Four Seasons Hotel at the entrance to Stanley Park and rechristen the area All Seasons Park. Harold Hedd, by cartoonist Rand Holmes, debuts in the *Straight.*
JUNE The paper's application for a $15,000 federal Opportunities for Youth grant is approved, then cancelled following pressure from the B.C. Liberal caucus. The *Straight* reports on the racial problems of East Indians in Quesnel and how zoo animals are driven insane by captivity. Also, Engledink Birdhumper reports on the Kosmic Baseball League: "The best chatter of the game award goes to the Moose Valley farmer who said, in heated debate, 'How can I lie? I take LSD!'"
AUGUST The *Straight* reviews *Hamlet,* starring future Vancouver Playhouse artistic director Larry Lillo. A Smoke-in to protest drug arrests is staged on August 7 in Gastown. Police attempts to

disperse the crowd of 2,000 result in the Gastown Riot. At least a dozen citizens are hospitalized and a *Sun* reporter claims he was beaten. *Hair* opens at the Queen Elizabeth Theatre.
OCTOBER An inquiry into the Gastown Riot finds police overreacted. Smoke-in organizers are also criticized. An estimated 10,000 local high-school students gather outside the U.S. consulate to protest nuclear testing at Amchitka.
NOVEMBER The *Straight* returns to weekly publication. Staffers vote 21 to 8 that Dan McLeod relinquish his legal ownership of the *Straight* and become an equal member of a co-operative. He declines this invitation.
DECEMBER Tom Campbell is re-elected mayor, despite the efforts of another Tom Campbell—Andrew Thompson Campbell—who garnered 4,922 votes. The upstart Campbell is charged on the night of the election with assault and selling LSD to a policeman, but he is eventually found not guilty.

1972

JANUARY About 15 staff members take over the *Straight* offices after Dan McLeod refuses to turn the paper into a legal collective. While the breakaway staff produces the more political *Georgia Grape*, McLeod and the remaining staff publish from another location and beat the *Grape* to the streets.
FEBRUARY McLeod gets a court injunction and reclaims the paper's office. Both the *Straight* and the *Grape* continue publishing. "The real tit is so much more interesting than the shape fashion decrees that it's hard to believe that it is a rational motive which persuades us to march them in uniform A, B, 32, 34."—Germaine Greer in the *Straight*. Nixon goes to China.
MAY *Greenpeace III* sails for the French nuclear test site at Mururoa Atoll. Governor George Wallace of Alabama is crippled in an assassination attempt.
JUNE Twenty-one police are injured in a disturbance outside Pacific Coliseum during a Rolling Stones concert.

"I found the vertical architecture of the Big Mac more pleasing than the sprawling wasteland of the Quarter Pounder."

Burglars are caught breaking into the offices of the Democratic National Committee in the Watergate Hotel.
AUGUST B.C.'s first NDP government begins 1,200 days in office. Daniel Wood writes in the *Straight* on the "withering" of Greenpeace. The last U.S. ground troops leave Danang.
SEPTEMBER Mayor Tom Campbell decides not to run again. Team Canada wins its summit hockey series against Soviets. "When I scored that final goal, I finally realized what democracy was all about," declares Paul Henderson.
NOVEMBER Nixon and Agnew are re-elected. The *Straight* reviews McDonald's: "I found the vertical architecture of the Big Mac more pleasing than the sprawling wasteland of the Quarter Pounder."
DECEMBER Michael Kluckner writes on the Fairview Slopes redevelopment as part of the *Straight*'s civic-election coverage. *Life* magazine stops living.

JINGLE JAZZ WITHOUT CHRISTMAS

RABID CATS WELFARE REDNECKS

IKE AND TINA AT BACEDA'S

CONCRETE POETRY PICKPOCKETS

LOUSY, CHILDISH MELLERDRAMA

PART TWO
1973–1985

ENVER HOXHA DUNGAREES

MAHARISHI DOLLARTON CRAWL

NAKED ACTORS SEAL KILLERS

SLOB ICE AND THREE CHERRIES

JOEY SHITHEAD HELP WANTED

TOUGHEST MILKMAN U-J3RK5

★ **"Taking Care Of Business" with Bruce Allen – An Interview With Mr. B.T.O.**

GEORGIA STRAIGHT

25¢ OUTSIDE B.C. 35¢

Vol. 9 No. 391 April 24—May 1, 1975

WALKING ON THE WILD SIDE

20th-Century Amazons: Ike & Tina at Baceda's

BY ROB GELDOF, AUGUST 1–8, 1974

Michael Jagger once remarked in regard to Tina Turner that it was "nice to see a chick doing it once in a while." Jagger treads the marshy soil of universal fantasy—he knows what he's talking about. But where Jagger advocates the ageless arts of sensuous subtlety, the carnally knowledgeable sneer of awareness, the sulking pout of innocence, and the uncertain aura of danger, Tina Turner employs the almost theatrical art of sexual overkill—subtle she is not. Tina Turner does, however, embody a whole unisexual family of fantasies. She is the lusting, available housewife/whore, nymphoid of a billion male dreams, and she is possibly the personification of an equal quantity of female alter egos. There were at Baceda's on Thursday night as many moans as there were sighs.

Tina Turner's power lies in her ambitonal mouth, an orifice she uses not solely with regard to her singing. It is a voice that is at once brutal, rough, soothing, and experienced, and were Tina to stand on stage and merely sing, that alone could be classified as an experience. But the open-mouthed wonder and silent drooling sexuality of her audience is not a product of the voice alone, rather it is the result of the strenuous stage calisthenics of Tina and her Ikettes. If exaggeration breeds excess, and excess is blood brother to decadence, then Tina Turner learned her lessons well from her Imperial Roman forerunning sisters. The extravagant use of body in general, and facial gesticulation in particular, afford not the least sexual mystery, so lovingly taught us by the flood of "How To" books currently inundating the drugstore stands. Tina does not beguile, she claims and demands forthright, but her insistent charm appears to lie in the fact that she panders to the male obsession and lets them believe that any one of them can satisfy her apparent needs. The female aspects are amply catered to by the odd knowing wink and constant invocations to her fellow "sisters." To identify is to belong....

There were, of course, the now-famous "mike moves" of Tina, handling, touching, and oh so softly biting the steel microphone stand. Her male audience sat transfixed while she crooned and panted her way to the grand finale. It stopped short of ridiculous with the domestic and familiar asides from Ike, who every now and again would create the most ludicrous slurping and licking sounds that Tina professionally ignored. Although it did not appear to be obvious to the audience, Ike and Tina were definitely and very amusingly parodying themselves, and in fact making a lot of fun out of the slavering crowd. At times it was all she could do to keep a straight face. The show ended abruptly amid much strobe-lighting, crescendoing, and general stage histrionics.

Really a very short show but energy-wise on the expenditure of a three-hour bash. Many tight-lipped older women later, the crowd rushed from a packed Baceda's, some of the male members (of the audience, smart-ass) walking with a noticeable limp.

SFU Prof in Sex Play?

BY JOHN L. DALY, AUGUST 21–28, 1975

Vancouver's suburbs are hotter than the ads at the back of this paper. Everybody knows that. What dispute there is over sexuality is mostly about presentation; how one comes to grips with it, so to speak.

I know one successful suburban couple who swing so far their bedroom walls need frequent repair. He's a mildly withdrawn type (a banker) and she is a wonderful mother of two robust young children. All her family and friends know her for her excellent knitting. You'd never expect to find *Playboy* on their coffee table, let alone a ribald, raunchy, get-as-much-as-you-can orgy with two other couples in their bedroom.

But that's exactly what they're into. They invite a few friends over for drinks, put on a little music, and get honest with their feelings for each other's husbands, wives, and all the combinations. Painful pleasure, kinky clothes, and sex paraphernalia are not reserved for British aristocrats and government officials.

Sqrieux de Dieu is a new play about just such leaping libidos on the cocktail circuit right here in Vancouver. That it is mostly funny really says that the material will be presented in a generally acceptable way, inoffensive to most.

Most, but perhaps not all; playwright Betty Lambert has written a full-length farce about the shifting sands of social and individual values. It could be criticized as not dealing with the heavy feminist problems inherent in the leisured lifestyle of suburbia that surface particularly in the sexual mores of that group. But it is supposed to be funny, and after talking with Ms. Lambert, I have high hopes. Could she have done both—written a funny play and still dealt with the sexism, oppression, of the situation? That wasn't what she set out to do.

She's written a play about a swinging university professor (at SFU?), his mistress, wife, and mother-in-law. The curriculum she has outlined for them includes adultery, masturbation, homosexuality, sadomasochism, and nude therapy. Will there be much nudity?

"Not an awful lot," says Betty. "But what there is is 110 pounds and very nice."

Probably there will be crowds waiting to audit the course.

Reading Between Those Classified Lines!

LETTERS, FEBRUARY 26–MARCH 4, 1976

BLK FUNUAL GAY SEEKS W END

Now what does that mean in the jargon of *GS* classified ads? Such nonsense is not the result of a secret code, but of old-fashioned censorship. The *Georgia Straight* censors or rather Bowdlerizes its classified ads. Oh Heresy! How can this be true?

If you read the ads carefully you will never actually see the word "SEX." *GS* staffers carefully replace the letters "SEX" with the letters "FUN" wherever they appear. Thus "OVERSEXED" becomes "OVERFUNED" and "SEXUAL" becomes "FUNUAL."

Another rude word you will not see (except in extra-cost boldface) is the obscenity "HUNG." It is replaced with the confusing "ENDOWED" or even worse "END."

In these liberated times it is considered impolite to be concerned with race. Thus "BLACK" and "WHITE" are replaced by the unpronounceable terms "BLK" and "W."

Even numbers are candidates for censorship. Besides the obviously indecent number 69, the numbers 16 and 17 are changed to a genteel 18.

Even the innocuous euphemism "GAY" is completely censored out of communal housing ads.

Without understanding these substitutions, you might be convinced that your average advertiser (namely me) had the intelligence of a mature toaster.

Roedy Green

Vancouver's Male Strippers Let It All Hang Out

BY DONA CRANE, JULY 21–28, 1977

Male stripper: To simply mention the words is enough to disturb the machismo of any self-respecting man in this town. "A male *what?*" "A male stripper, you know, someone like you, *except he takes his clothes off for a living.*"

Witness a typical after-dinner scene down at Jerry's Cove. The table right inside the door holds 25 pints of beer and an ashtray with several cigarettes burning away. There sit 13 blind, jimmied people, three women, 10 men, and they're all pals. All the guys either slouch forward into their suds, or lean back in their chairs, crossing their arms and puffing up their chests. They're all ex-hippies, who've quit doing acid and reading *Lord of the Rings.* Now they've discovered the joys of working-man life: building construction, drinking beer, living with an old lady, and digging women strippers in the bars and pubs.

They're all laughing and yelling, "Shit, man," and "Come on, now," because the three chicks are making a last stand for women's liberation and defending their right to enjoy naked men dancing on a stage. They've never had the opportunity to see such a spectacle, unlike one of the guys here, just over from Victoria. Now he's up and demonstrating—trying hard to gyrate his hips and flutter his eyelashes, waving his arms, and flipping his wrist.

His act is met with shrieks of laughter from all who can see.

Later, a girl called Jeannie hands me a copy of *After Dark* magazine. This theatre-oriented glossy is full of pretty Adonises clad in straps and leotards and ripped T-shirts. Jeannie also has stacks of *Playgirl* and *Cosmo.* The former shows her what it is, the latter tells her how to go and get it.

Coming from Jeannie, with her Bowie-esque style and nose ornament, the male stripper scene in Vancouver sounds completely underground and campy. And yet the media tells us how established the concept is in most other big cities—those guys who love to tease the middle-aged women in the audience. The hard-core brassy ones who yell requests at Tom Jones to throw them his panties.

Jeannie makes a few phone calls and returns with the information. Amateur night for the male strippers in Vancouver is Wednesday, at the Foxy Lady on Beatty Street.

The Foxy Lady used to be the Egress. Cover charge is $2, and we don't get any odd looks from the management as we waltz in, two vulnerable young females. After all, this is *not* the Smilin' Buddha or the Penthouse.

I'm disappointed. The clientele here is not sleazy, or kinky. Most of the tables are filled with young, well-dressed women. Maybe they work in banks or offices. There are a few university types, along with their residence boyfriends. All here for a laugh and a thrill.

A guy comes around with two scoresheets and politely explains the point system of amateur night. At the end of the night, the amateur with the most points gets the most money. I feel like I'm playing bingo.

Round #1. The first contestant is a magnificent creature called Michael. His role is that of hippie-intellectual—he keeps his wire rims on through the whole performance. Michael tries hard—waving his long arms in front of him; flinging his hair. And he doesn't smile when he undoes the laces of those white pants.

The second contestant is a well-formed black, laden down with tribal jewellery. His name is Granville, and I've heard his name mentioned far and wide—most recently by a belly dancer at a Greek restaurant. They've all been saying what a good dancer Granville is, that he's been classically and jazz trained. And sure enough, he does steal the show, leaping, twirling, doing steps more apt for *West Side Story* than for the disco hit *Carwash.*

I rate him a nine-and-a-half out of a possible ten.

When I look back up at the stage, I'm in for a surprise. There's a real live turkey up there! He's no classically trained dancer, this guy who's big and burly with a dark moustache and he-man hair sprouting all over his chest. Dr. Guy is dressed in a backless patient's gown, kneesocks, and a doctor's cap. The women are screaming with hysterical laughter as he exposes his cock, packaged sweetly in a crochet penis warmer. Dr. Guy leaps, sneers at some of the girls, and directs his cock like a marionette with little strings attached.

Things are getting to be fun. Jeannie's eating her lasagna, bopping her head back and forth as she ogles alternately at both male and female strippers.

"I can really feel the sexual atmosphere in here," she purrs.

The last dancer in Round #1 is Paul. He has the sultry looks of movie star Belmondo and the ballet-style steps of Granville. His gimmick is ripping a T-shirt off his body, shred by shred.

Exquisite.

Attempted Murder on the Ice

BY PAUL WATSON, APRIL 28–MAY 5, 1977

Greenpeace anti-sealing campaigner Paul Watson gives his personal account of the greed and brutality in no-man's-land off Newfoundland's frozen shores.

MARCH 15TH, 1977

0700 hrs: The morning of the Ides of March. The slaughter of innocents has begun. Fifty miles east of our base camp, the clubs are even now rising and falling. On the frozen barrens of Belle Isle the confrontation squad members are completing final preparations. Our three JetRanger helicopters are presently en route to us from our rear base, 85 miles to the west of this position.

0800 hrs: A whining, whirring chop-chop sound is audible. The first of our choppers comes into view. After a few moments, the last machine alights with a crunch upon the hard crusty snow. Two minutes later, our supply plane, a brilliant-orange single-engine Otter, performs a hazardous landing on the uneven terrain before our encampment. The roar of her engine dies slowly down, the prop becomes visible then stops. The side door opens and a dozen journalists from Europe and North America step out, most of them pale and shaken. The last occupant bounds out the door, a smirking superior smile across his jolly mustachioed Québécois face. Our Otter pilot is the personification of all the decades of romantic Canadian bush-pilot legends. He tells us that he would be happy to put us down on the floe ice himself but that he has not been able to find a piece of floe ice large enough to land on. The ice is more broken and more dangerous than last year.

0830 hrs: Our confrontation crew begins to board the helicopters. Deputy expedition leader Al Johnson of San Francisco explains our heretofore secret tactics to the members of the press.

"Our intention," he begins, "is to attempt to shut down a sealing vessel. We are prepared to put our lives in jeopardy by placing our bodies in their way. Between club and seal and before and behind the ship itself. The future of an entire species is at stake. Ultimately the future of our own species is at stake. We must take the step of committing ourselves to this serious and drastic effort to interfere."

0845 hrs: The immense expanse of salt "slob" ice sweeps by 2,000 feet beneath us. The ice looks extremely unhealthy. On the other hand, mother nature has blessed us with a clear sky. After nearly a half an hour in flight, the bloody armada of 11 Norwegian and Canadian sealing ships comes into view.

Behind each vessel lies a trail of scarlet gore. For the second year, I am witnessing the icy blueness of pack ice besmeared obscenely by young baby seal blood. My stomach feels like heaving and my anger is almost beyond control.

0920 hrs: We circle and descend. We scan the ice for signs of seals. The Fisheries officers are in the area waiting to pounce upon us if we violate their absurd "Seal Protection Act." If we land within a half mile of any seal, our helicopters will be subject to seizure. We finally find a place and settle down on the largest pan of ice we can find. The pan is about 40 feet across. We are over two miles from the nearest sealing ship.

The surface of the ice is surreal. An eight-foot swell is rolling the ice field like a constant earthquake. There is no security in this lack of solidity. There is room on our floe for our second helicopter, but the third is forced to land on another floe some 100 yards away. From where we sit, we can watch the third machine disappear with the rise of each swell.

I know that if I allow my mind to dwell on the apparent impossibility of trekking across this frozen hell that I won't be going anywhere. I find myself shouting above the noise of the blades.

"Everybody out!!! Let's go!"

A stretch of water separates each pan. We must learn to wait for the swells to push the pans together and then jump. Progress is painfully slow. We cannot see the ship only two miles away. I have taken a compass bearing from the helicopter before we landed. With a hand compass our zigzag hike across the ice will hopefully not lose us completely. Nine of us have started out. We left two media photographers back with the helicopters. Both of them felt that their jobs were not worth the risk of a hike across these treacherous ice fields. Somehow I can't really blame them, but I feel perturbed that they cost us two spaces in our helicopters.

1230 hrs: We have lost four of our original nine crew members. Our documentary photographer and two crew members have turned back from exhaustion. Our deputy expedition leader, Al Johnson, has severely injured his ankle during a jump. He also, with great reluctance, turns back.

Aside from myself, there are only two other confrontation crew members, Al Thornton from Greenpeace England and Peter Ballem, our legal advisor, a lawyer from Vancouver, and two documentary crew members. The responsibility for halting the ship now rests in our hands. We are relieved that cameraman Fred Easton and soundman Michael Chechik have kept the pace, thus assuring that the world will be able to bear witness to our protest.

We are now among the seals. The incredible beauty of these animals renews my confidence in the necessity of our campaign. The air here is filled with the happy sounds of new life. We are still far from the killing grounds. Mother seals watch us curiously and warily. Even here, the seal nursery is not the safest place for the newborn seals.

I can hear a cry just off to my left, louder and more desperate than the hundreds of other cries that surround me. Ten feet away, two ice pans have moved apart. A pup has fallen into the crack and is now struggling helplessly in the frigid water. The sides of the pan are too high for him to regain the security of the floe.

I drop my day pack and within a moment I have reached the edge. The ice pans are now closing together with the rise of a new swell. With a few inches to spare, I grasp the little flipper and pull the frightened pup to safety. Setting the pup down in the centre of the ice pan, I give his little head a pat. The pup gives me a bewildered look, raises his head, and cries. The pup's mother is crossing the pan toward her infant. The baby safely by its mother's side, I turn and continue the trek to the ship.

1445 hrs: Peter Ballem advises me that we have come too far. We will not be able to return to the helicopters before dark. The helicopters must be off the ice and returning within the hour. The helicopters cannot and it is illegal for them to fly at night. Should we return anyway? We have a vote. Everybody is in agreement: we stay.

We are all thirsty and tired. Our legs are sore and our faces sunburnt by the glare from the ice. We have taken turns dragging the inflatable boat and we have been tempted to ditch it many times. We need it, however, to cross the wide leads, and we will need it once we reach the ship.

1510 hrs: At last we have reached the killing grounds. There is blood upon the ice everywhere. The happy, innocent baby cries that we have been hearing all day have been transformed into fearful screaming. The air stinks with death, and the atmosphere of barbarism-induced fear among the seals is thicker than the ice beneath our feet.

The first sealer we reach is a burly brute of a man. His hands and face are plastered with dry rust-red blood. His clothing is black with gore, his eyes are hidden behind reflective sunglasses. The glasses reflect the carnage, the devastation he has wrought with club and knife. He is bent over the body of a seal pup, knife in hand. He is coldly and efficiently removing the pelt from the warm little body.

He has placed his club on the ice. I walk slowly behind him. He is pretending to ignore me. I reach quickly down, grasp his club, bring my arm back, and hurtle the weapon into the open lead. I leave him to retrieve his floating club.

The next sealer seems to be in a bit of trouble. He is on a pan which has only one available jumping-off point. His problem is Alan Thornton, who is firmly seated on the only spot he can jump to. The sealer is gazing about for help. He has with him a length of rope with a seal pelt attached to it. Before he was interrupted he was in the process of dragging the pelt to a pile for retrieval by his ship.

After a few minutes, he decides to jump at another point. He tosses his rope to the next pan, takes a running leap, and manages to make the jump. During his jump, however, I took the end of the rope that he had thrown and tossed it back on the floe from which he had just left. He jumped back to retrieve his rope and found himself in the same predicament as before. Alan stays to guard him, while Peter and I proceed to the next sealer.

We can see two helicopters coming rapidly across the ice, 15 feet over the heads of the seals. They land and a half-dozen Fisheries officers are on the scene to come to the rescue of the sealers we have been hassling. We retreat toward the sealing ship.

The *Martin Karlsen* is actually moving toward us. I take up the bow position and Alan Thornton manoeuvres to take up the stern position. It is all so sudden. The ice pans are being pushed before the sealer's bow. I attempt to stand firm on a small pan some 100 feet before her. Alan is pushing the inflatable into the water to prevent it backing away from me, if I am able to stop her. The cold red bow is looming larger and larger before me. I feel the ice shudder as the bow strikes the pan. I stumble but I am able to regain my footing. I am being pushed before the *Karlsen*'s bow and fearful of being capsized. My God, I wasn't aware that they would go this far. My pan is pushed along for about 30 feet and then pushed aside to drift past the hull of the sealing ship. On her decks, almost two dozen sealers are jeering at me and making obscene gestures. I wave to and rally my crew.

1600 hrs: The *Martin Karlsen* has stopped some 100 yards from us. She is beside a pile of pelts and some sealers are busily engaged in securing the pelts to a winch line which has been paid out from the starboard side and over the ice. An idea flashes and I can see an excellent opportunity to shut down the ship. We begin to move toward the activity by the pile of pelts.

The four sealers stop their work as I approach. They are prepared for me to shout at them; they don't expect our protest to go beyond the verbal attack. I have no intention of wasting my time talking with them. I have already attached a pair of handcuffs to my belt. I walk directly over to the winch line and, with a quick flick of the wrist, secure myself with the cuffs to the line.

The sealers stare at me speechless. The sealers on the deck of the ship begin to chant "Haul ta bye in" and "Giv ta bye a right cold swim." I feel elated that the ship is unable to proceed. Surely they won't attempt to haul in the line and risk killing me. The sealer beside me mutters, "Ye are right daft, bye, we's will killya fo sure."

My heart almost stops when I feel the first tug. The wire line is taut. The two dozen shipboard sealers are cheering and urging the winch man on. I am being pulled off my feet and across the ice. Across 20 feet of jagged ice. My parka and pants have been ripped on the sharp ice. Suddenly, beneath me there is no longer solid ice. I am being hauled through a thick sludge of slush and water. I feel the line pull upward and my body leaves the water and slams against the side of the steel hull. Ten feet above the water I'm hoisted. The line stops, slackens, and I fall back to the water, jerked to a stop while waist deep. Immediately the line tightens again and once more I am hoisted upward. Once more the line slackens and I fall, this time plunging into the water up to my neck. Again I am hoisted, again I am dropped. I'm a mouse on the end of a string being treated as a plaything. On the fourth pull, my belt breaks beneath the strain and I find myself falling five feet, into and under the frigid waters of the north Atlantic. The shock immobilizes me. I can't move my legs, my arms are numbing, my chest feels as if it's on fire. I scream up to the deck, "For God's sake, throw me a rope."

Some turn their thumbs down, others jeer. One sealer yells down to me, "Drown, ya bloody bastard."

Andy Bruce Trial Opens: Convicts Are Fuel for "Justice" Industry

BY TOM SHANDEL, JANUARY 20–27, 1977

The story begins on June 9th, 1975, when three prisoners seize a number of hostages at knifepoint within the B.C. Penitentiary in New Westminster, and ends 41 hours later with the killing of Mary Steinhauser—the most dramatic incident in a series of incidents of prisoner rebellion and acts of defiance within the Canadian penitentiary system.

The Canadian Penitentiary Service and the federal government are under extreme pressure, publicly and politically, from a sudden abundance of inquiries, public and private, in courts and in the media, regarding the conditions for prisoners and guards within maximum-security prisons like the B.C. Pen.

Incredibly, the motive for this exposure has not come from a concerned public or government department but from within the prison walls, and actually from within another prison within the Pen, the super-maximum Solitary Confinement Unit, a small concrete coffin 11 feet by 6 feet, where for violations of prison rules various human beings spend 23 ½ hours for days on end without charge, trial, or appeal, and worst of all without ever knowing how long it will last.

The fear of going back to solitary, where he had already spent 793 days, prompted Andy Bruce's desperate bid for freedom, he testified. Later in December 1975, Bruce was one of eight prisoners who Appeal Court of Canada Judge D.V. Heald found had suffered "cruel and unusual punishment" in contravention of the Canadian Bill of Rights when held in the Solitary Confinement Unit of B.C. Pen.

In the light of all these exposures, a comprehensive examination of our entire prison system is imperative. But on closer examination, the prison system is revealed as just part of a larger system which is the spinal structure of our body politic, our society, our culture.

From the people come the politicians who write the laws in Parliament for the police to monitor and apprehend abusers of public or private property, person or thing, for the Courts of Law with their Lawyers and Clerks to arbitrate over, and for those found a danger to the community, the Prison System will provide the cell, the buildings, the classrooms and shops, the guards and rehabilitation staff, the exercise yard and the dining room, all the amenities necessary to sustain the minimal half-life allowed for people buying their way back to normal life by spending their precious time.

What's a prisoner worth? Four hours for a judge; 50 hours for the lawyers; a hundred hours for the police; an eight-hour shift for the guards every day of the sentence; part of the career for the administrators and criminologists. The prisoner is also an appetite for food suppliers, dry-goods salesmen, drug dispensers (legal and un) to satisfy. The prisoner is an automatic maker of hard news which feeds the entire media machine. When you think the B.C. Pen holds only about 400 to 500 bodies, each prisoner represents a lot of productive employment for many people.

If the justice industry is seen as radiating rings, then right where the pebble drops, right at the heart of the organism, is the super-expensive uranium rod powering the entire reactor, especially caged and carefully guarded in concrete vaults behind bars, locked behind doors locked within locks, right there resides the most unmanageable, unrehabilitatable creation of the justice industry, the state-of-the-art triumph of this technology, the nothing-left-to-lose super convict.

Bruce, Wilson, & Lucas are on trial this week at New West courthouse on charges stemming from the hostage-taking of June 9, 1975. Since the guards involved in the shooting have been cleared and no charge laid, an attempt is being made to charge these three with felony murder, an unusual charge which must prove that the three were guilty of murdering Mary Steinhauser by virtue of keeping her hostage and causing the assault which lead to her death.

An heir to the local Army & Navy Stores fortune was recently convicted of possession of 23 caps of heroin and a gram of cocaine and received a $500.00 fine; on the same day a street user with a record charged with possession of a couple of caps got 10 to 20 years at the Pen.

The Kiss

BY BRITT HAGARTY, JULY 28–AUGUST 4, 1978

It was Christmas Eve of 1972, and I was in Oakalla Prison Farm outside of Vancouver serving two years for possession of heroin. In the afternoon I had an appointment with the dentist down at the hospital, so my supervising officer drove me down in the pickup truck. I was in a restless mood, having spent almost a year in prison already, and I was hoping to get an answer from the parole board within the next few weeks, so when I was let inside of the holding cell outside the dentist's office, I was pleased to see

Jeanne, one of the transvestites from tier three, the cell block across the hall from mine. She was the finest "queen" in the entire prison, and I'd been attracted to her for quite some time. Originally she'd had waist-length black hair, but when she'd been arrested she'd cut it off shoulder-length, and now she had cute bangs which complemented her big blue eyes. When she'd first arrived she'd had enormous breasts, but once she'd been cut off her hormone injections they had slowly started to shrink, but they still looked plump and sexy. Legally she was a man, but she'd had her testicles removed by a doctor in Vancouver, so she had a high feminine voice, and she didn't have to shave. Her complexion was soft and womanly, beautiful, and the velvet choker around her throat and the slight make-up on her eyelids and lashes made her seem even more desirable.

"Oh hi, Jeanne. How's it goin'?"

"Not bad," she said, looking up from the bench where she was sitting with a group of "goofs," inmates, mostly new arrivals, who didn't form a part of our strange subculture. They were wearing tattered baggy pants, baggier shirts, and muddy work boots, while I was wearing a rusty-brown denim jacket, a clean white T-shirt, well-pressed pants, and shiny black loafers. Custom-made to accent my athletic physique, my clothing was made by my friends in the tailor shop because I was one of the "solids," the tough men who formed the upper echelon of the prison hierarchy.

"What a way t' spend Christmas, eh Jeanne!"

"That's for sure!"

"Have you seen the butcher yet?"

"Yeah. He pulled one of my molars already."

"Is he drunk?"

"Nah, he ain't bad today."

As I stared into her eyes I couldn't help but feel attracted to her obvious femininity. I hadn't even spoken to a woman for a long time, and as I felt the sudden glow of lust undulating through my body, I was pleased to see that same desire reflected in her features.

"Hey, c'mere for a sec, Jeanne," I said impulsively, grabbing her hand and drawing her to her feet. I led her around the corner into a small recess where the radiator was situated, almost entirely out of sight of the shabbily dressed goofs. I put my arm around her waist and pulled her tight against my chest. "How about a Christmas kiss, Baby?" Her face was only inches from mine, and it emanated a strange androgynous beauty, which to me, however, was entirely feminine.

"Well, I don't see why not," she said coyly, smiling. We both closed our eyes, then our lips drifted closer together, and as our mouths met, waves of ecstasy radiated through my body. Suddenly her tongue pushed its way gently into my mouth, and I felt her arms pulling me closer to her embrace. For a few seconds our world of iron bars, steel cages, and sneering, violent inmates disappeared, and we lived, beyond time, in the world of sexual delight.

Suddenly the door opened behind us, and I heard a guard's voice bark out, "Sean Gallagher?"

"That's me," I said, stepping back from Jeanne, but still holding her small hand. For a second I looked into her eyes, and I felt as infatuated with her as with any

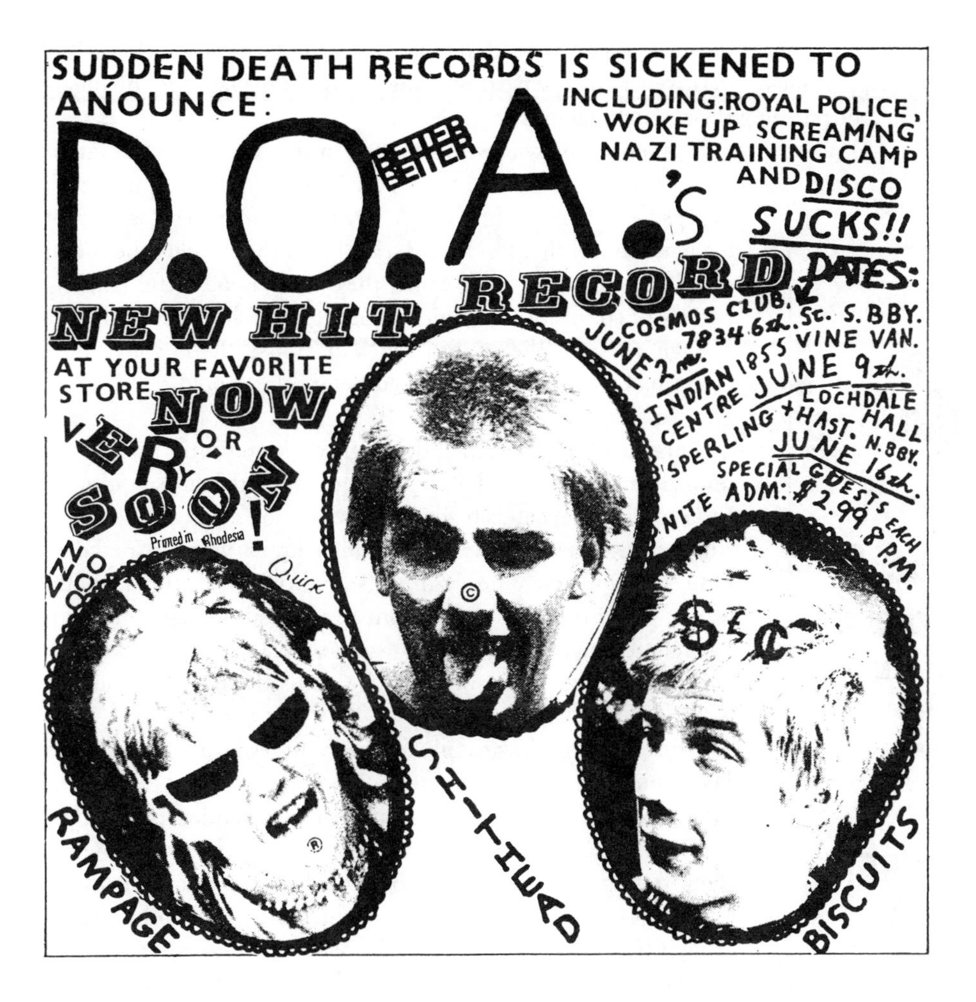

woman I'd ever known. For a tiny moment, we both knew, and saw it in each other's eye, that we had just cheated the guards for a portion of our penance, had left that prison for one brief slice of eternity, and had transcended, not only our personal problems, but time itself, which as I released her hand and turned to go, once again held us cruelly in its cold, uncaring, vicelike grip.

Britt Hagarty first entered Brannen Lake School for Boys in 1965. In 1968 he was sentenced to a year in Haney Correctional Institute for possession of marijuana and trafficking in LSD. In 1971 he was charged with possession of heroin and sentenced to two years less a day. His novel, Prisoner of Desire, *from which this story is extracted, will be published by Talonbooks.*

D.O.A. Alive or Dead?

BY ALEX VARTY, DECEMBER 14–20, 1979

In a move that left fans stunned and drew low moans of relief from parents, policemen, and civic officials across the continent, Vancouver's D.O.A. has apparently decided to call it quits. Manager Ken Lester phoned me on Monday night with the news that guitarist Joey Shithead, bassist Randy Rampage, and drummer Chuck Biscuits had come to a relatively amicable parting of the ways, and that all three members would be pursuing their individual musical projects.

D.O.A. has been together for almost two years, and in that time they had established themselves as Canada's finest and one of North America's best punk-rock groups. At their peak, D.O.A. created a merciless assault of dynamic sound that's indelibly seared into the frontal lobes of all who heard them. At their worst, they made a god-awful jangling barrage of confusion and unintelligible gibberish that was still raw enough to scare the uninitiated and amuse the devoted. The group had the good sense to fold before they could seriously be accused of being boring.

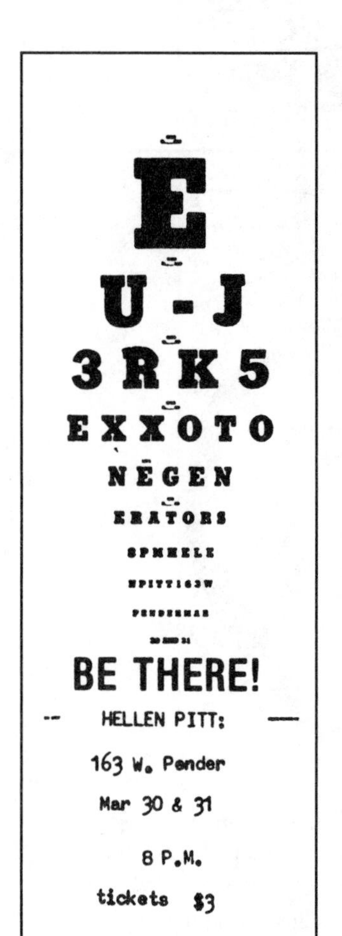

I first saw D.O.A. at their debut gig on March 11th, 1978, at the now defunct Japanese Hall, home to many of the city's best punk and experimental bands before city fire marshals closed it down on trumped-up charges. Frankly, I didn't know what to make of D.O.A.'s hyperactive heavy-metal sound, which featured a solid wall of guitar noise, crashing drums, and vocals force-fed through a barely adequate public address system, so I carefully picked my way through the hordes of spikey-headed kids and went home to listen to Roxy Music.

After catching the group a few more times, it became obvious that something a little more serious than beer-drinking and hell-raising was at work. The group's first extended-play single confirmed that view. It bore comparison to the seminal English punk-rock groups of the year before while showing a distinctly Canadian hard-rock influence, introducing the call-and-response group vocals that lifted the band above the one-dimensional sound of other local new-wave groups. While a lot of latecoming posers have seen punk as just a way to shock older people while wearing funny clothes and consuming vast quantities of alcohol, many of D.O.A.'s public pronouncements have been overtly political. Their first record jibed at our image-conscious but none-too-scrupulous RCMP, while sticking the first pin into the now nearly deflated disco balloon.

The month that followed the ep's release found the band giving one of their best concerts ever at, of all places, the Body Shop, courtesy of the first *Georgia Straight* Battle of the Bands. D.O.A. didn't win—all the record-company representatives and radio jocks made sure of that—but to my mind they gave the most satisfying performance of any band in attendance.

After the Body Shop, D.O.A. packed up the token $300 snare drum that Chuck Biscuits won as a consolation prize and headed off to the States. Joey won instant notoriety and a place in San Francisco's punk hall of fame by pissing off the stage of the Mabuhay Gardens into the drink of a loud and obnoxious glass-throwing female heckler. That's the sort of stunt that a lot of D.O.A.'s public image has been based on, but those who dismissed the band as musical terrorists just out to shock were ignoring the fact that by this time D.O.A. had developed into a really tight unit.

After a long tour of Canada and the States, the group returned to Vancouver for a concert at UBC's Student Union Ballroom that would turn out to be an amusing but less than grand finale.

It was a bizarre show from the beginning. The student promoter began by making ridiculous demands and by showing a total ignorance of the new-wave ethos. The bands involved sat by feeling thoroughly cynical about the whole confusing business. Everything was untangled and the concert went ahead as scheduled, but from the moment D.O.A. hit the stage the tension in the air was evident. On one hand there were the punks, out for a good time but not necessarily prepared to stick around for a long time. In contrast, a platoon of red-sweatered, hired goons from the Engineering Society were out to maintain their concept of law 'n' order on their home turf. Their blow-dried hackles were visibly raised by the sight of all the leather, dirty denim, and haywire haircuts.

At first, D.O.A. played well, but as soon as a fan attempted to climb onto the stage—not an uncommon or an unwelcome event at punk concerts—half a dozen amateur rent-a-cops submerged him in a heaving scrum of bodies. This happened a couple of times before Biscuits blew up, knocked over a drum or two, and stormed offstage. The volatile drummer was quickly subdued. The concert went on with the band's manger doing the bouncing with a bit more subtlety and tact.

After a while the seething engineers piled en masse onto a hapless fan who seemed too close to gaining the stage. Biscuits threw down his drumsticks and joined the fray, whereupon a score or so of D.O.A.'s followers and unconnected punk fanatics stormed the stage. In the ensuing clash, the band's drum kit was thoroughly trashed, some large stage curtains came tumbling down, and the chastened engineers were run offstage. I later saw them sheepishly licking their wounds in a nearby Chinese restaurant.

But before the big altercation, D.O.A. had played some of the most magnificently angry and powerful music of their career.

If D.O.A. really has broken up for good, I have to congratulate them on their timing. Punk rock has been the single most significant musical movement of the decade, because it's cleared out some of the cobwebs and dope-induced fantasies that threatened to make rock 'n' roll just another entertainment industry. But it's an inherently confining musical style, bounded by negativity, two or three easily repeated riffs, and an unwillingness to progress that's just as stultifying as the lack of forward motion found in the offices of the big record companies. D.O.A. was caught between its individual members' creative desires and its commitment as a group to the sound of London, 1977. The breakup is probably the best option for both their listeners and the musicians themselves, even with commercial success just over the horizon.

ALTERED STATES

Drama

BY TOM CRIGHTON, AUGUST 5–12, 1976

The Douglas fir stood majestic, immovable, pointing Godward, like a finger of truth as I clung to it, trying hard not to throw up.

Getting drunk in the Cecil is fine, but getting drunk at a Sunday-afternoon picnic is quite inexcusable. It was the most dramatic thing that happened all week. Sunday was one of those days when I didn't really want to be me. I would have felt much better as Lord Killanin or Jim McQueen.

Buntzen Lake is a B.C. Hydro reservoir in Ioco. Ioco is not an Indian word meaning "the place where the waters meet." It's an acronym of the Imperial Oil Company. Other important acronyms are radar, nylon, and Fiat.

Lord Killanin is not an acronym; he is an anachronism. Jim McQueen is neither. He is a wonderful actor who will be seen in *Chinamen*, by Michael Frayn, opening at the New City Stage August 11th. Lord Killanin plans to spend the next four years in hibernation.

They don't allow power boats on Buntzen Lake, which is very thoughtful, but they do allow you to get drunk, fall over children, frighten dogs, throw Frisbees into people's conversation, and make cutting remarks (from a distance) about torquey little tattooed men from Coquitlam. I should have stayed home and tried to get an interview with Jim McQueen.

Canoeists are funny folk. They truck around these great long canoes looking for lakes, spend hours preparing and unloading hundreds of dollars' worth of bright-orange equipment, and, eventually getting it all together, paddle around for ten minutes and then go home. I suspect they also go to golf courses and play one hole.

Of course, the only way to enjoy the great outdoors is to take as much of the great indoors with you as possible. For this reason they are now building Winnebagos with basements. I think it was Voltaire who said "Marriage is the only adventure a fool can partake of." I would say camping is another. Campgrounds are designed to make people look ridiculous. They should have big signs outside saying "No Overnight Cynics."

The opposite of a campground is a theatre. Theatres are designed to make people look intelligent. This is achieved by getting them to sit quietly in the dark. Any trace of lunacy, which would be very obvious in the afternoon sun, can be hidden quite well in the still of the back row.

That beautifully sedate German gentleman sitting behind you is the same nutcase who will kick footballs into your salad, rearrange the picnic tables, and sing hiking songs till half-past three.

The theatre is a tranquillizer, if not a downer, for most people. Their behaviour improves, they become much more self-conscious and eager to please. The hedonistic anarchy of the campground is nowhere to be found. They stand patiently in queues, applaud at the right times, don't smoke, and buy drinks in the intervals. Over the years I've probably sat beside cannibals, communists, murderers, and social workers without ever feeling any fear or prejudice. It's amazing what a little darkness can do....

Catnapping at the All-Canadian Drive-in

BY JOHN HASLETT CUFF, JUNE 9–16, 1977

Once a year my lady and I make a pilgrimage to a drive-in movie theatre. It's usually a spur-of-the-moment decision when I'm desperate and in need of fodder for the column, but sometimes it's strictly for fun.

Last Sunday we went to the Lougheed Drive-in for both those reasons and one other, in the long run probably more important.

In six weeks' time we are moving to Toronto, taking a leisurely trip across the country in an Econoline Super Van.

We will be accompanied by two cats, both eight years old, one a male and one a female. So last Sunday we had the brilliant idea of going to the drive-in to see *Garden of the Dead* and *Rabid*, utilizing the excursion to acclimatize the two cats to motor-vehicle travel.

The male cat, who once previously suffered a minor nervous breakdown, was easy to corner and load into the van. He immediately sought out a dark corner and cowered there for the duration of the first movie, *Garden of the Dead*, before emerging to order a hotdog and a large Coke. The female, however, put up a helluva fight and inflicted savage lacerations on my forearms before being subdued and bundled into the van. Once inside, though, she relaxed immediately and lounged regally on the built-in bed, occasionally checking out the action on the screen.

Frankly, the action on the screen was rather less interesting. *Garden of the Dead* was happily truncated to placate the raucous Sunday-night crowd, which sounded diesel horns and wolf whistles in disapproval for its entire length.

The film concerned a camp of formaldehyde-sniffing convicts, a number of whom escape, are shot, and then return from the dead to terrorize their former companions. The scenes in which they suck and snort the formaldehyde vapours were funny in a campy way, but the rest was a predictable imitation of *Night of the Living Dead*.

Rabid, the main feature, starring Marilyn Chambers of *Behind the Green Door* notoriety, was a cut or two above *Garden of the Dead* in concept and execution.

Miss Chambers is a surprisingly wholesome girl who reminds one of the bionic woman, Lindsay Wagner. She is nearly killed in a motorcycle accident and miraculously brought back to health with injections and skin grafts which have the unpleasant side effect of turning her rabid. The victims she infects with a bloody penis-like extension which emerges from a wound in her armpit grow bloodthirsty and foam at the mouth.

Of course it is all rather silly, and not at all scary. But production values are higher than you'd expect, and there are a lot of snappy camera angles that lend the show some veneer of class and professionalism.

The only thing that makes the film [directed by David Cronenberg] interesting besides Miss Chambers's participation is the fact that it is a Canadian production partially financed by the CFDC and Famous Players Corporation.

The producer is Ivan Reitman, who first rose to the surface with a low-budget flick called *Cannibal Girls*, which proved that Canadian films could make money if they were gory and exploitative enough.

They Got Plenty of Nothin'

BY TED LATURNUS, DECEMBER 23, 1976–JANUARY 6, 1977

Behold the jazz fan. Discerning. Suspicious. Eccentric. Head cocked to one side, jaw piously thrust forward, critical faculties and sensibilities at the ready to sniff out any missed key changes, sloppy linkups, or improper improvisations. Alert and determined to pick up on every note, nuance, subtlety, melody, and theme. On this occasion, being the first annual Jingle Jazz Festival, there were over two dozen of these musical stalwarts in attendance at the Planetarium auditorium.

Behold the jazz musician. Desperate. Cynical. Hopeful. Broke. Axe resting familiarly in hands that have driven countless cabs and eked out untold millions of C notes, modal improvisations, and D7th diminutives. Wallet at the ready to snatch any meagre returns that may capriciously float his way. Sensibilities and dreams continuously bludgeoned by the sour realities of the music biz. Still he plays on.

Behold the jazz reviewer. Hardened. Moody. Hounded. Pen poised to jot down any development, statistic, or movement. Deadlines, editors, and debtors hovering overhead. Personal prejudices and musical standards endlessly at odds with each other. Threats by disgruntled fans and musicians rumbling around in his subconscious.... "Jingle Jazz; what the hell can I say about THIS number?? It's Christmas, for Chrissakes!! How DO these guys make a living??"

The Nights Before Christmas

BY D.M. FRASER, NOVEMBER 24–DECEMBER 1, 1977

It's beginning again. Here it comes, only six weeks ahead of schedule, the Season to be Jolly, relentlessly jolly, expensively jolly, jollier than thou. About two thousand years ago, according to legend, some otherwise unremarkable kid in the Middle East had messianic delusions and a terrific Public Relations team, and as a consequence a perfectly innocuous pagan festival—the Winter Solstice—got transformed into the annual debauch that's already merely 30 shopping days away. (Aside: what, exactly, is a Shopping Day? "Mummy, can we go to the zoo today?" "No, dear, it's a Shopping Day and I have to shop.") Anyway, since it's categorically impossible to ignore Christmas, I've decided to do the next best thing, for your benefit and mine, and get it over with a few weeks before it actually happens.

All right. Lately I've been getting a bit of flak because the last couple of columns have been "negative" and depressing, and isn't the world shitty enough without my reminding people of it…and so forth. So I'm hell-bent and determined that this piece is gonna be cheerful, uplifting, inspirational, affirmative, and as positive as a pregnancy test; let's see those smiles stretch all the way from Woodward's to Eaton's. Let's start practising niceness now, because with only 30 (count 'em) shopping days left, and professional shoppers being notoriously not-nice at the best of times, there may not be an opportunity later. You really want to have a Merry Christmas, don't you? You can hardly wait for that transcendent moment when you truck over to the parking lot and pick out your very own stunted spruce, haul it home, drape a variety of nonrepresentational art objects on its branches, and plug in the lights, thereby providing yourself and your loved ones with (take your choice) a fire hazard, an eyesore, and a great many dead needles on the carpet. You like nothing better than addressing Christmas cards ("Jerry and Suzy? They didn't send *us* one last year, let's cut them off"); of course, since you read the *Straight*, your cards will be in impeccable taste, no Santas or reindeer or Baby Jesuses for you; no, you'll have artwork from underdeveloped nations and native peoples, and every card you mail will put another penny in the Old Man's Hat Fund. You're grateful for Christmas because it gives you a chance to kill two touchy birds with one stone: you can buy up all Aunt Judy's hideous pottery, relieving your familial conscience and making her happy; then you can wrap it up and give it away to your friends, solving the perennial problem of What Do We Give to the Whatstheirnames This Year. Without Christmas, the whole delicate fabric of western society would surely unravel.

How dearly we love illusion, and this is the season in which we pay it homage. Christmas is the largest and most unrepentantly foolish of our ritual non-events; and it's an orgy of illusions. One of the memorably insignificant crises of my own childhood was realizing, not that Santa Claus didn't exist, but that I couldn't tell my parents that I didn't believe in him—in case *they* believed in him. Years later, in Vancouver, lacking the inclination or means to buy the real thing, I fashioned a Christmas tree out of stolen wire, managed to make it look vaguely tree-shaped, and hung cut-out squares of cardboard from its metallic limbs, each one with a word on it: "ornament," "candle," "light," "tinsel,"

"star." It sufficed. The illusions one creates oneself, knowing them for what they are, tend to be more serviceable than those one borrows or inherits. 'Round about now, the churchy folks are going to be telling us, as they can never resist doing, that Christmas has become too commercial, that we ought to put the Christ back in it, etc. They're wondrously wrong. Christ is, and always was, no more than a convenient pretext, an attractive figurehead to open and bless the parliament of commerce. When we achieve the perfect Consumer State, we can easily dispense with him, though we may keep a little of the symbolism around to appease diehard sentimentalists.

Among whom, reluctantly and nervously, I have to include myself. The primary reason for writing about Christmas now, rather than when it happens, is that by the end of November I'm sufficiently sell-shocked to loathe the whole idea; anything I might have to say on the subject by then would be mean, nasty, cynical, and utterly out of keeping with what we're supposed to think of as the Spirit of the Season. By the time the Hare-lip Angels have sung their millionth carol, by the time the 20th overpackaged hausfrau collapses under the weight of her generosity in the basement of the Bay, I won't have any opinions about Christmas. And that's too bad.

It's too bad because most of us, whatever absurd roads we've taken in our lives, have probably at least once felt *something* around this time of year. A certain amount of traditional bullshit piles up in our emotional backyards no matter how diligently we try to shovel it out. Think of it as a fertilizer, of a kind. We wouldn't perpetuate these ridiculous festivals unless, at some level of ourselves we're incapable of comprehending, we desired them, needed them, depended on them. Gross as they've become, these occasions are our major functional excuse for...solidarity. So you might as well list me with the sentimentalists, right now.

In other words, pageantry is a requisite of history: events in the world, in our lives, are defined more often than not by the manner in which the knowledge of them is preserved, not by their own intrinsic character. Every culture invents and evolves symbologies the purpose of which is simply to freeze and store a particular aspect of its own sense of itself. So we have our holidays, of whatever nature, and invest them with the trappings of myth and fantasy, which are infinitely more satisfying than any plausible reality; and while in truth our celebrations may be as mendacious as the child who just *pretends* to believe in Santa Claus, the pretence is essential to the ceremony: it's the reason for it.

We can take other examples at random. The Grey Cup. Who gives a howling fuck about the actuality of two crews of steak-fed anthropoids making mock-warfare over a dead pig? You'd have to be crazy to care, but care we do, and surround the pitiful occasion with as much pomp as circumstance can afford. (Lest you suppose I'm being snotty, I want to tell you that I absolutely intend to watch the complete goddamn circus, and will scream and yell with unqualified enthusiasm for whatever side a flip of the coin decides I'm on.) Or there's your birthday, on which—if you're lucky—people give you congratulations and presents in honour of the prodigious achievement of having been born. Or there are funerals, by which the dead get a last chance to comfort the sort-of living. Or weddings, which a few people still use to legalize their lusts and consolidate their property. Or...make up your own. In any event, the meaning resides in the observation, not in the thing observed.

Given the situation as it is, then, we may as well try to be jolly for the next month. Deck the halls, and the pissoirs too. String up those strings of pointy little lights, hunt through your neighbourhood Bargain Mart for edible plastic mistletoe, and bear firmly in mind that *Ho-ho-ho* is only three syllables removed, linguistically, from *Ho-ho-ho-chi-minh.*

Workers Rejoice for TV Listings!

LETTERS, DECEMBER 8–15, 1978

Congratulations, Brothers and Sisters!

Workers everywhere may rejoice at your courageous decision to resume publication of the weekly TV listings. Such service to the people is welcome in a newspaper that some have criticized as having succumbed to the tawdry lure of decadent bourgeois diversions.

As you may recall, I last wrote you slightly more than a year ago, protesting the discontinuation of those TV schedules. While long overdue, the decision to resume this valuable service is both progressive and correct.

Continue your program of rigorous self-criticism and do not fail to catch *Leave It to Beaver*, five days a week at 5 p.m., Channel 11. June continues to caution Ward that she is worried about the Beaver.

Long Live Enver Hoxha,
Elmo Knit

bill bissett

EXCERPTS FROM AN INTERVIEW BY ALAN TWIGG, JUNE 2–9, 1978

Vancouver's bill bissett is a poet, painter, publisher and pacifist.

Representing Canada at an international gathering of sound poets in Glasgow earlier this month, bissett was the toast of his colleagues. He is the most sought-after poet for readings in Canadian schools. CanLit critics Eli Mandel and Warren Tallman have sworn up and down that bissett is a precious and nonrenewable cultural resource.

No matter. In the federal Parliament bissett has been the subject of a six-month-old brouhaha over the fact that Canadian taxpayers have been subsidizing his allegedly profane poetry.

"It's lousy, it's childish, and it doesn't say anything," Tory MP John Fraser (Vancouver South) has said of bissett's work.

Led by Tory MP Bob Wenman (Fraser Valley West), a nucleus of Conservatives have been urging their constituents to complain to the Canada Council about its support of bissett and his "blewointmentpress."

In a form letter titled *Sex. Filth. Smut. Dirt.*, Tories Arnold Malone and Jack Ellis have claimed, "One poem is merely a succession of four letter words dealing with slander against religion, speaking of body excretions and sex acts."

Besides espousing the limitation of Canada Council autonomy and offering to distribute copies of bissett's work without the author's permission, Malone and Ellis claim, "Talonbooks has received at least $74,000 for the publication of obscene literature."

Criticism of bissett surfaced in December, coincidental with the publication of *A Legacy of Spending*, by Vancouver's CJOR hot-liner, Ed Murphy. The Murphy book, which has sold over 30,000 copies, contains bissett poems reprinted without permission.

Perhaps bissett's popularity in the public schools has alarmed the Tories? Perhaps they fear bill bissett is the reincarnation of '60s idealism and dissatisfaction, a potential Pied Piper preying on the rapidly dwindling vestiges of liberalism?

Make no mistake about it, bill bissett's poetry is political. The man is an absolute pacifist. How much more subversive can you get? In our uptight, money-tight '70s, any poet who declares "iam not aftr anything" and obviously means it is going against the grain of our production-oriented materialist society. The man is either a saint or a fool. So he must be dangerous.

Twigg: When you started blewointment, was it the starving-artist routine, eating potatoes and Kraft dinners?

bissett: Yeh. Living on welfare and stuff like that.

Twigg: Then you got busted?

bissett: Then me and this folk singer from Seattle got busted. We were like the second bust in Vancouver. It was really a hot thing. A big deal and shit like that. I was going to make this movie with the CBC after that about how grass is good for you. The social workers were trying to take our child away. The police were coming all the time and I was getting beaten up. It was getting really bizarre.

Twigg: How come you got all this persecution laid on you?

bissett: There wasn't that many people into it yet.

Twigg: So that was your first hassle with the authorities?

bissett: No, before that they took our daughter away from us a couple of times. Because she didn't have pants on or something. We got hassles because we were artists. The police used to come in and say why do you paint like this? Weird shit like that. We were pre-hippie, post-beatnik. They didn't know what destruction we might do. All we were doing was painting and writing and living and smoking a little dope.

Twigg: You got busted again in the '60s, is that right?

bissett: For possession. It was another big hoopla with a two-year trial. But it was like old times for me. Things got raging in the '70s with a bit more council support. This year blewointment got a $2,000 increase, so we're printing nine books on $6,800.

Twigg: Compared to other publishers, that's not much.

bissett: It's the fourth-lowest block grant in the country. Me and Allen (Rosen) are running $7,000 in debt all the time. You keep hanging in there and conditions eventually improve. The dope thing isn't so heavy anymore. No one is frightened by paintings anymore. Concrete poetry doesn't scare people so much now.

Twigg: But when you look around now, don't you see the pendulum in society swinging back to the right, away from all that '60s energy?

bissett: Yeh, a conservative backlash. But that conservative backlash is funny, because the revolution never got off the ground. We're having a backlash without even having had a revolution! It's very Canadian!...

Artists Are Bums

BY DOUG COLLINS, DECEMBER 15–22, 1978

Artists—meaning actors and such like—have always been bums. Some of them have been bums who bring a little light into our lives, and others have been bums plain and simple. In pre-Elizabethan England, there used to be laws against them, it frequently being felt that to have the actors around meant you stood a good chance of having your pocket picked.

The bums plain and simple are still at it. Through the Canada Council, through the Secretary of State's office, through the city (any city), and so on. And only the other day there they were on the steps of Vancouver courthouse, whining away like mad because the feds, responding to taxpayers' howls and viewing with alarm the forthcoming election, have decided to tighten up a bit. Doom. Gloom.

Their piteous cries are heard all over. No doubt even Toronto has had to endure them, since one hears about something like the 1812 Committee digging in in that Athens of the North, apparently eager to save their grants come what may. But if *our* bums are to be believed, the Vancouver performance was prologue to a movement that is going to sweep the country. Yea, even unto the halls of Parliament itself.

Their show was full of mellerdrama. Take away the Canada Council grants, the National Film Board cushion, cut the CBC budget, and Vancouver will become, "culturally speaking," a ghost town, it was averred. And what the Philistines were really saying, we were told, was that "Canada doesn't really want a soul." Adding enjoyment to the performance (for the likes of rednecks like me, at any rate) was the statement that unemployed artists should register with Manpower so that their numbers could be counted. Hell, half of them are on the pogey already, which is where they've always been. Counting them up would be no trouble.

The fact is that our artistic pickpockets have had it too good for too long. Take the CBC, for instance (and, if you wish, take it right out to sea). For years and years it has been an actor's welfare agency. I'm not talking here about the odd good play or ballet that that fat old lady puts on, but about the black hole of CBC Radio. It still puts on *plays*, for God's sake. And when did *you* last listen to a radio play? Exactly. And *why* does the CBC put on radio plays? Because it has an actors' union breathing down its neck all the time and doesn't have the guts to tell it to screw off and get honest work. Not when it can reach into the public purse to continue its bad ways, that is. If the CBC had to balance its books, it would be Hail and Farewell to the good old world of radio plays, all right.

As with CBC Radio, so in large measure with the Canada Council and other national welfare agencies. In the 20 years of the council's existence, it has managed to get rid of about $400 million, rising to a crescendo in the last financial year of about $64 million. People have become used to being subsidized, and when the Big Milk Cow in Ottawa fails to squirt every time, anguished yells are heard on the courthouse steps. Well, let them yell. Better still, let them hold a bake sale or put on a bingo bonanza, for it is worth noting that private financial support for the arts has decreased in proportion to the increase in government funding. But the old private donors would never have given a cent to four-letter-word-so-called poets like lower-case bill bissett, who has done very well out of the Canada Council, thank you.

Or poetry, for that matter. It is not, you understand, that this writer hates the theatre. He is frequently seen gaping at the wonders of the stage. But he sees no reason why the state welfare system should be extended to village arts. Did Dylan Thomas, the greatest lyric poet in English of the 20th century, get any grants? Did Bill Shakespeare put the touch on Queen Elizabeth to keep the Globe Theatre going? Hell, those guys thought themselves lucky to stay out of jail.

Sunstroke

BY TOM SHANDEL, JULY 28–AUGUST 4, 1978

Wreck Beach is a hard place to try to write an article? A beach and theatre don't mix? Hah! Wreck Beach *is* theatre. Everyone plays to the sun.

Folks just love to do their turns, show their licks. The male gays are parading like bronzed mannequins, noticeable only by their razor-trimmed blown-dry hair, their gleaming teeth, and gold neck chains. The surviving flower children, pigtails flouncing with special proprietary abandon, still hoping that the nudity they think they discovered in 1968 will uncover the world and give peace a chance, are busy at Frisbee.

I love them all: the clowns, weirdos, freaks, and plain folks with kids and lovers, hanging out in the all-together.

Wreck Beach is definitely the absolutely best place to be on a hot July afternoon for a sometime drama critic, especially midweek, when all the unemployed, including most actors, directors, and writers, are also exposing themselves.

Naturally I never look, closely. Wreck Beach is for allowing the sun to blind the outer eye. The scene is interior....

It's a Bird! It's a Plane! No, It's the Maharishi!

BY BOB MERCER, JULY 7–14, 1978

The Maharishi Mahesh Yogi, high-flying prophet of Transcendental Meditation (TM), may soon be grounded, if Swami Vishnu Devananda has his way.

The swami has asked B.C.'s Ministry of Consumer and Corporate Affairs to investigate TM for apparent violations of the Trade Practices Act following an ad campaign in which the Maharishi offered, for a price, to teach the secret of levitation.

"The Maharishi," says the swami, "is giving religion a bad name.

"To me, it is the same as it would be to you if someone claimed to have a copyright on the Ten Commandments, was charging $4,000 to teach them, and claimed that knowledge of them would give the power to walk on water like Jesus."

Whether or not the Maharishi has the secret of human levitation—and presumably Swami Vishnu Devananda's legal action will settle that question—the blatant hucksterism of the TM pitch serves to bring into focus that weakness within some of the New Age seekers which American theologian Harvey Cox calls "spiritual gluttony."

"We've all been raised in a society where that propensity to gluttony is pervasive, and it fastens on different things," Cox told *East-West Journal* editor Sherman Goldman. "Now, since we have almost all the things we want materially, we go to the acquisition of spiritual goodies; adding up groovy experiences, ecstatic experiences, wonderful teachers, all of that."

Spotting Trends: Time for a New Highway into the '80s, an Energy Lifestyle Exposition at the PNE

BY DONNA STURMANIS, MAY 17–23, 1979

You were just getting into gear when the '60s turned into the '70s and already it's the '80s. How are you supposed to keep up with Time, man? Look for a sign.

It's not long before you see it—a brilliant coloured mandala composed of lions' heads and hands holding jewelled objects. Back comes that old but familiar rush of acid trips and hot Santana nights, and you know you must go where it tells you: "Trends '79—Energy Lifestyle Exposition" in the Showmart and Food Buildings at the PNE.

Soon you are standing at the entrance of a huge hall. Giant banners and streamers suspended from the mile-high ceiling billow in the cool wind which blows from the depths of the building. You read excerpts from the guidebook in your hand: "TRENDS '79 is for you and me today, to help us make the most of tomorrow...we have a number of professional and/or eccentric people who'd just love to get their message across to you. We'll show you everything, but most of all we'll show you how to have a good time and a great life!" You never knew it would be this easy.

And so you begin your journey among the displays: you're pleased to know the artisans of the future will still be making sandals, batiks, pottery, and hash pipes.

If you could jump into the '80s on this Sundance trampoline, you could also fly into it on that unreal Aurora candy-striped hang-glider over there. But your New Age Debut must not be merely physical, but spiritual as well. Take the path of total awareness with Eckankar; get to know the complete, integrated system of Polarity therapy; listen to John Denver talk about the Hunger Project at the est booth.

Life in the '80s could be a rugged mountain journey in a Suzuki four-wheel drive, a lazy Windjammer Barefoot cruise, or a gig in Sunshine Recreational Paradise. Perhaps a swim in a solar-heated pool, a massage in a jiggling chair, a rest on a waterbed. And it will be easy to keep warm with all that insulation and a new fresh-air fireplace. Thing is, the only money you've got is a carefully folded $10 bill which you are saving for when you get the munchies later.

You drift over to the workshop area and take in Marcus Bell, who is doing an illustrated talk on self-composting toilets. At least these guys have their shit together.

After momentarily spacing out on the pyramids of golden B.C. honey, your quest brings you to the table of Edible Dried Goods, from Penticton, B.C., manufacturers of a product called fruit leather. You try some for free, and realize how neat it would be to have some Apple-Raisin hiking boots made.

Then you hear mysterious music—sax and xylophone—and are drawn irresistibly toward it. Will you find the Kublai Khan, Alice, or the Wizard of Oz? Only Trends Exposition and Marketing Ltd. knows for sure....

Out Tramping Where the Runways Were Never Built

BY GEORGE WOODCOCK, FEBRUARY 2–8, 1979

I have always had a special feeling for the islands of the Fraser Delta—always, that is, since I first came to live in Vancouver from the Island 26 years ago. I remember them when they were almost entirely occupied by vegetable farms and market gardens and a few dairy holdings. A remarkably high proportion of Vancouver's vegetables and bush fruit was grown there, in those days before we became so wretchedly dependent on Californian agribusiness, and a weekly expedition from early summer to late autumn was devoted to buying produce at prices that now seem unimaginably cheap; one often completed the trip by going on to buy salmon for 40 or 50 cents a pound on the wharves at Steveston.

It only endeared me more to the delta islands when I realized that the largest, Lulu Island, was named after Colonel Moody's friend, the actress Lulu Sweet, who in 1859, in high gold-rush British Columbia, softened the misogynist heart of Amor de Cosmos with a vigorous yet "chaste" presentation at the Theatre Royal in Victoria of *Lucrezia Borgia*!

But recently, since the developers have crowded the truck gardens of Lulu Island down toward the southerly dikes, we have tended to wander instead to Iona Island, to watch the great assemblages of seabirds in marshes redolent of the fragrance of Vancouver's not especially efficient sewage plant, and to the northern side of Sea Island, which is a quarter of an hour's drive from my home over the bridges and along the fringes of the airport, though when I am there, strolling beside the north branch of the Fraser, I can imagine walking over the water to the horse farms of Southlands and reaching the escarpment where my home is built in no more than 14 minutes.

On Sea Island, between the airport fence and the river, stretches one of those familiar areas—former farms and suburban lots—whose owners a few years ago were victims of one of the great unnecessary battles with the Department of Transport when they were dispossessed to make new runways for a growth of air traffic that has not materialized. The farmers ceased to cultivate their fertile alluvial land, took the derisory compensation offered, and departed. The buildings were razed. The farms have returned to hayland. Now not even the hay is cut. And the runways have never been built, partly because they are not really needed, partly because of the protests of environmental and other citizens' groups over the prospect of even larger jets using the airport, and partly because of the recent cuts in government expenditure. Good

houses have been destroyed; good land is going unfarmed, and all to no economic purpose or social benefit.

Yet there is one way in which social outrage has produced a kind of magical regeneration, an example of the way nature reasserts itself even on the edges of the city once it gets the slightest chance. In the deserted gardens the trees and shrubs grow at will in their natural shapes, with great cascades of roses falling in early summer into amethyst lakes of blossoming thistles, and fruit hanging in gemlike abundance—smaller and sourer every year—on the unpruned apple and pear trees. It is like one of those yearning romantic gardens that appeared in French films of the 1940s, or like Swinburne's "A Forsaken Garden."

We go there to pick walnuts for pickling, to gather mint, to collect filberts in season, to pluck the roses and sturdy lilies that survive among the couch grass: a writer's household engaged in a parody of pioneer scrounging, with due deference to Catharine Parr Traill.

And, as Mrs. Traill would have done, we watch the vast bird population that has returned with the passing of man. The thistles attract big wandering flocks of gold and purple finches; companies of bush tits flutter and dangle in the bushes, their voices needle thin; flocks of robins gorge on the tiny cherries; pheasants and red-shafted flickers yell across the ruined lawns; pileated woodpeckers tap out their Morse on the lichen-dappled power poles that have survived the destruction of the houses; the long grass rustles with voles; rabbits hop in and out of the unmown tussocks, the piebald offspring of escaped pets.

But nature strikes its own unaided balance. In the gardens the voles and young rabbits are preyed on by fat stray cats; hawks and harriers hover and pounce; and in the meadows an ecumenical congregation of predators gathers. One field is usually the province of great blue herons standing statuesque as they watch for the voles that seem to be a more predictable prey than the frogs who live among the floating beer bottles in the scummed ditches. In the next field, especially toward sunset, the owls emerge from the trees where they spend the daytime, mostly short-eared owls with gleaming golden eyes like cats, but sometimes the paler, more ghostly barn owls, swooping heavily over the tops of the tall grasses.

Most evenings we see the herons standing silently in their field, if they are not fishing out in the salt marshes, and the owls hunting or sitting on the fence posts in their own territories. But the night I am remembering we witness a dramatic confrontation. We turn the last corner through the treed gardens into the open meadows, and the gleaming evening sky is filled with the image of an avian battle. Returning to their nesting trees across the Fraser in the University Endowment Lands, four herons are crossing the owls' field, immense, black, primeval as archaeopteryx against the golden light. The owls have risen to meet them, clumsy as old Handley-Pages with their lumbering wings and great round heads. A hawk and two gulls have become elegantly involved in the complex gyrations.

For a moment it seems we are in another era; that the battles of humankind belong to an extinct species. The natural world has returned to its ancient hostilities. One expects carnage, owls speared on herons' lancelike bills, herons torn by the curved beaks of owls and the talons of hawks, predators destroying predators. But wisdom prevails, as presumably it must in the presence of owls. The herons go on to provide for their families a supper of half-digested voles; the owls return to terrorizing rodents; the grim harmonies of the world have re-established themselves.

It is doubtless human folly to seek a moral in all this, but since our minds are made that way, let me say that the thought I gained from it all is that nature manages its affairs superbly without unnecessary cruelty when it is left alone by Man, whose self-appointed role as Lord of the Universe is just about as irrelevant to the good of living beings (including himself) as the self-appointed role of the Persian King of Kings has been to the good of the people of Iran.

Al Neil: Music at the Centre

EXCERPTS FROM AN INTERVIEW BY ALEX VARTY, FEBRUARY 5–26, 1982

There's only one Al Neil. An obvious statement when one considers that all humans are unique and individual, but whether by freak of nature or through his own lifelong search for the true and the strange, Al Neil is more unique than most. Pianist, sculptor, composer, poet, diarist, recluse (reckless), philosopher, and tippler of homemade red wine. Al Neil is all these things in one. He ties his life and his art up into one multidisciplinary sack—not pausing to consider these divisions thought up by critics and casual observers—slings that bundle over his shoulders, and forges bravely out into a world where Coast Indian petroglyphs collide with Bud Powell's mad piano and Kenneth Patchen's poetry, where wine in the morning mixes with Taoist and Zen esoterica, where the cops on the beat, as ever, don't recognize true genius (crawling down the middle of the Dollarton Highway at 2:00 a.m.), where every day is an adventure of sorts to be savoured and later worked into the fabric of the man's living art.

I still remember the first time that I saw Al Neil play music. The experience is still vivid. This diminutive person of indeterminate age materialized from out of nowhere, dressed in a Sally Ann approximation of a Kwakiutl shaman's garb, and proceeded to play a program of solo piano which held me transfixed. The music swirled and spun around a lucent centre, interspersed with vocal commentaries which speared flashing moments of emotion with unerring poetic accuracy. I was new to the West Coast and felt I was being instructed in the hidden mysteries and moods of the rain forest, mountains, and surf by some primordial nature spirit.

In retrospect, that was the best Al Neil concert that I've seen to date. Some of his more recent appearances have been almost as powerful, but, on occasion, Al has been so looped that it was a struggle for him to stay on the piano bench, much less play to perfection.

Al Neil calls his piano meditations "half-assed pineal hallelujahs," and when he's off course that's about all they are. But, in his own inimitable fashion, Neil does live very close to the forces of nature, out there in his Burrard Inlet squatter's hideaway—waves at his feet, trees and granitic hills behind—and when he's on target, his music is a summation of an individual's private pact with these forces—and with his own internal demons.

LIVING IN A MATERIAL WORLD

They're Abuildin' at The Creek, Ma!

BY DANIEL WOOD, MARCH 24–31, 1977

"It's like motherhood. You've got a bunch of rusty tracks and ugly warehouses on False Creek. Who's against doing something nice with that?"—-a Marathon developer

Something is about to happen.

The old dredge belongs to Greenlees Piledriving and—for the past weeks—it has been unloading crushed rock from a barge tied up beneath the Cambie St. Bridge on False Creek's *north* shore. Just a two-man operation there, the dredge operator and a bulldozer driver who ploughs up mounds of rock for the dredge.

Shortly, however, in a few months (a second in the galactic time scale of urban development), the first of dozens of foundations will be poured there as Marathon Realty begins its 10-year program of filling the area between the Cambie and Burrard St. Bridges with 4,500 housing units, scores of buildings, 22 of them over eight storeys tall, the largest co-ordinated urban development this city has or likely will see.

It will make the south shore of False Creek—with its 900 mandarin orange–roofed units—sink into the turgid waters of the Creek by comparison. It will be—despite the rhetoric of Jim Lowden and John Webster, the present and previous planners of the site, despite the slightly wilted clichés like "neighbourhoods," "family environment," and "community"—nothing more than a beautified extension of the West End.

In selling, the buzzwords change, but the game is the same. By its nature, it's a dirty job.

THE THREE CHERRIES

Jim Lowden, the present planner for the 94-acre site, sits surrounded by dozens of maps and photos of "The Creek," the quaint, almost paternal rubric for Marathon's slice of the city. He has seen it from more angles, seen more plans come and go than your geriatric spinster aunt. He has heard all the excuses.

"If," he says through a Ben Ginter beard and a fog of pipe smoke, "if the three cherries come up on the old machine, we could have 550 units started in the Phase One section by the end of this year. We've got to generate that critical mass on The Creek to sustain that area by the Cambie St. Bridge. No less. Nope. No one wants to live in 162 units in a quasi-industrial wasteland."

In your hands you're holding a 1974 brochure that says Phase One would be almost finished by 1977. You imagine Lowden, his hand in a heavy-duty Watson glove, taking *one more* tug on the slot machine, hoping the cherries start dropping.

"We need that lift, you know?"

The first cherry has already appeared. And Lowden knows it. In early February this year Vancouver city council approved the permit for the initial 162 units. Sometime in April Coquitlam's council will approve a rail agreement on a 277–acre site directly beneath the western approach of the Port Mann Bridge. In a grand game of musical chairs, with multimillion-dollar floor prizes, the CPR, the present residents of the northern shore of False Creek, will remove itself (almost!) from those 94 acres downtown and relocate out there in Coquitlam in what will be called Mayfair Industrial Park.

It's a good move for the CPR. Despite grumblings from those trainmen who work down on False Creek, the economics of that location are poor. One doesn't need $200-a-square-foot property to repair diesels, wash the transcontinental, or unload Harry Hammer's furniture on. The new Coquitlam industrial park, tied in to the recently announced "major shopping centre" in Coquitlam with adjacent Woodward's and Eaton's stores makes a lot more than sense. Ask any realtor.

I did.

"There's nothing to build, nothing to sell. Condos and apartments? Nope. The office market? Bloated. Residential sales? Down. Way down. Only industrial land is selling."

By the end of the summer, Vancouver will have approved the development permit covering all aspects of the Phase One site—parks, sewers, pavements—and the building permits specifically for the two high-rises (eight and 15 storeys) and the fan of four-storey low-rises which will fill the waterfront between the new marina and the Cambie St. Bridge.

"That'll be our flagship, Marathon's way of demonstrating that it *believes* in The Creek." For Lowden, this would be the second cherry. And he doesn't like losing.

"Myself and two friends just bought a sailboat. A Peterson One-Ton," he says.

I guess I'm supposed to be impressed. "You sail?"

"We don't sail. We *win*. It's a fuckin' racing machine. *The Good, The Bad, and The Ugly*. That's its name." He pauses, the raconteur at work. "I'm The Ugly. I used to ski competitively. You've gotta have these releases, these institutionalized successes, placebos for modern, competitive man. If I couldn't go out and win at something, I'd go mad at this job."

Lou, his Malamute office partner, drops his head on his paws as if he's heard the story before.

It *has* been eight years in the planning, the northern shore of False Creek. And—despite the seemingly endless recession which has severely torpedoed the once lucrative housing market—the grapevine says the third cherry will fall.

"Right now, as you probably know," Lowden explains, "condos aren't selling, especially expensive condos like the ones we've planned for the Phase One section of The Creek. The drift has stopped of east coasters to the West. The population of Vancouver is actually shrinking. And the 'empty-nesters' have decided not to sell their homes for something easier like a downtown apartment. West Vancouver. Shaughnessy. Hell! Even on the south side of The Creek. *They* aren't selling either!

"But Marathon's a big company. Unlike the little guy who's got it all riding on a 24-suite apartment house in North Van, we can hold onto that land if it doesn't sell; we can survive long enough on other assets.

"If it does go ahead, the best things will likely be cut. The brick courts would be asphalt. The planting, lighting, fountains, the public infrastructure will—because they're expensive—go."

"Look," says Ron Dies, the head architect on The Creek, "the project is *so* far along. To be cancelled would be very unusual. If the local guys at Marathon say it's okay, the board back east will approve it."

His voice is so soft, his manner so at ease that one wants to curl up in its lap. It would be an apostasy to question the ministerial Anglican tone. I felt like I'd just gobbled half a bottle of Nytol.

"Look," says John Webster, the former Marathon planner, pointing out the window of La Raclette toward the Vancouver skyline, with its columns of light an illuminated bar graph of the recent construction boom downtown. "It's obvious. Obvious! You see it, don't you? Downtown needs *more* people. The Creek will put 9,000 more people downtown. And it should be *twice* that to really move. But 9,000's a good start."

Developers at Marathon have not always felt so certain.

By 1967, the rail clerks–turned–executives at the CPR had traded their eyeshades and quill pens for a vision that included the 20th century. For someone had dimly perceived—after scrupulous inspection of their holdings—that the CPR was third only to the various governments and Indian tribes in amounts of Canadian land in its control. And land, so the vision explained, meant money.

That year—at what must have been one of the headiest gatherings in Canadian real-estate history—the new management of the newly conceived offspring of the CPR, Marathon Realty, sat around looking at scores of maps inscribed with red markings indicating CPR holdings no longer vital to present or future railroad needs. By the time the quill pens had scratched their last squiggles, Marathon had found itself—at its birth!—holding enormous tracts of lands, ready for sale, speculation, or development.

One tract—those 94 acres adjacent to the heart of downtown Vancouver—must have caused a few palpitations in the hearts of even the most stoic of developers. Ninety-four acres virtually downtown. Without a resident population or buildings to remove. Virgin land practically, ripe for a developer's thrust. Holy Tom Campbell!

Working for the Government

BY KERRY BANKS, SEPTEMBER 1–8, 1977

I am one of the more than one million out-of-work Canadians. This is nothing new. I have been unemployed before. So have a lot of you. Ours is a familiar story.

1. WE ENROL AT MANPOWER

At Manpower centres we are always asked to fill out forms. Under our social insurance number, we are asked to state our occupation. A lot of us don't have one. We are forced to make one up. A friend of mine used to claim he was a FOX TRAINER. I usually say that I'm a gardener. I planted flowers in parks one summer.

We are immediately assigned to a counsellor. The last counsellor to interview me smoked a golf-club pipe and kept a cowboy spur on his desktop. He kept asking me what it was I was looking for.

"A job," I'd answer, suspecting it was some sort of trick question.

This response irritated him. He puffed harder.

"No, I mean what is it you really want to do? Don't you really want to do anything?"

Of course I did. I told him that I'd like to write. He then informed me that this was a poor choice, since there was precious little call for writers at Manpower.

With that, he went off to yell at some Pakistanis who were lining up in the wrong line.

In the end, he decided to classify me as a "reporter," which was the closest thing he could get to a writer. It went down on my card. REPORTER—Code number R3342 in the Manpower Occupational Manual.

2. WE READ THE WANT ADS

There is always a demand for certain jobs. Hairdressers, for example, and Retail Department Heads. Yesterday's paper had these:

WANTED: Exotic waiters/waitresses.
NEEDED: Mature girl/boy Friday.
NEEDED: Tree Person.
WANTED: Worm Pickers.

Most jobs require experience. Ones that don't are "student jobs." These are some of the worst jobs, for the worst pay. So bad, in fact, that the ads never actually reveal what you'll be doing. They only hint instead at the marvellous amounts of money that can be made doing it.

Those applying to these companies end up selling vacuum cleaners or funeral plots.

3. WE COLLECT UNEMPLOYMENT INSURANCE

We all know the code:

NO
NO
NO
YES
NO

We begin cashing pale green cheques and open up $37.60 savings accounts. We imagine that we are working for the government.

4. WE SUFFER FROM GUILT

Once you're unemployed it's often difficult to converse with others who have jobs. They habitually inquire what you're "doing these days."

It seems foolish to say "nothing," so instead, we make up euphemisms. "I'm between jobs"..."I'm on vacation"...or "Just hanging around."

A person without a job can't be a success. Our families hover in the background looking for someone to blame. Mine seems convinced that an immigrant has stolen mine.

5. WE MAKE PLANS

Unemployed people are always talking about working on the pipeline.

We spend a lot of time thinking about being somewhere else. What, for instance, would it be like to be out of work in Rangoon?

Before bed, we make up a list of things to do tomorrow.

1. get up
2. have a shower
3. put on a green shirt
4. eat breakfast
5. read morning paper
6. read mail
7. clothes to laundry
8. buy stamps
9. buy ballpoint pen
10. don't worry

6. WE INTRODUCE OURSELVES TO RECEPTIONISTS

We all know about the value of creating a "good first impression." We practise in front of mirrors.

To land my job as a gardener, I got a shave and haircut and put on my best clothes. The employer who interviewed me was most interested in my physical disabilities. Did I have any allergies? He also wanted to know if I could drive a lawn mower.

My answers seemed to satisfy him. I added that I enjoyed working outdoors.

There was only one other thing he needed to know. "Would I get a haircut for this job?"

7. WE KNOCK ON DOORS

I once applied to an office that was in the business of selling Canadian Identity Cards.

The boss gave an assembled group of applicants his promotional pitch about how in the next couple of years, every Canadian citizen will be required to keep one of these cards with them wherever they go. Our task would be selling the cards door-to-door. Convincing the people who answered that they'd be doing both themselves and the police a favour by buying one.

As the meeting broke up, I asked the boss what Terry Evanshen's signature was doing on the cards. He seemed pleased by my inquiry.

"You're the first person who's recognized the name...Terry's very much behind this project," he explained.

Terry Evanshen is a wide receiver with the Hamilton Tiger Cats.

8. WE DON'T HAVE A QUITTING HOUR

Without a regular schedule, the unemployed tend to lose track of the rhythm of the week. Weekends lose their special sense of urgency. Saturday night is like any other night.

We have ways to deal with the boredom. We begin solving crossword puzzles and magazine quizzes. We read all the comics in the newspaper and even the ingredients on cereal boxes...first in English, then in French.

We watch too many late-nite movies and are lulled asleep by the hum of a test pattern.

9. WE EAT A LOT OF HAMBURGER

These days employers can afford to be selective.

The interview is with an English jam-and-biscuit importer. A Mr. Robertson needs someone to work in his warehouse. I have filled out an application form and am waiting in his office. There is a cocker spaniel calendar on the wall and a WWII stand-up radio in the corner with big butterscotch dials.

Mr. Robertson walks with a limp and speaks with an English accent. He scans my application and begins to describe what he's looking for in an employee.

He wants someone who will make an honest commitment to the firm and become a member of their warehouse family.

"We are all like one big family here at McVities," he tells me.

"I hired a young man about your age last year named Bob. At first, Bob seemed fine. But after a bit, he began showing up late for work. He was not always in a co-operative mood. I'm quite certain Bob had started taking drugs...Eventually I had to get rid of him. Bob was upset, but you simply can't run a business with irresponsible people."

Mr. Robertson stopped talking. I just looked back at him. I didn't even deny taking drugs.

He said he'd phone.

He didn't.

10. WE READ ABOUT OURSELVES

Every month, the unemployed appear as a growing, front-page government statistic. There are many follow-up newspaper articles. In these articles, we are called "...destitute, disheartened, angry, victims, and bums."

We sit outside and discover the eerie stillness of 2:30 on a weekday afternoon.

What Makes Bruce Eriksen Run?

BY JOHN FAUSTMANN, JUNE 22–28, 1979

Bruce Eriksen has made a name for himself by being a pain in the ass. In the eight years that he has been running the Downtown Eastside Residents' Association, Eriksen has been steadily accumulating enemies. Slum landlords slam doors in his face. Certain beer parlour owners have barred him permanently. Six years ago there was a contract out on his life and the cops had to hustle him out of town. And when he turns up at Vancouver City Council meetings, the aldermen squirm in their seats like the Israelites caught red-handed worshipping the golden calf. How does Eriksen feel about all this animosity? "It doesn't bother me at all," he says. "I have 3,100 people (in DERA) who can tell me exactly what's happening. I'll never be satisfied until this area gets cleaned up."

Centred around the corner of Hastings and Main, the area referred to could stand a bit of cleaning. On a hot early summer afternoon, the place remains curiously seasonless. The noisy traffic shimmers down East Hastings: Chevy Biscaynes packed with Chinese, dirty buses rolling toward Burnaby, whooping sirens as another ambulance returns to the scene of the crime. The sidewalks are jammed even tighter than the street. The junkies twitch and scratch their noses and wait for the light to change. The drunks, winos, and late-afternoon mumblers lurch along, often giving up and falling asleep at the edge of the sidewalk. Unshaven bristly-haired guys in topcoats stand by themselves at the bus stop, delivering vengeful lectures to the universe.

Home to 15,000 people, this is Bruce Eriksen's neighbourhood. He has lived here, in one skid-row hotel after another, ever since he was 14 years old. And though he may have enemies—this is his turf. Operating out of a storefront office on Gore Street filled with typewriters, secondhand furniture, serious-looking young workers, mahjong players, and a toilet with flushing instructions in both Chinese and English, part of Eriksen's job (besides putting out a newspaper called *Downtown East*, fielding tenant complaints, doing liaison work with the police, and investigating local problems) is dealing with the media. And part of dealing with the media is taking them on "the tour."

GEORGIA STRAIGHT

VOL. 9 NO. 383 FEB. 27 - MAR. 6 1975

25¢ OUTSIDE B.C. 35¢

•Alien Saves V-Con IV by Geof Gray-Cobb (pp. 12, 13)

•Freak Brothers In Mexico (p. 9)

Befitting his station as the "Skid Road Crusader," "Professional Conscience," "Crime Fighter," and several other labels the papers have hung on him, Eriksen is dressed for the part in a neat-looking pinstripe suit. Halfway along the guided tour, it's obvious his neighbours know him. The tattooed waiter in the Regent Hotel pub shakes his hand and says he'll be over to see him soon at the DERA office. Three inebriated Indians, sprawled on the postage-stamp lawn in front of the United Church, call to him as we walk by: "Hiya Brucie! Hey Brucie, keep fightin', eh?" Some of his neighbours are not that impressed, however. We stop to take a picture of Eriksen in front of the Carnegie Library. A Chinese gentleman dips his head so as not to spoil the shot, but a fat drunk in a blue T-shirt keeps weaving in front of Eriksen, getting in the way. He's not sure what's going on, but he knows he doesn't like it. He looks at Eriksen's clothing and snarls: "Some of us don't have no hundred-dollar fuckin' pinstripe suits."

Throughout it all, Eriksen keeps up a steady stream of chatter about what he calls the issues: decent housing, alcoholism, unscrupulous landlords, sleazy beer parlours that pour the suds into their customers long after they're totally drunk. To make his point on housing, he takes us into a place that the health department has condemned this morning as "unfit for human habitation." Stained mattresses on the beds upstairs, a broken toilet with a sign on it that says it is broken, tile peeling up from the floors, wallpaper peeling off the walls, and in one bedroom upstairs, a souvenir pennant from Beautiful Cape Breton still busy collecting dust. "Two-hundred-and-seventy-five bucks a month for this place!" says Eriksen, waving his hand around. "The landlord hasn't made any repairs on this place since day one. He doesn't give a shit that people have to live here—he just uses it as a goddamn tax shelter!"

After a couple of hours of being around Bruce Eriksen, it's easy to see why he rubs some people the wrong way. The guy is a zealot. It's as if he's perpetually angry—a one-man crusade against ignorance, discrimination, and sleazy opportunism. At least he comes by his anger honestly. Raised in a Winnipeg orphanage, he rode the rods to Vancouver in order to search for his father, and though he's been a crusader for the last eight years, he spent a lot more time than that as a victim. "It depends on the class you come from," he says. "If you come from a certain neighbourhood and you get into trouble, there's a hue and cry. If you're poor people, it doesn't matter. Nobody cares."

Eriksen learned that lesson when he was young. He still remembers what it was like. "I slept on bare concrete floors and in doorways and on the street. One day just blurs into the next. You wake up in the morning, flat broke, and you wonder where the hell you're going to eat, or if you're going to. You see nothing ahead of you. I drank so much that I was snaky," he says, "and then a policeman down here—I guess he was the best friend I ever had—gave me good swift kick in the ass and suggested I check into Riverview for three months. But you have to understand," he adds, "once you get a guy sobered up, he has to have something to go to. It's like letting guys out of jail in the middle of winter with their summer clothes on, and saying: 'Go out and sin no more.'" Eriksen sees it all as straight luck that when he got dried out, his brother got him a job as an ironworker. And he sees it as pure coincidence that in 1972, he saw an ad for People's Aid, the LIP project forerunner of DERA, and signed on as a worker.

"That was when I learned I had some rights," he says, and Eriksen hasn't shut up since. All his angry talk about issues, he maintains, has simply been directed toward informing people that they have some rights. Whatever his reasons, Eriksen's continuous strident crusade has brought him a lot of attention. The subject of countless newspaper articles and total media coverage, Eriksen built up DERA to its present 3,100 membership and ended up getting 30,000 votes in the last civic election. Such popular support has unnerved the local politicians, who have accused him of "being too political." And it has laid him open to charges of being a demagogue.

DERA co-worker Jean Swanson labels the demagogue accusations as nonsense. "Anyone who has ever been to a DERA meeting and watched the crowd go to sleep when Bruce gets up and launches into one of his tirades would know he could never be a demagogue," she laughs. And having interviewed Eriksen, I'd have to say that it was virtually impossible to get the man to talk about himself.

The important thing, he kept maintaining, was the issues he was fighting for, and I kept hearing those issues repeated over and over again. Eriksen made it sound simple: he loved his neighbourhood, he wanted to make it better. He understood the people that live there—after all, he was one of them. "Look," he said, "we've got old-age pensioners, handicapped, and other people down here that are just poor. They're not drunks. They've got an 8-by-10 room and they've got a bed in the room, period. Maybe they've got a sink, but no refrigerator or bugger all. If they're single, they get $175 a month, and maybe they go down and get some bread and baloney, until they're broke, and then they just hang on, sitting in the park until the next cheque comes."

In a bid to improve the social life of people like these, DERA battled for years to save the Carnegie Library—so people could have somewhere to go besides beer parlours. The inevitable link between poverty, old age, and alcoholism was spelled out clearly by Jean Swanson, who used to work as a waitress in a downtown hotel. "I'd be serving customers," she said, "and I'd go up to the bar and say: 'Give me five.' The owner would say: 'Take 10.' If you came back with beer still left on your tray, you wouldn't be working there very long. One old guy in his 80s used to come in there, and after two beers he'd piss himself. So I had to refuse him service. One night he got angry and yelled at me: 'Where else can I afford to go and meet my friends? I haven't got anywhere else to go!'"

In the liquor laws of this province, the term for pushing beer like that is "overservice"—giving the customer two when he only wants one—and Jean summed up that practice neatly when she said: "The owner of that place took the staff home one time for a party, and he had a beautiful house, with a sauna and a swimming pool and everything. He was a nice guy. It's just that he bought his swimming pool by turning old-age pensioners into alcoholics."

In their licensed-premises checklist reports, the Police Department describes the beer-parlour scene in another way, not bothering with adjectives or summations: "Dec. 29, 23:10 hours, many intoxicated people staggering around beer parlour. One male ejected by staff. Jan. 5, 23:55 hours, 2 males in washroom sniffing glue: 00:45 hours, 4 males fighting—I arrest PDW waving knife at manager. Feb.3, 23:00 hours, gents washroom filthy, urine all over floor. Feb. 10. 23:30 hours, plainclothes P.C. jumped by two males, music so loud other P.C. 20 feet away could not hear call for help."

All of this adds up to a pretty damn poor way of life, Eriksen likes to point out. He adjusts the steel-rim bifocals he wears and lights another Sportsman cigarette, settling back in the one comfortable chair in his Main Street apartment living room. I think for a minute that I have worn him down, and that after all this talk about the issues I'm finally going to get him to talk about himself. After all, he did run in the last civic election. Is this guy with the Grade 3 education just looking for a job on city council? Will he run again?

"Yeah, I'll probably run again," he says, "but what I'd prefer to happen would be for the people we've elected to do their goddamned jobs. Given that they're not going to, I'm going to run until I'm elected." I try a few more questions, trying to dig out the man behind this story. Eriksen bats them away. "Look," he says, "never mind the personal crap. Let's talk about the issues. That's the important thing here."

Time to Say Good-bye to the Angus Garage

BY FRED PEAR, APRIL 28–MAY 5, 1978

On the corner of Davie and Nicola Streets there squats, like an enormous brown toad, one of the last remaining mansions in the West End. It was designed in 1901 by the prominent residential architect Samuel MacLure for Benjamin Tingley Rogers, founder of the British Columbia Sugar Refining Company Limited. Some residents of the West End refer to the Rogers mansion as "the sugarplum palace."

Behind the mansion sits the Angus Garage, its cheerfully antiquated pumps painted bright red and blue. The red pump, so it says, dispenses premium ethyl fuel, the blue pump, for a few cents less, regular. Originally, the garage was the Rogers mansion's carriage house.

Lately the mansion has sat empty and recently it has been announced that it will be refurbished and opened as a 150-seat New Orleans–style restaurant, under the auspices of Hy Aisenstadt of Hy's steak-house fame.

The Angus Garage will probably suffer a worse fate.

The Vancouver Heritage Advisory Committee has ruled that the former stable is of no heritage value. The Housing Corporation of British Columbia plans to tear down the garage in May, to make room for a 100-unit apartment block. The Housing Corporation, a private company in which the province has a majority control, has recently been put on the block by Housing Minister Hugh Curtis.

The disappearance of the Angus Garage will mean that more than a dozen people will be looking for someplace else to work. There's Warren Seebach, the man who has operated the motor-repair shop and service station for the last nine years. There are his sons Larry, Murray, and Glen; and there is Chester, who helps out in the garage.

There's the Czechoslovakian couple who split shingles in a garage stall they rent from Seebach. There's Bert's Moving and Storage. There's the man who buys and sells articles at swap meets and stores his inventory from week to week in another of Seebach's stalls.

Upstairs, above the motor-repair shop, a potter, a mould maker, and an art student have their headquarters.

Warren Seebach wants to fight for the Angus Garage. In fact, he has started a group called the Appeal to Save the Angus Garage. Anyone can belong. Memberships are one dollar.

Someone inclined to take a Marxist line on these matters would have good grounds for saying that the demolition of the Angus Garage is a typical case of class oppression. The ugly, bloated mansion is to be preserved as an expensive eating place for the present-day bourgeoisie, while the carriage house, where the coachman and his family lived in a self-contained apartment next to the hayloft, is to be destroyed.

After more than three-quarters of a century the carriage house stands as straight and true as the day it was built, despite 25 years of neglect. It is a testimonial to the architect who designed it and the carpenters who built it.

Yet there is not one picture of the carriage house in either the Vancouver City Archives or the Public Library Archives. A pen-and-ink drawing, signed by Samuel MacLure, is all that will be left when the garage is torn down.

MOVIES TELEVISION CONCERTS CLUBS & LIVE THEATRE GUIDE

CBC RADIO TIMES

Georgia STRAIGHT

JACKBOOTS IN THE KOOTENAYS

By George Woodcock

NO MORE FLIES FOR ME!

TAMAHNOUS GIVES YOU VD SEE P 10

WHAT'S WRONG WITH PICKING WINGS OFF FLIES?

By Doug Collins

THE CLASH

REID FLEMING

SCAPEGOAT

INSIDE

LAURIER LA PIERRE

URANIUM HEARINGS

YOU ASKED FOR IT

Let Them Eat Concrete

BY BOB MERCER, OCTOBER 13–20, 1978

There they stood, those tired and testy taxpayers, jealously eyeing the rows of empty seats set aside for the no-show big-wigs who rated an invitation to this official opening of Robson Square but who never came. The Vancouver Fire Department Concert Band was playing a medley of Elton John hits when, midway through "Good-bye

Yellow Brick Road," one elderly woman groused, "It looks like the chairs are not for the ordinary people."

"No," muttered her friend, "I guess not..."

Your editor affects the style of the hard-bitten, cynical newsman, but, really, Mrs. Mercer raised a good boy. As soon as I had scratched down that poignant exchange, I got up from my seat at the press table and offered it to the old woman. I couldn't see anyway, for the charming hostess standing right in front of me.

It was 12:30. The grand opening was 15 minutes late. Another woman, small and grey-haired, leaned over and complained to her companion that these damn things never start on time and now everyone on their lunch break would have to go back to work without a glimpse of the Premier.

But hold on. With a skirl of the pipes, there appeared out of nowhere four charming little highland lassies, dancing, so it seemed, with another four frantic TV cameraman out for a homey angle. The crowd warmed. Here comes the parade.

Maybe. But does Bill Bennett appear in public in a kilt and sporran? With Gary Lauk on his arm? No, he doesn't, but Alex MacDonald does and there stood Alex at the top of the stairs proclaiming, "On behalf of the people of British Columbia, who made it all possible, on behalf of our children unborn...on behalf of the building trades, the designers, and artists, in the fruits of whose labour we now rejoice, I hereby declare Robson Square officially open, for the pleasure and profit of the People of British Columbia..."

Alex wasn't supposed to open Robson Square. In fact, the Socreds—through oversight or ill-manners—hadn't even invited him, or any other members of the former NDP government, which had initiated the current project. But if the Socreds could be so rude as to try and steal all the credit, surely Alex MacDonald could presume to show up early and open it in the name of the People.

The NDP is sore. They would rather that the taxpayers remember that it was they who scaled down W.A.C. Bennett's dream of a 55-storey office tower to the current "three-dimensional park" with Arthur Erikson's "human scale" architecture.

The NDP should keep its big mouth shut. With any luck at all, the voters will hang this ugly $160-million boondoggle on the Socreds and pay them back come election time.

It is, after all, a pretty shoddy effort for $160 million. For his $1 million architect Arthur Erikson could have come up with something more imaginative than another cement and steel rerun of Simon Fraser University. He seems to have figured—rightly—that if Gordon Shrum fell for it once he'd fall for it again.

Let me admit it. I have no more than the slightest conception of what $160 million means. But I suspect that it is still a lot of money. The $40–odd million spent on our new civic park could presumably buy quite a few acres of parkland if scattered around the city. Forty million would probably pay for an adequate refurbishing of the Jericho hangars.

At the very least, that kind of money should buy better than the poor workmanship that has gone into Robson Square. Go see for yourself. The straight lines in the inlaid floors aren't straight. Quibbling maybe, but still, don't we look silly crowing about the architectural and engineering achievement of this overblown shopping mall?

Of course, I'm out on a limb. Everyone from Alex MacDonald to Grace McCarthy just loves Robson Square. Jack Webster loves it, even at $160 million. The *Sun*'s editorial page loves it. And given all this encouragement, so too will a number of Vancouverites.

And when the weather is perfect, they'll stroll through it to ponder the majesty of our justice system being administered just a spit from the Senor McTaco's concession. Or to gaze in admiration [at] the bevies of smug-looking lawyers "girl-watching" over cocktails at such pricey "people places" as the Old Bailiff restaurant.

When it rains, of course, the place will be deserted, because it offers so little respite from Vancouver's liquid sunshine. And when the real sun shines just a little too bright, they'll wander off dizzy from the glare of all that bone-white concrete. But that's the kind of appreciation that comes with time.

I'll make you a bet. Let's wait a year and see what you think of Robson Square after you've learned to live with it. Let's see if you don't agree with those anarchist demonstrators who rained on Bill Bennett's parade, drowning out his official opening remarks with cries of "Useless!" "Useless!" "Useless!" "Useless!"

...because every child has the right to smile
The Vancouver
FREE PRESS
With TIME OUT Guide
A Rare Interview
THE POPE AND THE COMMUNISTS
John Paul II Comes Home To Poland
PROMOTIONS
MOVIES TELEVISION CONCERTS CLUBS & LIVE THEATRE GUIDE
Georgia STRAIGHT
LADY IN LIGHTS BETTY CHABA PAGE 11
ISSUE NO. 600: THE LAST
INSIDE

FACING PAGE:
Dan McLeod with the "last" *Georgia Straight*.

CHRONOLOGY 1973–1985

1973

JANUARY California Governor Ronald Reagan vetoes marijuana decriminalization bill. Mayor Art Phillips shatters tradition by not wearing his chain of office in council chambers. MP Ron Basford announces the Granville Island redevelopment; False Creek will follow. The treaty ending the Vietnam War is signed.

MARCH Police raid the *Straight* bookstore and seize 3,200 copies of 26 different underground comics; some 400 are returned, but obscenity charges are laid against the paper, Dan McLeod, Greater Vancouver News Ltd., *Straight* distribution man Lloyd "Sharkey" Robinson, and the owner of a Victoria Drive grocery that sold two titles. Mainstream press "lies" about the American Indian Movement's occupation of Wounded Knee are examined in the *Straight*.

MAY Jimmy Pattison purchases the Philadelphia Blazers and moves them to Vancouver.

JULY The French navy boards *Greenpeace II* and assaults Capt. David McTaggart.

OCTOBER Spiro Agnew resigns in the wake of "damned lies." Henry Kissinger receives the Nobel Peace Prize. Nixon refuses to release audiotapes of White House conversations. Wanis Kouri reviews the Inbal Dancers of Israel—the headline reads: "Let My People Go-Go."

NOVEMBER The English underground newspaper *Oz* ceases publication. Dr. Henry Morgentaler is acquitted in Montreal of performing illegal abortions. Daniel Wood contributes "Memoirs of a Male Chauvinist Piglet" to the *Straight* and admits, "At 13 I went crazy, thinking of nothing but nudity for three weeks."

DECEMBER Rohans Rockpile nightclub opens on 4th Avenue. Seized comics are declared obscene and a $3,500 fine is imposed. An unbylined *Straight* editorial promises the paper will fight the ruling to the Supreme Court:

"After almost seven years of harassment by dumb, insensitive, bigoted assholes, we are fed up."

1974

FEBRUARY Patty Hearst is kidnapped by the Symbionese Liberation Army. The first issues of the *Straight* are distributed at UBC after student society efforts to ban the paper fail, but they are immediately carted away by staff of the *Ubyssey* student paper. Bob Cummings defends preserving the Orpheum from redevelopment for the "posh nonsense" of its interior.

The paper's appeal on the comics obscenity charges sees five of the six dropped, and the fine reduced to $200.

MARCH Chilean President Salvador Allende is killed in a military coup. The Beach Boys' Dennis Wilson and Mike Love streak during their Pacific Coliseum show.
APRIL Two street musicians are charged under Vancouver's new anti-panhandling bylaw.
MAY Co-op Radio is granted a broadcast licence. Soccer's Vancouver Whitecaps debut at Empire Stadium. The *Straight* reports the closing of the five-year-old Vancouver Free University, which offered courses ranging from traditional academics to "creative lovemaking."
JULY Illegal alien Bob Geldof, who began working at the *Straight*'s warehouse in midwinter, is now entertainment editor. In a review of John Denver's *Back Home Again*, he reveals other ambitions: "He's charming, has that ultra-brite smile, wholesome features, and the all-important boy-next-door quality, but if that's all it takes, why ain't I a star? I'd love to be a star. I think I'd be an excellent star."
AUGUST A three-day festival marks the opening of the Granville Mall. Richard Nixon resigns.
SEPTEMBER U.S. President Gerald Ford announces an amnesty for draft dodgers and a pardon for Nixon.
NOVEMBER Art Phillips is re-elected mayor, defeating Mr. Peanut, among others.
DECEMBER The *Straight* reprints an article from the *Ann Arbor Sun* on the dangers of aerosol spray cans and the disappearing ozone layer.

1975

JANUARY John Lennon interviews himself in the January 16 *Straight:* "I went to a party in L.A. just to look at Liz Taylor, was I thrilled to meet her, and on top of everything, who, but, who, do you think was all over her armpit? None other than the great, great show, David the Bowie! Wow! Was I thrilled to see that they were both smaller than me!"
FEBRUARY The *Straight* says goodbye to Bob Geldof, who heads back to Ireland. The paper's appeal on the comics obscenity charges sees five of the six dropped, and the fine reduced to $200.
APRIL "If you're the kinda person that likes to be beaten then I guess that I'm domineering," Suzi Quatro tells the *Straight*.
MAY "There's one professional in this town and everybody hates his guts too, and that's Terry Jacks. He's a dink. Well, if he's a dink why is he rich?"—promoter Bruce Allen in a *Straight*

interview with Nicholas J. Collier.
JUNE "If you list that Webster's a hash smoker, I'll come around and kill you personally."—broadcaster Jack Webster to the *Straight*'s Alan Earle. On June 11, Mary Steinhauser is killed as police end a B.C. Pen hostage-taking. Future *Province* music critic Tom Harrison debuts in the *Straight* with a story on Alice Cooper breaking three ribs in a fall from the Coliseum stage.
JULY *Greenpeace V* returns to Vancouver after intercepting Russian whalers.
SEPTEMBER Gastown Days marks the completion of the Gastown beautification project.
OCTOBER *Saturday Night Live* debuts. The executive producer calls *SNL* "the post-Watergate victory party for the Woodstock Generation."
DECEMBER *Straight* astrologer Geoff Grey-Cobb predicts Dave Barrett and the NDP will win the B.C. provincial election. He's wrong.

1976

JANUARY The Montreal SPCA opens the world's first blood bank for dogs. Karen Magnusson tells the *Straight:* "Hell, I'm no princess." The Downtown Eastside Residents Association proposes the disused Carnegie Public Library be turned into a community centre. Bill Vander Zalm, new Minister of Human Resources, tells the *Straight:* "I don't think a person should be allowed to refuse doing something he doesn't like so that he can be helped by others, who might very well be doing what they don't like but are forced to."
FEBRUARY "I do not kiss people's asses. I may go as far as their wrists or something."—local impresario David Y.H. Lui, just before the opening of his theatre (now Richard's on Richards nightclub).
APRIL The *Straight* reports that the Vancouver Spring Festival (the Be-in's new name) suffered poor attendance, bad weather, and too many drunks.
JULY Ben Metcalfe begins a long-running column slagging the mainstream media and denouncing the likes of the mysterious Tri-Lateral Commission.
AUGUST *Straight* food writer Jack Moore calls the new Egg McMuffin "filling and tasty."
SEPTEMBER CJOR Radio sports director Denny Boyd begins an acerbic sports column in the *Straight.* The paper costs 35 cents as of September 16. Following years of controversy, council votes to retain the property at the entrance to Stanley Park as parkland.
OCTOBER The lost history of women in B.C. is documented in the *Straight* by Johanna den Hertog, while George Woodcock examines the Doukhobors and Nick Collier reports on the cultural feast of Commercial Drive. The paper moves to 2110 West 4th Avenue.
NOVEMBER "Only with sadness is the death knell of the Committee of Progressive Electors rung, but the time has come."—Sean Rossiter, debuting in the *Straight.* On November 15 the separatist Parti Québécois is swept into power in Quebec.

1977

APRIL A gala performance by the VSO marks the official opening of the refurbished Orpheum Theatre.
MAY The *Straight*'s 10th anniversary is commemorated by a Jim Cummings cover illustration, a short editorial, and little else.
JUNE Perryscope Concert Productions sets up shop in Vancouver. The *Straight*

reports on (Gasp!) stock fraud at the VSE. Cover price of the paper hits 50 cents.

JULY Terry Glavin reports on the continuing arrests of protesters (154 to date) at Washington State's Trident submarine base. Dave Boswell's comic Laszlo, the Great Slavic Lover debuts; it soon spawns the character Reid Fleming, World's Toughest Milkman.

AUGUST The Savoy opens as a jazz club. The first Space Shuttle test flight occurs. Elvis Presley dies on his toilet in Memphis.

SEPTEMBER Canadian highway signs begin the transition to the metric system. Bob Mercer becomes *Straight* managing editor.

OCTOBER A cover story on the Skulls declares: "Remember how your mom hated the Rolling Stones? That's how you're gonna hate...Punk Rock!" The Skulls drive a few guests out of the *Straight*'s belated 10th anniversary party at the Commodore.

NOVEMBER Brian Platt reviews Bob Geldof's Boomtown Rats debut, saying, "These guys ain't sociologically or scatologically important enuf to be punk."

1978

JANUARY Activist Stan Persky runs against timber baron J.V. Clyne for the chancellorship at UBC.

MARCH The Ad Hoc Coalition for Disarmament persuades Mayor Jack Volrich to declare March 31 as Disarmament Day.

APRIL Leonard Schein reopens the Ridge Theatre as a repertory cinema. Vaughn Palmer becomes the first full-time rock critic at the *Sun*. Alex Varty begins writing a jazz column in the *Straight*.

JUNE The *Straight*'s own rock band, the Explosions, with Bob Mercer, Alex Varty, Tom Harrison, David Lester, and Jamie Baugh, debuts at Cambrian Hall after recording the single "Wilson, Lucas & Bruce," then fades almost instantly into obscurity.

SEPTEMBER New *Straight* rock critic John Mackie's first assignment is to review a band called D.O.A., formed in March from the wreckage of the Skulls.

NOVEMBER Pacific Press goes on strike (again), this time for eight months. "I'm pretty well writing out of a trench," Leonard Cohen tells the *Straight*'s Alan Twigg. "Trying to get my nose and eyes over the edge of the trench to see who's shooting at me."

DECEMBER Strikebound *Sun* columnist and professional curmudgeon Doug Collins debuts in the *Straight*. Book reviewer Alan Twigg and theatre critic Tom Shandel leave the paper over the hiring of Collins.

1979

FEBRUARY *Straight* staffer Bob Cummings leaves to work for Greenpeace. Sid Vicious, charged with murdering his girlfriend Nancy Spungen, dies of a heroin overdose.

APRIL "Pierre slugged me. He's given me a black eye....He got all his hostility out and he hasn't paid me so much attention in years."—Maggie on Pierre in the April 13 *Straight*.

MAY Issue 600 calls itself the last *Georgia Straight*. The paper, faced with falling circulation, tries to shed the negative connotations of its history by adjusting its focus and changing its name to the *Vancouver Free Press*.

JUNE The K-Tels win a *Free Press* Battle of the Bands. Former contributor Stan Persky returns to do a column called

The Last Word, and mainstream syndicated comics begin appearing.
JULY The Arts Club's 100th production in its 16 years is Noël Coward's *Private Lives*, staged in its new theatre on Granville Island.
AUGUST Bob Mercer leaves the *Free Press* and publisher Dan McLeod takes over his responsibilities. Sandy Price reports that the Granville Island Public Market is now open and says "parking is plentiful." Style section proclaims "Hairstyles softer, more natural."
SEPTEMBER The *Free Press* cover story is "The Perfect Girl" on Bo Derek, and the paper prints a leaked copy of Swan Wooster's doomed $12-million plan to reduce erosion of Wreck Beach cliffs by covering two kilometres of beach with a rock berm.

1980

JANUARY "The general moral, economic, and spiritual deterioration of our way of life is likely going to go on," Malcolm Muggeridge tells the *Free Press*. Ken Lester is named *Free Press* managing editor; he lasts six months in a period of high staff turnover.
FEBRUARY "The thing we're doing could be big for TV," says Raoul Casablanca, announcer for North Shore Channel 10's shoestring rock-video show *Nite Dreems*.
MARCH Jean Swanson reports on inadequate welfare rates and Les Wedman begins a column on the growing B.C. film industry.
APRIL Coquitlam's Terry Fox begins his cross-Canada Marathon of Hope in St. John's, Newfoundland. Jean-Paul Sartre continues his investigations into existentialism by dying. Sorelle Saidman reports that, by show time, scalpers were selling tickets for The Who's Coliseum show for $1; afterward, the band shows up at Rohans and jams.
MAY "We tried fitting them, but they would not ejaculate. No way."—researcher Alexander Jakubovic to the *Free Press*'s Bill Tieleman, on his and Socred science minister Pat McGeer's attempts, using plastic vaginas, to get sperm samples from laboratory rats injected with doses of THC.

Says Geldof of working for the *Straight*: "It was the second most enjoyable thing I've ever done in my life, working there, at first."

AUGUST Southam Inc. buys the *Vancouver Sun* from F.P. Publications and purchases Thompson Newspapers' 50-percent interest in Pacific Press Ltd.
SEPTEMBER Mayor Jack Volrich falters in his re-election campaign and will lose to challenger Mike Harcourt. "Tamahnous is at its collective best," writes Alan Twigg, on the theatre company's 10th-anniversary production *We Won't Pay! We Won't Pay!*
OCTOBER "I had no faith in the Pistols that amounted to anything other than a damp fart," former Sex Pistol Johnny Lydon tells the *Free Press*.
NOVEMBER Ronald Reagan and George Bush are elected.
DECEMBER On December 8, John Lennon is murdered. On New Year's Eve, media guru Marshall McLuhan dies of his own accord.

1981

MARCH On March 13, the *Free Press* mysteriously disappears. There are none of those flashy "we're redesigning to serve you better" ad campaigns, not even an editorial explanation. Circulation of the 50-cent paper has fallen below 10,000. The *Georgia Straight* nameplate returns and the move toward all-entertainment, mostly music-oriented content continues. The cover features Bob Geldof, interviewed by Alex Varty before a Coliseum show by the Boomtown Rats. Says Geldof of working for the *Straight:* "It was the second most enjoyable thing I've ever done in my life, working there, at first." U2 makes its local debut at the Commodore, tickets are $5.99.

Amid calls for a general strike, 40,000 pinkos rally at Empire Stadium to protest the Socred government's restraint program.

JULY The a cappella group the Nylons closes the Cave, the only club in North America decorated in stalactites and stalagmites.
AUGUST MTV goes on the air 24 hours a day. The first clip is "Video Killed the Radio Star."
OCTOBER Rohans closes to make way for a retail-apartment complex. "I thought I'd died."—Chief Dan George in the *Straight* on sex with Jayne Mansfield.
DECEMBER Bryan Adams and Kickaxe ring in the new year at Outlaws.

1982

APRIL Bill Bennett announces that Vancouver will host Expo 86. The End the Arms Race Rally attracts an estimated 30,000. The first Vancouver International Film Festival is held.
MAY The *Straight* celebrates 15 years of independent publication with three nights of music at Pharoahs nightclub. Stalwart music writer Steve Newton debuts with a Krokus interview. The New York Islanders defeat the Canucks in four games to win the Stanley Cup.
JUNE The *Straight* incorporates *Contact Magazine* and begins to publish *Inside*, a Western Canada music-industry supplement. The experiment, one of several doomed efforts to generate revenue with other products (including a sex-related personals tabloid), lasts about a year.
SEPTEMBER The September 17 edition marks a move to free distribution, a strategy to raise circulation and thus improve advertising income.
NOVEMBER The roof is inflated on B.C. Place Stadium.

1983

APRIL The *Straight* publishes an Academy Award–nomination checklist, a harbinger of the following year's introduction of the Oscar Challenge competition, and movie features begin to increase in prominence.
JUNE *Straight* jazz critic David Grierson writes that compact discs should be available by year's end from most major record companies.
JULY Film critic Ian Caddell begins an eight-part series profiling independent movie theatres.
AUGUST Amid calls for a general strike, 40,000 pinkos rally at Empire Stadium to protest the Socred government's restraint program. Operation Solidarity falls apart, though, in a fit of name-calling between union leaders.
SEPTEMBER Bob Mercer returns to the *Straight* to do design work and becomes art director the following March.

1984

JANUARY Michael Jackson's hair is ignited by pyrotechnic devices during the filming of a soda-pop commercial. *Soundproof*, the North Shore's no-budget, no-format community-access video show, beats MuchMusic to the airwaves by seven months.
MARCH "We think with our dicks, basically," says Nikki Sixx of Mötley Crüe to the *Straight*'s Steve Newton.
APRIL The Recording Industry Association of America announces that cassette sales have surpassed albums for the first time. The Vancouver peace rally draws 100,000. The Soft Rock Café, 4th Avenue's only proper coffeehouse, closes.
JUNE "Home is where I hang my hair," a wiggy Dolly Parton tells the *Straight*.
AUGUST Canada wins 44 medals at the Soviet-boycotted Los Angeles Olympics.
SEPTEMBER Brian Mulroney is elected with the biggest parliamentary majority in Canadian history.
NOVEMBER The Connaught (Cambie) Bridge is closed. "I'm 88 years old [and] I'm making movies," George Burns tells the *Straight*. "I've got it both ways. I'm a senior citizen; I can see my movies for half price." Movie features now dominate the *Straight*'s covers. Senior citizen Ronald Reagan is elected for a second term, while Mike Harcourt wins his third term as Vancouver's mayor.
DECEMBER The Bob Geldof–organized Band Aid single "Do They Know It's Christmas?" is released. Wayne Gretzky, 23, scores his 1,000th NHL career point.

1985

JANUARY The *Straight* begins a tradition of mocking the previous year and reporting its unfortunate quotes and absurd news stories.
FEBRUARY Bob Mercer becomes managing editor and starts to broaden the paper's scope.
APRIL "It's been a great disappointment that punk rock just cleared the way for the likes of Spandau Ballet," Billy Bragg tells the *Straight*'s Ellie O'Day.
MAY Amid much hoopla, New Coke is announced to a soon-to-be-angry public.
JUNE After three years reviewing for CBC Radio, Alan Twigg returns to the *Straight* as theatre critic. The play *Talking Dirty* has its 1,000th local performance.
JULY The Live Aid concert is broadcast throughout 160 countries.
AUGUST Illustrator Rod Filbrandt's single-panel comic True Life debuts.
SEPTEMBER The first Fringe Festival of theatre takes over the Mt. Pleasant neighbourhood.
NOVEMBER The B.C. Lions win the Grey Cup in Montreal, beating the Hamilton Tiger Cats 37-24.
DECEMBER Parents fight their way into the stores to buy ugly and expensive Cabbagepatch dolls.

LIBERACE'S LIVE RATS TWIG ART

AND GREY BACON EXPO LINES

WACKY BENNETT TAXIDERMY

FREDDY'S ARTLESS *SUN* SEQUEL

HAPPY PAPER PR MASTERS

PART THREE

1986–1996

BRIDGE DREAMS WONTON FLIPPERS

CECIL TOURISTS WHITE CRIME

CHICKEN BATTER BY THE GRAM

CELTIC HEALING BILL'S BABY

TRIGGER-HAPPY DRUG COPS

CLAYOQUOT BROWNSHIRTS

FREE

VOLUME 30 • NUMBER 1500 • SEPTEMBER 19–26, 1996

VANCOUVER'S NEWS & ENTERTAINMENT WEEKLY

THE • GEORGIA

straight

ISSUE #1500 OUR BIGGEST EVER!

BABZ CHULA • BLACK CROWES • TAP DOGS • GUERRILLA GIRLS • BRUCE DERN

TRULY VULGAR COWBOY SHIRTS

User-Friendly Expo Guide

BY DAVE WATSON, AUGUST 1–8, 1986

Expo 86. You've heard of it. With this guide you can survive it. It will enable you to avoid the awful, transcend the mediocre, and pinpoint the worthwhile. The uselessly egalitarian official guide will not do this for you. It will tell you that everything is equally great. It just ain't so.

This guide will also suggest to you the proper Expo attitude. With the right attitude you can be transformed from one of 100,000-plus people going to Expo on a given day to a professional doing Spo.

There are four classes of people at Expo. The Elite Class consists of somewhat important people (SIMPS) whose money and/or connections have gained them preferred status at the fair. Petty problems like lineups don't exist for these people. The Worker Class is made up of those blue-coated employees. Some are very helpful, but many are annoying. There should be a law against giving a 17-year-old $4 an hour and authority over thousands of helpless and confused adults. Sheep make up the largest class. Individually, these people are fine, but pack them together and they become stupid. There are two phenomena that demonstrate this. One is the Lineup Effect, the tendency of the unwashed to join any lineup that's forming—even if they don't have the slightest idea what it's for. The other is the Cluster Phenomenon. Just stand in one place staring at something and soon a crowd will gather and stare with you.

You don't want to be a sheep. You want to see Expo as a member of the Cool Class. Don't be drawn by bright colours or flashing lights. Be confident. Walk quickly. Size up pavilions before entering. (It's up to you to decide if the people who crash the exit doors are cool.)

Above all, use this guide to avoid lining up for boring nationalistic displays of automobiles, video display terminals, and telephones. While the pavilions are the core of Expo 86, a lot of them are rotten. The fair's biggest problem is that someone forgot to tell most of the exhibitors that the transportation and communication theme need not be as dull as it sounds. A whole swack of pavilions simply sell you the native version of a hotdog, show you where the national airline flies, and give you a brochure that invites you to drop around sometime. Who wants to go to Expo and be told that they should have gone to Bandar Seri Begawan?

Almost all the pavilions suffer from the fact that they are official government-sanctioned exhibits given to every form of dishonesty and propaganda that governments are known for. You will look long and hard before you'll find any fascinating history about crooked railroaders or press censorship. Only in a few corners, such as in the Northwest Territories pavilion, is there any hint of the damage that the evolution of transportation and communications systems can create.

If our guide is occasionally brutal, it is because we do not believe the fair is an invalid that needs nursing. Expo is a behemoth and the average visitor needs protection.

The site itself has a kind of pleasant ambience if you don't mind crowds and have a certain fondness for purple. The monorail only looks like a good idea. The best thing

Expo 86 taught Vancouverites how to line up.

about Expo is the entertainment. Vancouver has never had it so good and probably never will again. The wise Expo visitor would do well to size up the dozens of free shows happening in any given week and make one the focal point of a visit to the fair.

Hints on being cool at Expo: Don't even stand near a Minolta Photo Tips sign. People who need this kind of simple advice on photography should do everybody a favour and buy postcards. Do not mistake the Royal Bank kiosks for pavilions. Watch out for tourists with portable video cameras. Many seem to think they are important Hollywood directors. Travel west to east. Most people go the other way. Don't tell the tourists that they needn't slather their bodies in insect repellent. It reassures them and reminds them that they are on vacation.

And don't let Expo warp your view of reality. Remember, there are no purple or green zones in real life.

Nightshift

BY JOHN ARMSTRONG, JUNE 6–13, 1986

The great balancer of all things decrees that for proper order in the universe a series of trade-offs must be made. For every William Faulkner, a Mickey Spillane. For every Van Gogh, black-velvet toreador paintings. Lou Reed, Steve and Edie.

God alone knows what brilliance Liberace is paying the bill for. But on Monday (June 3) 4,000 people paid $22 a head to see a man dressed as Dr. Strange play the piano at the Expo Theatre. He was driven onstage in a 1937 Auburn boat-tail coupe chauffeured by his valet. At first glance he appeared to be wearing a tent made of live rats, later revealed to be 100-plus pounds of virgin fox.

After the ritual touching of garments by the audience, Liberace and a small orchestra began to play. The first selection was a medley of Gershwin hits, which was received with enthusiastic nods of approval from a sea of blue-rinsed heads.

The odd under-40 could be spotted among the floral-print pantsuits, but I swear I have never seen a more identifiably Canadian crowd. It may have been flown in from Hamilton for the event.

As the show progressed from the tribute to Eddie Duchin to the classics, it became clear that Lee is a pretty good pianist. How good, I don't know. His playing is embellished with so many ruffles, flourishes, and glissandos that the actual song is sometimes difficult to hear.

But the quality of his playing is not that important. There are certainly any number of pianists who play as well as he does, but few of them would appear wearing a cape topped with a gold lamé clamshell. I enjoyed it much the same way I enjoy a truly vulgar cowboy shirt, or seeing a group of middle-aged Shriners riding mini-bikes.

There is only so much really good stuff in this world, and as a great man once said, if you don't learn to appreciate trash you are in for a very dull time.

Twig Art, Grey Bacon, Talking Heads

BY ORAF, DECEMBER 4–11, 1987

Department stores play a big part in our consumer society, especially during the last months on the calendar. It might be helpful if we started thinking of art galleries in the same way: they're where we "shop" for visual information and experiences. The Vancouver Art Gallery, our local big-name art department store, currently has five shows on its four levels.

In the main-floor Children's Gallery, near the Hornby entrance, Doug Coupland, Vancouver's journalistic answer to New York's Stephen Saban and Michael Gusto, has an installation called "Floating World." Coupland, who has a degree in Japanese "Business Science," makes reference with "Floating World" to a part of 18th-century Edo, now known as Tokyo. Floating World was the home of the Japanese underworld where the unemployed samurai, bandits, artists, prostitutes, and gamblers lived in a self-contained world outside the very rigid structure of Japanese society. The Japanese woodblock print is the most famous product of the original Floating World.

If Mr. Coupland, by conjuring this image with his title, makes any reference to that societal fringe in his messy, overwrought, badly designed store-window display, then it has escaped. The only other art reference left out of this chaotic, preciously placed jumble of objects is the Crucifixion. Do you know the trick picture where you try to find the hidden object? Well, the same sensibility is at work here. Has anyone ever seen a grey piece of bacon? Good luck, kids!

Dave Crosses Over

FROM UNDERCURRENTS, BY DAVE WATSON, JUNE 3–10, 1988

Jaywalking. What kind of a crime is that? Not a very important one, but big enough to be ticketed $15 for. What a stupid law. Millions of years of evolution went into the development of our acute senses, clever minds, and quick reflexes. Eventually we became the most powerful and dangerous species on the planet—and for what? So that a *lightbulb* can tell us that it's safe to cross the road? I think not....

Why did the critic cross the road? The answer to that would entail a metaphysical discussion, and life's just getting too short to bother with metaphysics. The fact is I *did* cross the road, and now I have a blue piece of paper to prove it. The subject is closed....

The Socred Stonehenge

FROM UNDERCURRENTS, BY DAVE WATSON, SEPTEMBER 9–16, 1988

This column is brought to you after a week of screaming failures, not all of them entirely my fault. The worst aggravation was SkyTrain's failure to proceed properly on the evening of September 1, once again screwing up my life on one of the very few excursions I make to New Westminster. SkyTrain. The official transit system of Hell.

It's the McDonald's of public transit—a garish place with uncomfortable seats, well-designed for thoughtless mechanical efficiency, but very poor for any sort of human enjoyment. You can't even relax on it, because every seat faces another. It must be a terrible place for borderline paranoids. I'm not saying that the Socreds are gullible, but I know *I* wouldn't pay a billion dollars for it....

Dave Goes Skiing

BY DAVE WATSON, FEBRUARY 12–19, 1988

What is it about this skiing stuff? You can't avoid it. Skiing touches all our lives, and it's a sport that everyone in town has an opinion on. Scratch Vancouverites in the wintertime and they'll hit you with a ski pole. They'll also tell you how much the pole cost, where it was purchased, why it's the best ever made, when the best time to buy ski equipment is, and where to get a ski-rack for a 1974 Volvo.

They'll tell you about boots, bindings, and goggles. They'll try to sell you some old ski equipment they don't need anymore. Don't misunderstand: it's really nice, and they'd keep it except that they need the money for lift passes or this darling new digital Ski-Dometer that records average and highest speeds, distance travelled, and time spent in weekend lift lines.

If they find out you don't ski, they'll give you ski advice, because everyone who's ever slid down a 10-degree slope on a piece of wood is a self-proclaimed ski expert. The sacred name of the best ski run on the best ski mountain might be uttered conspiratorially.

"Do leg exercises. Hamstring stretches," they tell you sagely. "Wear a tuque and bundle up," my mom offers. "Ski on an empty stomach," some say. "Ski on a full stomach," say others. Then you hear, "Don't ski on your stomach at all. Ski on a mountain. Wear skis."

Skiing looks so glamorous, especially if you watch James Bond movies or beer commercials. It is the heart of several Olympic sports—downhill slalom, 90-metre freestyle jump, and that weird blend of cross-country skiing (which some wag recently derided as nothing more than a Swede's way of going to the 7-Eleven) and target shooting. Who thought up that one? A survivalist?

Skiing is reported to be incredibly great, even by people who admit to not having skied for a decade. It sounds so good that it should be illegal. Take the snow reports, which sound more like *Miami Vice* cocaine-seizure statistics than anything else: base, powder, crystal, etc. Not to mention the healthy per-capita ratio of Porsches at trendy ski lodges—those people can't *all* own McDonald's franchises. Where does the money come from? Skiing is expensive, even if you do pack a lunch.

Despite all the data people will give you about skiing, there are things they won't say. They won't tell you that tow ropes on the bunny hills will eat a pair of $70 Italian gloves in less than a second. They won't tell you how embarrassing it is to forget to get off the chairlift (after a ride that is about as much of a thrill as I can stand in a single day) and thus trip the idiot bar, shutting the whole thing down and annoying absolutely everyone on the mountain.

Nobody really properly explained falling down an incline to me. (I'm from the Prairies. We had lots of snow, but no hills.) They said, "You might slip once or twice and land in a big pile of snow, but don't worry." Didn't seem like anything to be concerned about, but I fell down and tumbled with impressive momentum more than three dozen times on my first two runs. If I had known that was to be the case, I would have done some practice falls at home in the tub, where 25 percent of all accidents rightfully occur.

If you don't ski but want to know what it's like without actually having to go anywhere, risking getting lost, and being the subject of a massive search effort, begin with bruising exercises, perhaps a preparatory whelp-down with a bamboo stick to simulate appropriate rib and buttock pummelling. Tie four-foot lengths of two-by-fours to your least comfortable shoes and fall down the stairs while practising silly walks. Pour cold water down your pants while shredding money. Then pay $20 for a six-pack of beer and brag about what a good time you had. Build a little mountain with the empty cans.

Of Taxidermy, Gospel Tents, and Dixieland Bands

BY JAMES BARBER,

JULY 26–AUGUST 2, 1991

One fine day, the Socreds are going to dig up Wacky Bennett, send him to a good taxidermist, and stand him up on the platform at all their conventions, with a recorded message playing the party policy out of his desperately smiling, stuffed face.

That was about the only thing missing from the Socred leadership convention last weekend. Every time W.A.C.'s name was mentioned, there was applause. For Bill Bennett, too, and even for the other celebrated William—Mr. Vander Zalm—they all switched on the automatic response. Nobody said "Hallelujah," not out loud, but the teeth came out of the faces just the way they used to for Jimmy Swaggart, and the hands came together in the same flaccid ecstasy.

Swaggart, on the other side of town at the Gospel tent in Empire Stadium, drew his 400-odd faithful, while the Socreds had close to 2,000. Apart from the numbers, there was a lot of similarity between the two events.

Nobody said they were sorry, and at neither event did anybody come flat out and admit anything. Nobody spoke of the heritage of deceit and corruption and hypocrisy, and both spoke loudly of vision. Swaggart offered hell and the Devil as the only alternative to not following him, while the Socreds frightened themselves with images of the NDP, Mike Harcourt, and the everlasting flames of socialism.

This was not just a leadership campaign. It was a job interview. The Province of B.C. has had a management crisis. The CEO, publicly disgraced and (to an unbiased observer) either crazy or very stupid, has had the keys to his office taken away, his assistant has been temporarily taking his calls, and we've been looking for a new boss, maybe a new board of directors. But not one of the applicants was telling us much more than "Trust me."

As employment references, they were offering Dixieland bands, coloured umbrellas, and assorted party favours. There was talk of a new, improved product, a better product that will win the hearts and votes of the shareholders, but there was not even the slightest acknowledgement of anything ever being wrong with the old product.

Five candidates made virtually the same speech. Grace McCarthy spun some evangelical passion ("I received a gift, it changed my life, I want to share it with you…"),

ERNIE POOK'S COMEEK By Lynda Barry

AT NIGHT I KEEP SAYING BIG DEAL, BIG DEAL, IT'S JUST A STUPID BIRD. BUT IT TURNS OUT THERE'S NO SUCH THING.
IF YOU TELL ANYONE, I'LL BASH YOUR HEAD IN.

but it was a screech as much as a speech. Rita Johnston gave it a lot of desperation—she wanted the job, and if she had to stand on tiptoe and scream into the microphone, then that's what she had to do. And she did.

Mel Couvelier, normally a bright, witty, thinking man (and the only sensible option for the Socreds), managed to look as sad as an abandoned bloodhound and sounded like a graveside eulogist. Norm Jacobsen and Duane Crandall, one after the other, lip-synched the words in best Toastmaster's style. Crandall (at 39, the voice of youth in the party) did have the novel idea of "not only balancing the books, but balancing them as low as possible," but he also thought a stuffed white wolf displayed at his turf in the candidates' village would be a vote-catching idea.

They all addressed the delegates, but nobody really addressed the issues. The future—bright, rosy, and Socred—existed in a world untroubled by anything but the horrors of not being free enterprisers....

There were two agendas. One, open and declared, was to beat the NDP. The second, publicly unspoken but privately of primary importance, was to spite somebody else. It was a convention of petty spites, of paying back, of getting even, and it was a convention of personal and party confusions.

Rita Johnston got herself elected because there were so many long knives out for Grace McCarthy. "Revenge is a dish best eaten cold," says an old Arab proverb, and while McCarthy had everything going for her that the party stands for (real free enterprise, success, no special privileges for women—anybody can do it), these are precisely the things the party can't stand. And it took its revenge.

Grace McCarthy was simply too much for them. When Mel Couvelier dumped her and made his pledge to Rita, close to 30 of his delegates left the convention. "Rita's nothing, but Grace is unthinkable," said a Victoria delegate, "so I'm leaving." "There's no difference between Lillian Vander Zalm and Ray McCarthy," said another. And finally, in obvious glee (she may have been nursing the line for years), another butted in, "We'd better get the second ballot over before Grace's face slides off."

In addition to spite, there was a lot of confusion. The Socreds have a serious identity problem. The Christian ethic, fundamental to the party, seems to be getting pretty selective in regard to goodness and virtue.... Bill Bennett, with a face like a very old, very tired and rotting plum, was walking the floor without shame (and without Herb Doman). Robert Bonner, W.A.C.'s attorney general, doing a remarkable imitation of George C. Scott, was holding forth on truth and honesty, apparently having forgotten the 707 days in which his ministry kept the lid on Robert Sommers' bribery shenanigans, for which Sommers got five years. Phil Gaglardi wasn't there, but Bernie Smith (Socred president at the time of the dirty-tricks scandal) was getting a lot of exercise, trying to shake every hand that attempted to pass him.

The convention floor was littered with ex–cabinet ministers, which may have contributed to the confusion littering the minds of many of the delegates. "If there wasn't welfare, then all those women wouldn't be leaving their husbands," said a Jacobsen supporter. "Why should we help them? We have to have free enterprise. Anybody can make it in this province if they've got the will. My husband and I have worked side by side for 32 years, and we've made it despite our differences." I asked her what particular field of entrepreneurship they were engaged in, and she told me they were both employed by the DND—the Department of National Defence—that well-known private-sector institution totally unsupported by our tax dollars.

Somehow, all this confusion made itself obvious to the convention organizers. "I have to tell you," said Les Petersen (the party's permanent concession to intellectualism, who seems to have recently taken elocution lessons from Clyde Gilmour, the CBC's long-time voice of the living dead), "that delegates should be careful what they say. A certain television station [and here was a long and significant pause] has resorted to concealed microphones, and your remarks may well appear on television. *Without your knowledge....*" Another pause, for expressions of shock, and cries of "Shame." "And I will tell you that it was British Columbia Television...." More cries of shame, but it didn't seem to make a lot of difference. At least half of the people in the room must have fervently hoped they would be on TV, just to wave at the folks back home.

It was that kind of convention, with all the spontaneity and desperate gaiety of New Year's Eve in the old folks home, with hats, streamers, and brass bands. There were fewer than 1,000 seats occupied during the candidates forum, and there were 1,847 eligible voters. "I don't want to listen to that stuff—my mind's made up," said one man, energetically pumping a "Win With Grace" banner up and down while riding up and down on the escalators. "And if you print my name, I'll sue you."...

If one lesson came out of the convention, it was that being Socred today is to be confused. The party philosophy has always been one-dimensional (us against them), but there is now a big *them* in the party itself—them in the city, them with the money, them with friends in high places, them who ain't pro-life, them that are the Zalmoids, them over there, them, them, them.

And if Johnston's going to heal this, she's got to accept one basic premise—that free enterprise doesn't mean a licence to live in yesterday and govern from a time capsule.

If she doesn't heal it, then disinterring W.A.C. Bennett might be an insufficient fall-back position. Apart from being a little insensitive (and a little unsanitary), that one stuffed replica just might not be enough. Perhaps Lillian Vander Zalm could be persuaded that some of the $20,000 in the infamous briefcase at the Westin Bayshore was really for a shipment of life-size W.A.C. inflatables, one for every member.

Swaggart sells videos, inspirational cassettes, and selected writings. He just might be available—as a free-enterprise consultant?

Of Punks, Peach Crumble, and Pitiful Puns

BY IAN GILL, DECEMBER 6–13, 1991

There was a movie playing in town this past fall season called *Freddy's Dead: The Final Nightmare.* I didn't see it and I hope I never meet anyone who did, but if I'm not mistaken, the basic thrust of the *Freddy* movies—in sequel after awful sequel—is that yon Frederico is a bad piece of work and, kill him as they might, he somehow manages a rebirth that's more hideous than the last.

There was a new morning newspaper playing in town this past fall season called the *Vancouver Sun.* I saw it, and if I'm not mistaken, the basic thrust of yet another artless sequel in the *Sun*'s contorted career was twofold: to take the paper to morning publication and, in a concomitant strategy aimed at attracting more readers and more advertising dollars, to redesign and restock the editorial store. The word *rebirth* got tossed around a lot and, come the morning of September 16, so did copies of the new-look *Vancouver Sun.*

Two initial reactions: the paper came out early that morning and can thus be adjudged to have succeeded in its primary aim of becoming a morning paper. As for the refurbishing of form and content…at first glance, the reborn, pre-dawn *Vancouver Sun* appeared to be marginally less hideous than its immediate forebears. Now, in the months since its revivification, the *Vancouver Sun* has had a chance to reveal its true, new self. The swaddling clothes have slowly unravelled and, almost inevitably, the resurrection has begun to smack of false prophecy. Reborn, the *Sun* has gained weight without substance and, for all the hyperbole about what a signal event its going to morning publication would be, today's *Sun* turns out to be pretty much the same derivative, rebarbative idiot child that Vancouver inexplicably continues to tolerate as its newspaper of record.

And there's worse to come. Within possibly two years, definitely five, the *Vancouver Sun-Province* will be our omnibus morning newspaper—count on it. They still won't have killed the thing off, just joined it at the head with its sister. And you thought it was ugly now….

Vancouver Sun editor-in-chief Ian Haysom is one of those irrepressibly jocular types, the kind of guy you'd expect to find leading a sing-along at a church camp. Or, to borrow from Spiro Agnew, a sort of "nattering nabob of positivism." Given his track record at the *Province*, it is little wonder that Haysom's biggest challenge upon taking over the *Vancouver Sun*—to take the paper to mornings—was accomplished this fall in concert with a relentless "happification" of the newspaper. To the point that the paper is even less readable than before, and less relevant to the times. We were promised a morning newspaper, which to my mind really just meant that we'd get the same old rag, but with older news because they'd have to print it earlier. Instead, we now get old news, but it's old news made *happy* in an attempt to make it look more like new news. Or, as promised in a pre-launch brochure, the tone of the *Vancouver Sun* is now "more friendly and vibrant"—laudable qualities in, say, a piano tuner, but just plain irritating in a newspaper.

The *Vancouver Sun* went to morning publication in September on the heels of one of the most bizarre advertising and promotional campaigns this city has ever seen. Perhaps it was intentional reverse psychology that the paper's own advertising was at pains to highlight all the things readers might *not* like about the move to mornings. "If I wanted yesterday's news, I'd just buy a fish," read one of the paper's full-page ads. It then countered its own message with platitudes about how readers would now have all day to absorb the paper, that the *analysis* of the news would run so deep that it would never be dated, and that the features would "keep" all day long. The simple fact is, however, that the *Vancouver Sun* went to morning publication not to in any way serve the readers better, but because afternoon newspapers are dying in North America and the *Sun* was no exception....

The *Sun* anticipated a backlash against the move, such that Burson-Marsteller—the New York–based disaster spin doctors known for their work on Tylenol, Bhopal, Argentina's dirty war, the B.C. Forest Alliance, and other joyous turns of the globe—were hired to help steer the process. In the end, the move was hardly disastrous—even if the results were highly predictable.

Since September 16, the *Province* has been losing readers, especially sports fans who can no longer count on getting even box scores from the previous night, let alone up-to-date reporting. For its first edition, *Province* news reporters are filing their stories before the previous night's TV newscasts have even aired, so don't try telling *Province* readers that they're getting anything approximating news. That is, of course, unless you count the stuff that the *Province* can be accused of either making up or beating up. But such is the province of a tabloid.

As for the *Sun*, its circulation has been going up. The first figures I heard were that the papers basically exchanged 10,000 daily circulation at the tabloid's expense. I've since heard that the *Sun*'s gains have softened; it will be several more months before the Audit Bureau of Circulation issues reliable figures....

The readers were promised a great deal when the *Sun* moved to mornings in September. Certainly, as *Sun* columnist and media omnivore Stan Persky recently observed to me, there's "a lot more stuff" in the *Sun* these days than there used to be. But is any of it any good, and does it go any distance to fulfilling a mandate beyond providing Southam Inc. shareholders with a return on their investment?....

I guess it is somehow appropriate that in a country so paralysed by self-examination, the people who run a major daily newspaper might be similarly afflicted by the need to somehow "democratize" that process. Hence Nicole Parton, the *Sun*'s "community ambassador," and her absurd "citizen's advisory panel." Hence the *Sun*'s own town-hall meetings, where you get answers to that burning question: "What does an editor do?" Next, the *Sun* decides to alter its comics, and you, the reader, get to help choose the new ones. Kids have been invited to write movie reviews, among other things, for a page called Savvy. (Ooh, don't you just love it when newspapers talk hip?) There's now a Voices column on page three, where readers, otherwise unpublished *Sun* staffers (receptionists, worn-out editors), and the likes of Moira Farrow and Barbara Yaffe share their innermost thoughts with us.

Readers can win a travel bag and a beach towel if they send along a postcard from their vacation. One woman thought it would be neat to start a walking club, so she did what any self-respecting *Sun* reader would do: "I went to Ian [Haysom] with the idea and he thought it was great," she said, describing the genesis of the *Vancouver Sun* Walking Club. There's now a Community column on page B2 featuring, in

Nicole Parton's words, "the three As—adulation, applause, acclaim." A "happy news" column, in other words.

Likewise, readers are asked to send along suggestions for the paper's Best of B.C. campaign. And just in case readers weren't busy enough participating in all this self-congratulation, the *Sun* recently launched a Be a Sun Columnist contest, whereby readers get to write more stuff that will be published and maybe win them a prize in the process. Honestly, can we now be far from that crowning event, wherein some hapless soul is randomly plucked from the anonymity of readerdom, having won a contest to Be the Sun's Editor for a Day? Hand that person a beach towel!

The point is, what does any of this have to do with putting out an even semi-literate, moderately credible newspaper? A newspaper that seeks to be all things to all people ends up being everything *but* a newspaper. In its erratic attempt to deliver friendship and vibrancy, the *Sun* further erodes its slender authority. People don't want newspapers to be their friends. They look to newspapers to *tell* them what's happening in the world, not to ask them what they think is going on, then regurgitate unrepresentative and often uninformed opinion in endless artificial forums that live in the editor's sociological imagination as exercises in participant observation en route to reader empowerment.

More such cant-in-progress is evident in the recent demand for letters from readers outlining what they would like to see in the Canada Clause of the constitution. "It has become clear to Canadians that it isn't easy to define what it is to be Canadian," the *Sun* said. No easier, I'd hazard, than it is for the editors of the *Vancouver Sun* to define how it is one goes about publishing a newspaper. I don't know, maybe Joe Clark and Nicole Parton could engage in some sort of joint, liquid-free transmogrification that would answer both the big questions confronting society today. Question: What's a Canadian? Tentative answer: A *Vancouver Sun* reader. Question: What's a Canada Clause? Tentative answer: Nicole Parton with a beard and a red suit....

Sooner or later, all pretence at "competition" in Vancouver's newspaper market will cease, Southam will have a cash cow with just one teat, and the *Vancouver Sun-Province* will still want to be your friend. But that's a story for another day. We were, after all, brought here on the pretext of celebrating the *Sun*'s morning rebirth, and who better to encapsulate such a momentous event for us than the *Sun*'s resident bard, its wordsmith nonpareil, he who slathers words across a page like a dry-waller on Benzedrine. On September 16, under the headline (wince), "The sun rises and the *Sun* rises on a new morning," Stephen Hume masticated variously on the writings of Alphonse de Lamartine, on the observations of Monsieur de la Violette, on Richard Wilbur's morning air "awash with angels," before finally spitting up the following: "Here at the *Sun*, as our newborn morning edition greets your day, many of us will reflect on the setting of the evening *Sun*. A curious irony. In the very beginning, when the Vancouver we inhabit was barely a dream, the earliest progenitor of the *Sun* was named the *Saturday Sunset*. Yet this dawn also crowns our nostalgia with a celebration. It is the moment at which the past yields again to a new day." Quick, a *Georgia Straight* beach umbrella and a year's free membership in our crawling club for the first reader who can figure out what the hell he's on about. Chances are, whomever you are, you're not just a true *Sun* reader. You're probably a real Canadian, too.

Here We Are Now, Entertain Us

BY DAVE WATSON, JULY 17–24, 1992

Summer brings two great curses to Vancouver:

1. Teenagers are exempted from school and allowed to roam freely about the city with the normal people, who are thus subjected to unhealthy amounts of skateboarding and rap music.

2. The wave of tourists hits its annual peak, filling the sidewalks with meandering and relaxed bodies that aren't on their immediate way to someplace else, obstructing and provoking jealousy in those of us with firm agendas and full schedules.

There are several similarities between these two groups. Both proliferate in summer. Both actively loiter in public, like this was some kind of damn resort or something. Both are also sometimes clad in really ridiculous clothing.

Differences? Oh sure, a few. Tourists have money and cameras, which the teenagers could have but thankfully haven't worked up the gumption to take yet. And another comparison: a tourist usually won't start swearing at you unless you punch him, while a teenager usually won't stop until you do.

Also, the tourists are far more interesting. The teens are local, and just looking for a cheap place to sit around and compare acne remedies and algebra teachers. The tourists have selected this spot on the globe and invested significant money and time towards coming here. But if you live here, you tend to forget why people would do that—choose to hang out in the same mundane place in which we work, sleep, and shop for toilet paper. This phenomenon needs understanding.

Tourism Vancouver has just released a study of the economic value of local tourism in 1991, full of statistics, percentages, and bar graphs. The report claims that 5.94 million overnight visitors came to Greater Vancouver in 1991 and left an estimated $1.72 billion behind when they packed their bags. That's the third consecutive year overnight visitors have topped the 5.81 million–person mark set here in 1986, when we had Expo and staged somewhat of a breakthrough in tourism.

And what made them select a trip to Vancouver? A guidebook, perhaps? Those can be strange sources of information, as the Cecil Hotel has discovered. Parties of young Japanese women have shown up in the bar, which is a strip joint, apparently drawn there by some guidebook recommendation.

Frommer's Canada '92–93 is the least accurate, but is very entertaining in its inaccuracies. It begins with a near-poetic ode to the wilderness and diversity of the province, then describes Vancouver as "a place where mountains and ocean seem to have had a love affair and given birth to a city," which borders on civic pornography.

Robson Street is selected as the local "focus and orientation point," with the notation that "you can spend days strolling its length." Must be disappointing to come here and find out how short "Robsonstrasse" (as several guidebooks still refer to it) really is, or that people who live downtown mainly consider it a convenient location for London Drugs.

The criticism of Granville Mall begins well (too few benches, plants, and sidewalk cafés to make for a successful pedestrian mall), but then mentions that "portions of it have become rather tacky stomping grounds for teenagers, reeking of soggy chips and chicken batter." Yes, that skunklike odour of chicken batter, being sold by the gram.

SQW 92
CAFE
TRAVEL BACK
VANCOUVER'S HASTINGS STREET
TO THE GOLDEN AGE OF NEON

White Peril

BY TARAS GRESCOE, JUNE 16–23, 1995

As he walks past the small, carefully tended gardens of Strathcona, Vancouver's oldest residential neighbourhood, Mr. Sang Lee can recall a time when he didn't have to knock used condoms out of the rosebushes or flick syringes into the gutter with the tip of his umbrella. During the past year, the president of the Strathcona Property Owners and Tenants Association—one of Canada's oldest neighbourhood-rights groups—has watched drug-related crime hit the streets in earnest, an overflow from the incessant dealing at the nearby intersection of Hastings and Main. "The selling of drugs seems to be very active over the last year. Some people who are not residents of this area are trying to bring drugs and prostitution to this neighbourhood."

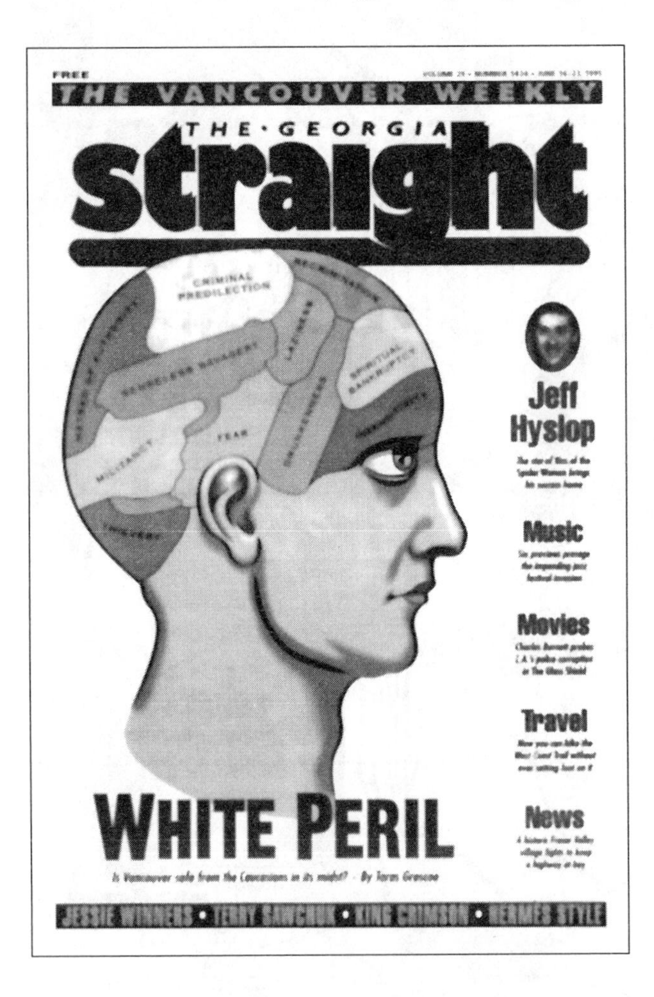

Who are these arrivals, the dealers, pimps, and burglars poisoning life for the residents of Strathcona? Mr. Sang Lee doesn't have to think twice. "Most people involved in local criminal activities are Caucasians."

It's one of the tragedies of Vancouver's urban geography that the city's oldest residential neighbourhood, peopled by the founders of the city—farmers from China's Guangdong province, whose families have prospered in the New World—is also bordered by one of Canada's hotbeds of white crime. On any given day, Mr. Sang Lee can watch Irish- and Scottish-Canadian dealers on Hastings Street peddling heroin outside the bars and welfare hotels. When their clients run out of cash for their habits (and statistics show that drug addiction in Canada is an overwhelmingly white problem), they break into the respectable homes of Strathcona—then sell what they've stolen to pawnshops on Hastings. Not coincidentally, many of these shops are owned by other Caucasians....

When Mr. Sang Lee came to Vancouver in 1967, he—like many other settlers—was looking for a safe and prosperous place to raise his children. But it's becoming clear that in this paradise on the Pacific, all is not as advertised. The tourist brochures and magazine articles that have attracted settlers from Hong Kong, India, and Singapore may dwell on the city's scenery, but they inevitably fail to mention that it is also home to a burgeoning Caucasian underclass. What's at work is a disturbing social trend: while 41,252 immigrants from around the world came to B.C. in 1994—by far the nation's wealthiest immigrants—almost as many, 38,649, came from other Canadian provinces. Many of these "in-migrants" were poor—and most of them were white. Alongside peaceful residential neighbourhoods, the city's swollen welfare rolls and overflowing skid-road bars are breeding a Caucasian criminal class with no scruples about the race of their victims.

It's long been a truism among criminologists that, in Canadian prisons, white faces tend to outnumber those of visible minorities. Statistics released by the Correctional Service of Canada show that Caucasian Canadians are regularly overrepresented in federal pens. In British Columbia's penitentiaries, where 2,114 prisoners are incarcerated, 1,573—or 74 percent—are Caucasian. People of Asian descent, who account for 11 percent of B.C.'s population, account for only four percent of the province's federal prisoners. Nationwide, the figures are even more telling: although only one in a hundred prisoners is Asian, fully 80 percent are white. These unsettling statistics are finally forcing observers and experts to ask some tough questions. Why do so many whites turn to crime, and in numbers out of all proportion to their representation in the population at large? Is it merely a cultural failing—a lack of morality in a group for whom family values and tradition are falling by the wayside—or, more ominously, is it something genetic, an innate propensity toward crime?

Can anything be done about these monsters in our midst?...

Letters

JUNE 23–30, 1996

Taras Grescoe's "White Peril" was an appalling read. Rife with racism and pandering to the pseudoscience of sociobiology, the article indulges in several disturbing conceits.

Reverse racism is not a tolerable practice. Although at first I was gratified to finally read an article that dispels the urban myth that new Canadians are responsible for crime in Vancouver, being Asian-Canadian, I was soon repulsed by the article.

Grescoe disingenuously quotes Elliott Leyton and Earnest Hooton to buttress his statistical observations and interviews. Hooton and Leyton, in the context of "White Peril," subscribe to sociobiology and genetic determinism. Grescoe quotes Hooton: "[The Celtic type] ranks first in assault, just as in red hair..."

It is a horrifying correlational statement that has the whiff of eugenics and ethnic cleansing.

Not only does "White Peril" buy into a lot of bunk, it also undertakes an assault on the Scots and Irish of Shaughnessy. It is snide, self-congratulatory, and smacks of liberal self-righteousness. Whenever the liberal media give free rein to reverse racism, it is the minority communities that suffer the backlash, not the liberal media.

James-Jason Lee
Vancouver

Thank you for the wonderful piece "White Peril" by Taras Grescoe. I hope the journalists and editors of our Vancouver media can see the errors of their racist ways. Their fear-mongering, stereotyping, and "exotifying" coverage of people of colour is

so painful and so tiresome. Perhaps through the humour of this clever satire they will get the message. Writing to them and pleading for sensitivity has been futile. Thank you. Thank you.
Valerie Jerome
Vancouver

Finally, a *Straight* article that does not treat Euro-Canadians as an amorphous group, but recognizes that they, too, are many ethnics with their own history of oppression and suffering. I am pleased that the dark secret of Canadian society, the plight of the Gaels, was highlighted.

I offer some of the public policy implications of Grescoe's research. The prison statistics are proof of rampant judicial discrimination against Gaelic-Canadians. I believe a separate Celtic justice system in which we could use the judicial practices of our ancient tribes, such as mutilation and human sacrifice, would be more culturally sensitive to our needs.

The burgeoning underclass of Gaels detailed by Grescoe shows the need for an equity program with hiring targets for Gaelic-Canadians. University places and funding should be reserved for Celts. UBC should build a traditional Highland castle (but with heat, water, sewage, and electricity) on campus as a place where Celts can gather. Government services, signs, and documents must be made available in Gaelic. Anyone convicted of a crime against a person in a kilt, because that person is wearing a kilt, should be subject to a harsher sentence.

The cultural healing can start with the CBC funding programs on the Duke of Cumberland's "pacification" of the Highlands and Cromwell's slaughtering conquest of Ireland. The government must lobby the English to issue a full apology (and a cash payment would be nice) so the Celts can start the healing process. The TV series *The Highlander* must be banned as a case of cultural appropriation. The Canada Council needs to fund "Writing Through Plaid" conferences in which Celts can be among their own and discuss being Gaelic in an oppressive Anglo-Saxon society.

Although these measures may seem costly, they pale compared to the cost to Canadian society if we lose another generation of Gaels.
Richard MacRae
Richmond

When Will the Mayhem End?

BY KEN HEGAN, MAY 16–23, 1996

Carey is an eight-year-old child born with neither gonads nor the vocal cords to complain about it. Carey has thumbless hands, floppy shoes, striped socks, bright-yellow pants, and a plucky, toothless grin. Carey is not like the other boys and girls. Little Carey is a mascot.

"Carey is a walking United Way logo," coordinator Lori Johnstone explained, "our ambassador who reminds us that we can instil hope of a better life by caring for one another and working together."

Sadly, Carey has learned how idle Surrey youths work together. In 1991, Carey was waddling around the city accompanied by the Royal Bank mascot, Leo the Lion.

Without warning, they were pounced upon by a pack of preteen boys who grabbed Carey's arms and tried to rip Carey apart. The boys punched Carey in the face and Carey ended up turtled, absorbing kick after kick. Leo the Lion ran away, but the youths soon caught him and punched his nose in. "The most disturbing part was the onlookers did not attempt to give any assistance," sighed Johnstone. "They just watched and laughed. On the positive side, during this whole unfortunate incident, Carey's smile never wavered. What a trooper!"

Isolated incident? Think again. Carey has been stabbed in the back with a stick by a 10-year-old boy, savagely bitten by a dog, and roughed up by a gang of teens who chased Carey into the National Bank of Canada. This last "wilding" was different. It happened at the Bentall Centre, downtown.

What's going on, Vancouver? Obviously, mascot abuse is not just a suburban phenomenon.

Consider the case of Bee Bop, the Vancouver Aquarium's mascot. Bee Bop is a gentle, smiling beluga whale with lots of blubber and fur for children to hug and stroke. However, during a recent Symphony of Fire fireworks competition, Bee Bop was viciously attacked by preteens on rollerblades. "As a mascot," said Brenda Nyznik, "there is nothing more upsetting than repeated blows to the head from unseen assailants."

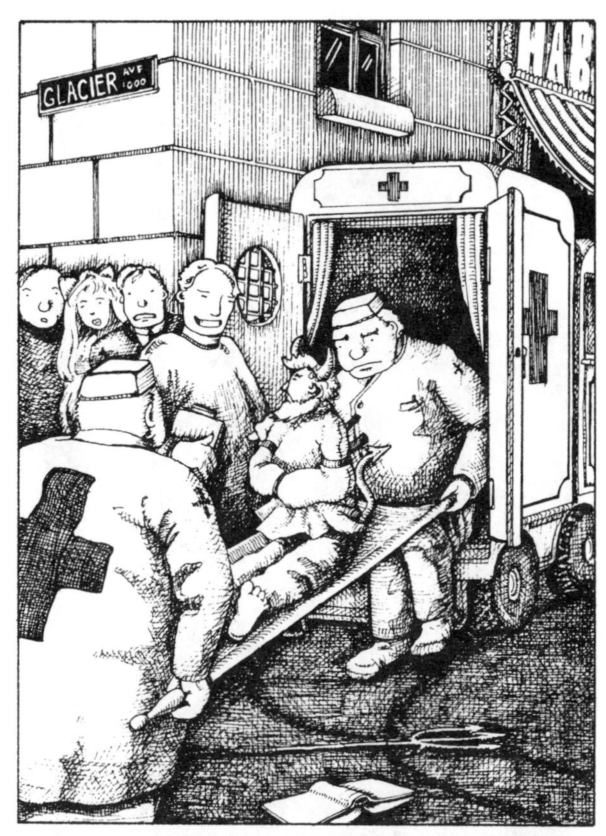

"Look, relax. This isn't the middle ages. If you really are the Devil, of course we'll release you."

Peach of a Dream Leads to a Trinity of Messiah Tests

BY BILL RICHARDSON,

DECEMBER 12–19, 1996

I dreamed I had a baby. Gave birth to one, I mean. As dreams go, it was very arresting. I was not alarmed, but I was sure surprised: surprised that this was happening at all, especially to me. It was the last thing I'd have expected. It was nothing I'd ever asked or hoped for. Also, I was surprised—and rather pleased—that it came to me so easily, this birthing business. My baby didn't have to fight its way out of any of the available holes or crevices, and there was no pushing or panting or straining on my part. I simply felt a stirring, looked down, and there it was: this welling fetus, growing out of the region of my navel, rising up like bread from a pan. The most benign of tumours. A ripening peach. Just at the moment it was about to detach itself—at which point, I had the impression, it would float up and bounce along the ceiling—I came to. I lay there in bed, inhabited by a slight throbbing in my thighs, as well as by a peculiar feeling of absence, and by the lingering suspicion that herein lay a message, a sign or portent to which I should pay attention. After all, miracles of an obstetric variety are known to occur at this time of year. If only I had remained somnolent for just another minute or two, I might have heard an annunciatory voice pronounce me—possibly in Latin—blessed among men. All day long I pondered these things in my heart. On the way home from work, I stopped at the drugstore to pick up a pregnancy test.

Whenever I browse the shelves of the local London Drugs, I get a bad case of vulva envy. Gals are so lucky! All that us fellas have access to is shaving supplies and a few varieties of condoms. But gals! Gals can choose from all those pads and panty liners and sprays and gels and deodorants and creams. There's row after row of something for every vaginal microclimate. So, I wasn't so very surprised to find that in this one quite small pharmacy there were no fewer than seven pregnancy tests. I decided to buy them all.

The pharmacist gave me the well-practised supercilious look of someone who is often asked for free methadone samples. "They're all the same, you know," she said as I set my septet on her counter. "They test for a hormone in the urine, and they're all the same." I gave her a kind of gosh-shucks Jimmy Stewart shrug, in order that she might think me a nervous father-to-be who wanted to leave no stone unturned in uncovering the truth of his happy wife's gravidity. "They're all the same," she said, more firmly, as I pushed them toward her. "What? All the same?" I asked. "All the same," she answered. She was beginning to wax quite tart, as if she didn't want me to have more than my share, as if she thought me greedy, even though the shelves were still groaning with a dazzling array of fertility prognosticators. "Fine, then. I'll just take three," I said, sensing that compromise would have to be brought to bear unless I wanted to do some pretty fancy explaining. I just didn't feel like telling her, as probably I ought to have, that when you think you might be on the cusp of parenting the new Messiah, you really can't be too careful and seven pregnancy tests is not a superfluity. She slipped my packages of Fact Plus, Answer Now, and Clearblue Easy into a discreet sack and said, "That comes to $50.79." I paid up and left the store. I couldn't wait to get home and try them out! En route, I paused briefly to buy and swill a litre of mineral water. By the time I got through the door I was fit to bust.

I danced a nervous jig in the kitchen while I opened the boxes. My dog danced along, thinking I might be unwrapping something edible from which she could profit. She jumped up to sniff the thin wand that slid from the Answer Now box, which in its foil wrapping is just the size and shape of an after-dinner mint we both favour. A similar contrivance lived in Clearblue Easy, while Fact Plus housed no fewer than three tenants: a plastic urine container, an applicator, and a hermetically sealed "test disk." Each kit came with a long sheet of instructions, and these quickly put the lie to the pharmacist's "all the same" reassurances. Although they share a common principle and end (pee, then wait to see if you're knocked up), they are administratively vastly different, one from the other. For instance, only the makers of Answer Now were thoughtful enough to incorporate an "easy grip handle" on their "one step tester." The purveyors of Clearblue Easy were scrupulous in their own way, providing a cap you can slip onto the "absorbent sampler tip" in order to prevent spotting on the bathroom counter, as well as specific directions that while peeing, one mustn't splash the windows in which the test results are displayed. Although Fact Plus—with its clinical sample cup and its urine dropper and the "test disk" into which the stuff is dripped—is far and away the most cumbersome of the three, it also provides the user with the suitably grave feeling of taking part in a carefully regulated scientific experiment. I found Answer Now the easiest to use of the three, and its pink answer to my question came up very quickly and distinctly. The robin-egg whispering of Clearblue Easy took longer to be heard, and was never as clearly articulated. Even though Fact Plus kept me in suspense just a tad too long, and left me with a cup full of cooling pee to deal with, it was the most fun of the three.

My trinity of tests showed a common result. In the fullness of time, all will be revealed. I'm not yet ready to spill the beans. In the interim, if anyone can tell me the name of the English insurance company that will pay 1,500,000 bucks to clients who can prove to have been impregnated by God (*Harper's* Index, December '96), give me a dingle. Late morning is best. Typically, the nausea eases up around 11.

HEALTH AND WELFARE

The Greenpeace Giant

BY MARTIN DUNPHY, SEPTEMBER 13–20, 1991

There always seemed to come a point in the old Andy Hardy films when young star Mickey Rooney would jump to his feet, smitten with brilliant insight, and declare: "I know, let's put on a show!" Right on cue, an equally young Judy Garland or Ann Rutherford would chime in with: "Sure, my dad has a barn!" It was corny, but they got the attention of the audience—and they put on the closest thing to a spectacle that those darn kids could produce.

Life imitated art in Vancouver in 1970. The scene: two frustrated Sierra Club members, Jim and Marie Bohlen, are sitting around the kitchen table mulling over effective ways to protest an upcoming U.S. nuclear test at Amchitka, Alaska. Cue Marie: "I know, let's put on a show! We'll get a boat and sail into the test zone, and everyone will watch!" Sadly, no one's dad had a boat, but those darn kids and their friends found the *Phyllis Cormack* and sailed into a spectacle the world's been watching ever since.

Greenpeace was born.

Of course, just as those films are gone forever, so is that method of starting up environmental organizations. Things have changed. Besides, Andy's dad today would have to be the CEO of IBM and Judy's dad would have to own international PR giant Ogilvy and Mather. Consider this Greenpeace media release dated August 29, 1991: "Today the Greenpeace flagship *Rainbow Warrior* leaves Kitimat, B.C., for the Kitlope Valley. A European delegation on board the *Rainbow Warrior*, including a Finnish Member of Parliament and a representative of the Swedish Samme people, will join with members of the Haisla people on a three-day fact-finding mission into the valley. The Swedish participants will remain in the Kitlope with a film crew from Greenpeace's Communications Division, which is planning a European documentary release of the footage this fall. They will return to Vancouver on September 2, and will be available for interviews."

Compare that release with the following, the August 4, 1976, edition of a daily bulletin distributed to crew members of the *James Bay*, a Greenpeace anti-whaling ship aiming to take on the Russians in the north Pacific: "*Recommended mental attitude:* Positive. Don't shit on anybody with your trip, especially if it happens to be a bummer. If you're feeling great and totally on top of it, tell everybody you see, especially poor, downed crew members who need to hear good news instead of problems, all of which originate in the individual psyche as projections of internal karmic ritual behaviour. *Scheduled departure time:* I beg you, please don't fuck everything up by mouthing heavily in every direction...Love each other for each of our heroic struggles. Love your brothers and sisters...Don't bug the skipper on this point, because of the personal risks involved. Period."

Even if people did still write that way, Greenpeace can't *afford* to sound like that anymore. The lean, green fighting machine that launched a decrepit 80-foot halibut seiner from Vancouver in its inaugural action in September of 1971 has become, as it prepares to enter its third decade, the largest and most influential environmental organization in the world.

The long-haired, bell-bottomed, *I Ching*–consulting karma commandos of the early days have been replaced by a worldwide network of professional administrators, scientists, expert fund-raisers, and media and communications specialists. A fleet of eight modern, globe-girdling ships, helicopters, and even a hot-air balloon have superseded the old fishboat and wooden sailing vessels of the first campaigns. A private communications network with satellite uplinks and an extensive database now does the work previously entrusted to rumours, word of mouth, and phones with several months' worth of overdue bills.

For those charged with the economic well-being of the organization, the hand-to-mouth, eternally in-debt status of its chaotic formative years has disappeared in the wake of well-organized teams of fund-raisers. Bummer trips and karmic ritual behaviour don't cut it in today's disposable-income scene.

It's the very size of Greenpeace today—coupled with fears that the organization has become fund-raising driven while overextending itself—that has led to charges of conservatism and a lack of results to show for such an enormous budget. Is Greenpeace in danger of betraying its grass-roots activist past? Has it lost the cutting edge that came with fearless eco-warriors throwing their bodies between harpoons and whales, between seals and clubs, between ice floes and ships' hulls?

There are, literally, thousands of other environmental groups in North America, many of them born out of the '60s and fighting long before Greenpeace or its predecessor, the Don't Make a Wave Committee, came on the scene. Greenpeace Canada executive director Michael Manolson says the proliferation of those groups points out the need for an organization like his. "Take Greenpeace *and* all the other groups put together, and we're just a drop in the bucket compared to the enormous forces arrayed against us."...

While it's certainly comforting to realize there are that many people out there who care about the future of this planet, the question is: are they all getting their money's worth?

Critics such as Paul Watson, an early Greenpeace activist who was heavily involved in the Save the Whales campaigns and the seal-hunt protests, don't necessarily think so. "Greenpeace lost touch with its roots a long time ago. It's lost its passion. It's a corporation, a multinational eco-corporation.... Other groups are doing a hell of a lot more than Greenpeace on a fraction of the budget, and they don't litter the U.S. with 48 million pieces of direct mail per year. I think it's hypocritical for an environmental organization to litter the world with so much junk. The problem is, Greenpeace is a feel-good organization. People join to feel good. It's a waste of millions of dollars."...

PR Giants, President's Men, and B.C. Trees

BY BEN PARFITT, FEBRUARY 21–28, 1992

On a grey day in late November 1990, a handful of senior executive officers with some of B.C.'s biggest forest companies gathered in a downtown Vancouver boardroom to hear a sales pitch from one of the most powerful public relations firms in North America.

It was not a happy time for the captains of B.C.'s biggest industry. Pulp, paper, and lumber markets were drying up, prices were falling, and a protracted recession was under way. On the international front, Greenpeace was mounting a sophisticated anti-chlorine campaign in Germany that threatened to cripple or sink some B.C. pulp producers.

Back home, ominous signals were emanating from a government-appointed commission—signals that said perhaps it was time big forest companies shared some of their publicly owned timber holdings. Amid these cannon shots, the captains found themselves drifting closer and closer to a reef with little wind in their sails to steer a new course. Years of expensive "Forests Forever" PR campaigning had failed to sway the public to their point of view. Fewer and fewer people believed the captains any more.

If B.C.'s big forest companies weren't in a state of crisis, they were dangerously close to it. The captains knew that, and that's why they had sent out an S.O.S. It was time for the boys from Burson-Marsteller Ltd., masters of crisis management, to spin a new tale for a beleaguered client.

The captains were obviously impressed with what they heard. And Burson-Marsteller was promptly awarded a first-year, $1-million contract. The boys from Burson had a simple notion—forest companies couldn't rely on themselves to solve their PR problems. Putting a company forester in front of a clear-cut mountain slope to say "What we're doing here is mimicking Mother Nature" wasn't going to sell. What was needed was an "independent" group of people—not seen as having any vested interest—to defend the companies.

Five months after the November meeting, just such a group was unveiled at a news conference at Stanley Park's Fish House. The B.C. Forest Alliance was introduced to the assembled media members by Burson-Marsteller employee and new Alliance executive director Gary Ley. Media representatives were told the new group,

headed by IWA Canada president Jack Munro, would bring reason and truth to forestry disputes dividing the province.

The question became whether the Alliance's directors, many of whom were hand-picked by Burson-Marsteller and 13 of B.C.'s biggest forest companies, could fulfil their mandate to maintain a healthy forest economy and forested environment. If circumstances required, would they be willing to risk all and bite the hand that feeds them? Those questions remain unanswered, and largely because the Alliance's initial moves were mapped out by Burson-Marsteller, not the ostensibly independent body it put in place.

Furthermore, when questions of Burson-Marsteller's past—its work for the former military junta in Argentina, for example—have been raised, the PR firm has displayed little, if any, regret for past actions and a genuine hostility toward the press for raising such issues. When *Vancouver Sun* columnist Stephen Hume wrote a series of pieces questioning the ethics of Burson-Marsteller working for a junta that was busy "disappearing" thousands of its own citizens, Alliance supporters suggested he should resign because the same PR firm had taken an account with the *Sun*'s publisher, Pacific Press.

Harold Burson himself even took the extraordinary step of flying from his Manhattan offices to Vancouver to tell his side of the story on Argentina in a pre-arranged interview with *Sun* columnist Trevor Lautens. But it's not just Burson-Marsteller executives who attack certain members of the press. The Alliance's directors have largely fallen in line with their creators, insisting the press is wrong to focus any attention on the PR firm's past and present actions.

Take, for example, University of British Columbia professor of forest policy Les Reed and his comments on my *Sun* article that disclosed that senior Burson-Marsteller employee and Alliance consultant Ken Rietz played an important role in Richard Nixon's scandal-ridden 1972 re-election campaign and was a key figure in Ronald Reagan's presidential nomination in 1980.

Quoted in a recent article in *B.C. Report,* Reed suggested I was little different than the late Senator Joseph McCarthy—he of the early-'50s Communist witch-hunt fame. "It would take a heavily biased mind like Ben Parfitt's to establish any connection at all!" between Mr. Rietz's involvement 19 years ago in the Nixon campaign and his work for the Forest Alliance, Reed said. *B.C. Report,* it should be noted, failed to point out Reed's directorship on the Alliance or the fact that his chair at UBC is paid for, in part, by the very companies who fund the Alliance....

Rietz is Burson-Marsteller's executive vice-president for North America. In 1972, he played an important role in secur-ing the youth vote for Richard Nixon. But, as was later revealed during the Senate Watergate hearings and in media coverage of the issue, Rietz was also associated with the so-called *dirty tricks* that marred Nixon's campaign and later cost the president his job.

In stories in the *Washington Post* and in Bob Woodward and Carl Bernstein's now-famous book on the Watergate scandal, *All the President's Men,* Rietz's hand in facilitating a spying operation on then-Democratic front runner Edmond Muskie was detailed. Those accounts note how John Erlichman, Nixon's chief domestic-affairs advisor, told the Senate Watergate committee how a Nixon campaigner worked undercover as Muskie's personal driver. Muskie befriended the spy, who returned the favour by secretly photographing the senator's mail. Erlichman said the spy was a former cab driver recruited by a friend of Rietz's.

The friend, according to an article in the *Washington Post,* was an ex-FBI agent named John "Fat Jack" Buckley. And Buckley was the man who received the photographs of Muskie's mail. "Like a couple of characters in a spy thriller, Rietz and Fat Jack would meet on street corners near the White House to transfer the clandestine negatives," the article said....

How Should We Police the Police?

BY MARTIN DUNPHY, DECEMBER 11–18, 1992

Daniel Possee just happened to be in the wrong place in North Vancouver at the wrong time. He also had the great misfortune to be plinking away with a pellet gun at a box of kitty litter when Cpl. Doug Bruce and Const. Tim Pollitt of the West Vancouver police stepped unannounced and in street clothes through the door of his basement suite that night of the 12th of May. Bruce found himself one metre away from a man holding what appeared to him to be a shotgun, and Pollitt opened fire with his semi-automatic 9mm handgun. The bullet struck the 22-year-old in the chest.

Neither the expected kilogram of marijuana nor the two people named in their search warrant—Possee's sister, Kelly, and her boyfriend—were in the apartment. The information used to obtain the warrant, approved by a real estate agent who also works part-time as a justice of the peace, was supplied by a confidential informant just three hours before the raid. Yet Kelly had separated from her boyfriend and moved out three days previously.

Daniel Possee's last words were "Oh, shit."

Three months before Possee's death, Feng Hua Zhang and Wai Shuen Wong—a 30-year-old food-factory worker and a 20-year-old student, respectively—were relaxing in their basement suite in East Vancouver on a Sunday afternoon. Zhang was sleeping and Wong was dozing off and on while watching TV in his room when the main door burst open and a heavily armed group of masked men poured in.

Terrified, Zhang ran to his room, closing the door. Wong, equally frightened, came out of his room only after repeated commands and threats of shooting by the gun-toting invaders, who turned out to be members of the police department's emergency response team (ERT). Wong says he was grabbed, dragged out of the house and roughed up, had his glasses flicked off, and was sprayed in the eyes with Capstun, a painful and incapacitating oleoresin capsicum (pepper) spray.

Meanwhile, Zhang, who understood no English and thought they were being robbed, was listening to heavy footsteps from the suite above his when his door was shot in (by a non-lethal, disintegrating projectile, according to police), introducing Capstun to his room. He ran to an open closet and cowered in a fetal position, from which he was grabbed by his hair and his arms, punched in the face and head, and dragged from the house to a lane. There, an ERT member sprayed him in the face with Capstun and he was kicked, punched, and handcuffed. The suite was left a shambles.

The problem was that the police had the wrong apartment and the wrong people. The beating in the lane was captured on videotape by a neighbour, and the assault was broadcast nationwide by news services.

Police said a tip had led them to believe a significant amount of heroin and cocaine was being dealt from the house and that the residents were in possession of two handguns. No guns or drugs were recovered in the raid; $10,000 was found in the upstairs suite. After an ambulance dropped them at St. Paul's Hospital to flush their eyes, Zhang and Wong had to borrow money from hospital staff to take a bus back to their ransacked apartment.

The fact that such tragic and traumatic incidents could, quite literally, happen to anyone was frightening enough. What was perhaps more frightening was the official police response to the two events: in neither case was an apology for its actions extended by the police department in question; no wrongdoing or mistakes were admitted; and both departments as much as stated that they'd do things no differently if given a second chance.

To John Westwood, executive director of the B.C. Civil Liberties Association, the botched police raids provide prime examples of the need for a mechanism for impartial review of incidents of police force resulting in death or injury.

As he puts it: "There appears to be a pretty significant gap between what the police view as acceptable and tolerable levels of force and what the public thinks are acceptable and tolerable levels of force."

The bungled raids weren't the only police actions to stir up public sentiment earlier this year. Two other police shootings of unarmed suspects in January and March, resulting in one death and one wounding, had focused public attention on the RCMP and Vancouver police. The RCMP corporal involved in the wounding had also shot and wounded another unarmed man during a drug raid two years earlier—what he had thought was a weapon turned out to be a TV remote control.

More than anything, Daniel Possee's father, Derek, says, it was the absence of an apology or admission of error on the part of the police that galvanized him to go public with his family's tragedy.

In October, regional Crown counsel Bob Wright decided it was reasonable for Const. Pollitt to have shot Daniel because the pellet gun he had been target-shooting with appeared to be a lethal weapon. Wright also mentioned Daniel's consumption of marijuana and alcohol immediately prior to his death as being among his reasons for not recommending charges be laid against the police. (Police found half an ounce of marijuana in the apartment.) Then, West Vancouver police chief Hal Jenkins compounded the Possees' anguish with the insensitive pronouncement that Daniel was "a casualty of the illicit use of drugs."

Just as in the public washing of hands by police in the Possee case, the final disposition of the Commercial Drive ERT raid lacks the stamp of any recognition of fallibility or—especially—humility.

A medical report on Zhang's condition after the raid, from Vancouver doctor Raymond Kwan to Det. Bob Cooper, listed the following injuries as a result of police actions: chemical conjunctivitis, a rib contusion, a kidney contusion, forehead and cheek contusions, and post-traumatic stress disorder. Dr. Kwan's list of Wong's injuries included: chemical conjunctivitis, traumatic perforation of the right eardrum, a genitourinary tract contusion, a forehead abrasion, and abrasions of the thigh, wrist, and leg.

Three months after the February 9 incident, special prosecutor Glen Orris announced that no charges would be laid against any of the police involved and that the force used during the raid was not "excessive or unreasonable." He also told reporters there was "absolutely no comparison" to be made between the famous videotaped beating of Rodney King by Los Angeles police and the tape of Zhang being beaten. In that, he was correct—at least with respect to the duration of the beating and police terminology. Det. Cooper described the actions of the two videotaped ERT members as "distractor techniques"; the L.A. police described the beating levelled on King as "a controlled application of baton strikes."...

Is Logging Threatening Our Water?

BY BEN PARFITT, MARCH 12–19, 1993

...From its inception in 1926, the Greater Vancouver Water District—under its first commissioner, Ernest Cleveland—strongly fought all attempts to open the Capilano, Seymour, and, later, the Coquitlam watersheds to logging. (The water district was then a separate entity, but today it is an arm of the GVRD with jurisdiction over water quality in the region.)

Cleveland (for whom the Capilano watershed's dam is named) maintained throughout his time as commissioner that logging and road-building greatly increased the risk that silt and other organic debris would be deposited in Vancouver's drinking water. Indeed, four years before assuming the post, he argued as provincial comptroller of water rights that any timber holdings in the watersheds should be taken from logging companies and turned over to city or district control.

"The pre-eminent objective to be attained is the maintenance of an adequate supply of pure water—all other considerations are subordinate: and to that end, the watershed should be preserved inviolate," Cleveland wrote in a report to the lands ministry on future ownership options of Vancouver's watersheds.

There were, of course, powerful provincial forces opposed to Cleveland, including then-minister of lands T.D. Pattullo. Pattullo, who often lobbied in Victoria on behalf of the province's burgeoning forest industry, proposed in 1924 that the Capilano Timber Company, which had been logging in the Capilano watershed since 1918, should be granted more logging rights in the area.

Then, as now, all sorts of reasons were given why the timber should come out. In a nutshell, it went something like this: The trees are old. If they aren't cut down, they'll be rendered useless for lumber production and, in all likelihood, burn in some cataclysmic fire, thus ruining Vancouver's drinking water.

In reply, John Davidson, a UBC botany professor, said the Capilano Timber Company had already logged significant stretches of the Capilano watershed, and that logging activity would increase the risk of flooding and erosion. The only reason the company wanted more cutting rights, Davidson said, was because logging had already deforested the valley from just below the reservoir's water intake at Capilano Creek, around Sister's Creek and the slopes of Crown Mountain.

"They want to go higher and higher up the watershed. Vancouver's water supply is of no interest to them; it's the timber they are after, and they mean to get it whether Vancouver survives or not," Davidson told Vancouver's Natural History Society in October 1924.

Cleveland died in January 1952. One month later, a consulting forester convinced the GVWD to hire a forester. By early 1953, C.D. Schultz & Company, a prominent forestry consulting firm, was hired to survey the state of the forests in all three watersheds.

Late in 1956, Charles Schultz submitted a report to the GVWD that later served as the basis for justifying a return to logging in the watersheds.... The twin forces of evil—bugs and disease—were cited as justification for logging.

"The danger from insects and disease is one of timber loss and increased fire hazard," Schultz wrote. "At this time, the chances of an outbreak of insects in the watershed(s) are considered to be average for the region. The chances of an epidemic will increase as the overmature stands become more decadent."

In short order, limited logging of trees alleged to have been attacked by insects began. By 1963, GVWD commissioner Theodore Berry asked B.C. Forests Minister Ray Williston to allow the GVWD to "protect or improve the quantity and quality of water" through a limited program of logging. By 1967, his request was granted. The new policy allowed for logging on a "sustained-yield basis for the purpose of developing, protecting, and improving the water-yielding characteristics of the lands."...

The Fight for Fish

BY TERRY GLAVIN, JUNE 25–JULY 2, 1993

...From the roof of my houseboat, I could still see the ridge above the place called Saint Mungo's on the far side of the river, across the roofs of the new complex of warehouses that had gone up beside the sewage treatment plant on Annacis Island. I was just a boy when I was first drawn by the wooded ravines that cut deep into that ridge, when it seemed to hover in the morning clouds above the great expanse of the delta and the bog. But now the Alex Fraser Bridge towered above the ridge, carrying tens of thousands of commuters from new subdivisions to their jobs in Vancouver, and the bridge abutments dug into the detritus of a fishing village the Musqueam called Suwq'eqsun'. It's one of the oldest-known sites of human settlement in Canada. For as long as 8,000 years, the people there harvested salmon and oolichan and sturgeon from piers suspended from pilings jutting into the river, and they lived in cavernous plank houses in those ravines. After the smallpox, the white fishermen who built their houses there, on the hill above the Saint Mungo's and Glenrose canneries, used to say that there were so many bones, they were sticking out of the ground, and when the winds were strong the bones would fall from burial boxes in the trees.

In their turn, the canneries fell idle, until all that was left were the burnt-out stubs of pilings sticking out of the mud. The great Fraser River salmon runs declined, and control of B.C. salmon fell into fewer and fewer hands. Today, only two salmon canneries remain on the Fraser—an Ocean Fisheries canning lineup by Deas dock and a small non-union line in Ladner. The Premier Cannery, Cleeve, Westminster, Wadham's, Harlock, and Wellington—all of them are gone, their pilings sticking up between the weeds, just as the ribs of the Japanese gillnet boats poked through the mud over by the old Annieville Dyke, where they had been rafted together after they were confiscated in 1942 and left to break up in the storms that spring.

And somewhere in one of those ravines were the remains of an old China House, one of the dreary barns where Chinese cannery hands were housed before the invention of a mechanical gang-knife eliminated them from the industry. The canning companies called the machine the "Iron Chink."

Upriver, the *Joy-Ethel*, the *Panther*, the *Slo-Poke*, the *Escorial*, the *Three Sons*, and all the other gillnetters swayed at their moorings. The view of the river that cold spring morning didn't leave much hope for their future.

Still, the descendants of Suwq'eqsun' have survived somehow. Although they are diminished, they live on at Musqueam and Coquitlam and Tsawwassen. Maybe there's a lesson in this somewhere for those gillnetters. Maybe for all of us.

The salmon have survived all this, too, if only in remnants. They survived 1913, when the railroad companies blasted the side of a mountain into the Fraser River at Hell's Gate. They survived the onslaught of the canneries. They have survived just about everything we have thrown at them so far, and in 1993 the salmon that are heading towards the Fraser River are believed to be massing in greater numbers than any year in a long, long time. More than 17 million sockeye salmon. More than 30 million pink salmon.

This is not about miracles.

What this all comes down to is survival, and the fact that there are still ancient cycles at work out there. There are forces that shape the way we live, and whether those forces are newsworthy or not, we flourish or we die by how well we understand them. Our chances of survival depend on how well we adapt to the changes they demand of all of us.

There will be more changes in the river in 1993. There will be problems in the Native fisheries in the Fraser River. There will be rumours, and there will be those who succumb to panic and allow themselves to believe just about anything they're told. Some of them will probably do just about anything they're told. Their chances of survival are pretty slim.

Much has been made of the miracle of Pacific salmon, the way they arise from gravel beds in glacier-fed streams splashing down from the Rockies, the way they tumble downstream to the sea and swim so far that they come within sight of the mountains of Kamchatka, and the way they find the route back home, somehow.

This is not about miracles. This is about survival.

If there is a miracle in this, it is that after everything we have done to them, they come home to us at all.

River of Doubt

BY DIRK BECK, JULY 23–30, 1993

On a spring day in 1991, Bill Schouwenburg cleared out his office at 555 West Hastings Street, or the "Triple Nickel," as it is known to employees at the Pacific regional headquarters of the Department of Fisheries and Oceans. After 32 years as a biologist in the public service, Schouwenburg was preparing for retirement. As he packed files and personal effects into cardboard boxes, he put one item aside. It was a certificate of commendation awarded to him in 1987 by the DFO deputy minister at the time, Peter Meyboom.

Schouwenburg had spent the better part of a decade studying the effects of Alcan's Kemano Completion Project (KCP) in northern British Columbia on the salmon of the Nechako River. He had guided the efforts of a dozen other scientists in the department's Kemano Completion Task Force—"the best minds the department could muster," he called them—and had edited the resulting 600-page report. If any one person could fully grasp the reams of research that had gone into the project, including Alcan's own 22-volume impact assessment, it was Schouwenburg. The commendation was meant as a ministerial pat on the back for a job well done. But for Schouwenburg, it was cold comfort.

In August 1987, a series of in-camera meetings took place in Vancouver under the mediation of UBC president Dr. David Strangway. Nine scientists, representing the DFO, the Province of British Columbia, and Alcan, sequestered themselves behind closed doors and emerged four days later with the Nechako Fish Conservation Program.

The agreement paved the way for Alcan to begin construction on the KCP. Tom Siddon, then fisheries and oceans minister, would later assure fishermen that Alcan had agreed to a "program of mitigation and, if necessary, enhancement, that ensures an increase in Nechako river salmon production." The deal, said Siddon, was based on sound scientific evidence; it had been agreed to unanimously by all scientists present.

What Siddon didn't mention was that Schouwenburg and several other senior biologists who had spent years studying the project had not been invited to the meetings. Nor did he mention that some of those who *had* taken part were given less than a week's notice—"a couple of working days and a weekend," recalls one of them—to prepare themselves for a decision on what had been called, in a 1984 DFO discussion paper, "the habitat issue of the century."

Siddon also neglected to mention that the water flows agreed to in the settlement (which Alcan would release into the river from its reservoir) were the same flows for which the DFO had been preparing to take Alcan to court. For more than a year, the DFO's team of expert witnesses had been preparing testimony to the effect that those flows were too low to ensure the protection of salmon stocks. Siddon's announcement, just as the court proceedings were getting under way, prevented the DFO's scientists from taking the stand.

All this was going through Schouwenburg's head on April 1, 1991, when he slid his commendation into an envelope and mailed it back to Ottawa. The accompanying letter, addressed to Meyboom's successor, Deputy Minister Bruce Rawson, reads, in part: "The DFO members of the Strangway working group were instructed (intimidated?) by your predecessor to ensure they came up with a resolution to the problems which were consistent or compatible with Alcan's objectives. Reputations built over a lifetime were sacrificed because small men with even lesser courage couldn't admit to the truth.

"I kept this award posted on the wall as a reminder of how much the politicization of the public service along with bureaucratic cynicism is responsible for the very low morale of the department's staff. Now that I have resigned from the public service, I no longer need such painful reminders."...

An Ancient Enigma and a Death on the River

BY TERRY GLAVIN, DECEMBER 3–10, 1993

The first call came in on Monday, September 13.

Annie Van den Berg phoned the B.C. Environment Ministry's regional offices in Surrey to report that something hideous and strange had washed up on the riverbank in her own backyard. Annie lives on the Fraser River at Derby Reach, near Fort Langley.

It was a creature straight out of *Jurassic Park*—a fish, more than 12 feet long. It weighed hundreds of pounds.

The ministry official who took the call was Marvin Rosenau, a 37-year-old biologist whose portfolio in the ministry's fisheries branch—a poor country cousin to the federal Department of Fisheries and Oceans—was more or less a grab bag of things nobody else wanted, such as urban streams, crayfish, and a sad list of rare, vulnerable, and endangered species that includes the Salish sucker, the Nooksack dace, and the Cultus Lake sculpin.

The list also includes the Fraser River white sturgeon, which was the species of beast that had washed up at the Van den Bergs'.

Rosenau had been quietly labouring away on the ministry's sturgeon file ever since he'd come back to Canada two years earlier with a Ph.D. from the University of Waikato in New Zealand. The Langley fish was *Acipenser transmontanus*, and one of the rare giants, at that. Obviously a real old-timer, probably 100 years old or more.

Maybe it got caught in a Native's gill net and died. Maybe it was just old and died of a heart attack. These things happen.

Rosenau noted the details and made plans to head out in a day or two to cut it up and have the lab look at the pieces. He didn't think much of it at first. Just an obscure creature from the past—a holdover from another age—dead on a sandbar in Langley.

Pushed to the brink of extinction earlier this century, the remnant population of Fraser River white sturgeon had not been holding its own in recent years. They had been disappearing from their old haunts along the Fraser for some time, and "alarming trends" indicating what scientists call recruitment failure—the term that comes up often in any discussion of the East Coast's northern cod stocks—were duly recorded in ministry reports. Still, there were studies under way and stricter conservation measures under review, and Rosenau was making headway with the salmon fishermen who catch sturgeon by accident and the few anglers who catch them for sport. Things had been starting to look up, but it was hard work made no easier by the obscurity of the beast in the scientific literature—biologists still don't know where or how white sturgeon spawn, and they know just as little about their feeding patterns and migratory behaviour. Rarely studied; rarely even seen. Half myth.

That's the way it's always been with these fish. The old Sto:lo sturgeon fishermen said that people who fell from their canoes and whose bodies were never found became sturgeon or lived among the sturgeon. The memory of these stories was fading, but what was sure was that sturgeon were somehow involved in the whereabouts of the souls of those who drowned and whose bodies were never recovered from the river.

The occasional dead sturgeon might not be cause for alarm, but as the days passed, more sturgeon started washing up dead—all of them giant old-timers. On Thursday that week, Dennis McKamey from Northside Cedar in Mission called up to report a dead 12-and-a-half-footer. It weighed more than 800 pounds and turned out to be more than 100 years old. The following Monday, Rosenau got a call from Todd Chapman, a platoon sergeant with the Lower Fraser tribal fisheries. An 11-footer had washed up dead at Katz Bay near the Chawathil reserve, just downstream from Hope. Something was happening in the river, and Rosenau didn't know what it was. His every effort was frustrated, and, for a time, the prospect of the white sturgeon's extinction loomed closer.

Something was happening down there and Rosenau didn't know what it was, how to stop it, or where it would end, and before it was all over he would find himself gasping for air, struggling against the violent rapids in the depths of the Fraser Canyon and fighting for his very life. He barely survived the ordeal, but there would be a death—a drowning in the river; a body not recovered....

Stupidville

BY JOHN MASTERS, JUNE 24–JULY 1, 1994

The Night We Disgraced Ourselves began, for me, at 9:30 p.m. as I was walking along Granville Street. Two girls, about 14, trudged by and one of them, without breaking step, hurled a beer bottle to the pavement. They didn't look happy, they didn't look mad; she just smashed the thing without any look at all on her face and they kept trudging.

My office is at the corner of Robson and Granville. Tuesday night, after the hockey game, I went downtown to do some work, thinking that things would be quiet. We had, after all, lost. There would be a Canucks-appreciation afternoon two days later at B.C. Place, and fans who wanted to cheer the home team one more time could do it then. There was, to my mind, no good reason to party that night.

But soon after 8 o'clock the first revellers hit the streets, honking and whooping. Four hours later, at midnight, about 150 stores, mostly along Robson, Granville,

FACING PAGE: **What really caused the Robson Street riot?**

OBSON
ST
1000

Georgia, Seymour, Alberni, and Thurlow, had been looted or had their windows staved in for the sheer joy of it. The streets were filled with broken glass and strung-out rolls of toilet paper, the stench of beer and piss and tear gas. We had become Stupidville.

A week later, new glass and short memories have already all but erased the blemish of that night. But the riot pointed up a problem that requires more than cosmetic attention, a few clucks over rowdy youths, and inquiry into whether or not the police should have used tear gas. The events of June 14 laid bare some fundamental shortcomings of how we do things here. There are fingers to be usefully pointed, I believe, and the first one is at ourselves.

What, exactly, is Vancouver? Say what you will about Toronto, it's a city with a very firm idea of what it is, and a great many people take pride in its achievements *as* a city.... It believes itself to be a compassionate city, and, more important, it has a long tradition of its inhabitants getting involved in civic politics because they care about the city and want to do their bit to make it a better place.

We in Vancouver can define ourselves by our geography and our weather, but not by very much else, not in positive terms. Yes, we have some fine arts festivals; yes, there's some outstanding architecture; yes, there are some lovely neighbourhoods—but, although they're good components, there's no bedrock they're built on, no irreducible ur-Vancouver. We're more of a staging area than a city, a place people start from to go skiing or sailing or hiking or to make money to take somewhere else.

Part of the reason for this has to do with media reinforcement. In Toronto, the daily media, and especially the *Toronto Star*, have a love for the city that is conveyed every day to its citizens. I've never gotten much sense of that here. The *Vancouver Sun* is an accurate gauge of the city only insofar as it reflects and amplifies the polarities of the citizens. Too often, its voice is appallingly negative....

When the *Globe and Mail* commissioned a study recently to see what people in the Lower Mainland thought of the local newspapers (the *Globe* was thinking of launching its own West Coast edition), it discovered, to its surprise, that many of us don't even think of the *Sun* or the *Province* when we're asked how we feel about "our" newspapers. We think of the *Courier* or the *West Ender* or any of a dozen other weeklies. *Those* are the papers that speak for us. But they speak only to their neighbourhoods. The big picture is missing.

The Saturday after the riot, the *Sun*'s top page-one story was the irrational behaviour of former football star O.J. Simpson, charged with the death of his ex-wife and her male friend. An unusual story, certainly, and on another day perhaps the top news story, but not four days after a major riot in downtown Vancouver. At the bottom of the page was a puff piece on how Robson Street is still a swell place to shop. Pushed back to page 4 was the first story we *should* have been reading and thinking about over croissants and cappuccinos. In it, [B.C. Supreme Court] Justice [Wallace] Oppal is quoted as saying that anyone who feels he or she was a victim of police heavy-handedness Tuesday night will have a hard time getting a fair inquiry into the matter, since the cops investigate themselves. "Let's assume you are down there and you are roughed up by the police," Oppal told the *Sun*. "You would go to the police station and complain. You can ask yourself: How objective is that?" How objective, indeed?

The *Sun*—and everyone else in town—should be all over this story, and should *stay* on it until fundamental changes are made.

Here is a good quotation from social critic Paul Goodman, the author of *Growing Up Absurd.* "The society in which I live is mine, open to my voice and action, or I do not live there at all. The government, the school board, the church, the university, the world of publishing and communications, are my agencies as a citizen. To the extent that they are *not* my agencies.... I am entirely in revolutionary opposition to them."

The crowd Tuesday night had by no means thought things through enough to call itself "in revolutionary opposition" to anything, but when the cops moved in and the looting started, its reaction to these events seems to me to speak clearly of a large group of citizens who *don't* feel that the society in which they live is theirs, open to their voices and actions. For many, I think, when the party turned ugly Tuesday, the fleeting feeling of having belonged to something was lost. The crowd that remained broke into two groups: those who merely feel disconnected from the city and can stand by and watch its stores being looted and its police firing tear gas, and those—a much smaller number, but not insignificant—whose simmering opposition easily becomes pronounced, who respond to an overt display of authority by saying "Fuck you" with a wrench through a window.

When the lawlessness started Tuesday night, there were three sides: the vandals, the police, and the audience. A fourth one said: "Hey, this is our city you're destroying. How dare you. Stop it." It was minuscule to nonexistent. My argument is that if we had taken a healthier interest in our city all along, there would have been no sides at all, and no riot.

When the official inquiries are made into the causes of our June 14th disgrace, Mayor Philip Owen and police chief Ray Canuel had better look seriously at ways to make the cops a part of the community instead of apart from it. And the rest of us had better decide what we want this community to be about, besides pretty vistas when it doesn't rain. What shared tasks can we undertake whose achievement will fill us with civic pride? What conditions are needed to come to unconditionally love this place, not for *where* it is but for *what* it is? "We are all reflected in what we see" was the elegant observation painted on the plywood covering the windows at Second Skin on Robson the day after the riot. It would be wonderful to find a way to repair the glass so the next time we look at it as we march en masse through our downtown streets what we see reflected back is something nobler than a mob heading to Stupidville.

The Green Shadow

THE FIRST OF AN EIGHT-PART SERIES, BY ANDREW STRUTHERS, JULY 1–8, 1994

Ten years ago, Tofino was a green tunnel with Chesterman Beach at one end and the Maquinna Pub at the other. I lived on the beach and I drank at the pub. When my little daughter was born in 1988, all I wanted was for her to grow up exploring that green tunnel. But right around that time I began to notice that the planet was spiralling into an ecological Armageddon, taking me, my daughter, Chesterman Beach, and the Maquinna Pub with it. Clearcuts like giant sets for TRAC II commercials were sweeping up the coast. Every year, more tourists returned than salmon. I had to act. So I checked out the local environmental group, the Friends of Clayoquot Sound.

I'm leery of groups because of my family background. Yeah, that's right—it's all my family's fault. See, when I was a kid there was this thing in my head called the "family fuse." When our little clan got stressed past its breaking point—when, for example, we arrived on a new continent and our stuff didn't, or when we got chased in a dugout canoe by an angry hippo in Lake Nabo Gabo, or when something really horrible came on TV, like a BBC documentary about mercury poisoning in Japan, someone had to flip out. That someone was me.

It was a simple deal: my mind blew first, and the family would "reset" by calming me down and fixing me up. I had the nightmares for everyone. And that's just the way I am. I cover the night shift. I take out the psychic garbage. Which was fine inside my family—we all had chores like that, and were good at them. But with a bunch of strangers? Yeah, sure.

For this reason, I approached the Friends with caution.

But it turned out they weren't really a group, any more than a bunch of people fleeing a tsunami are a group.

The leader by acclamation was a man called C.J. He talked like the Village People. He translated *The Wizard of Oz* into Latin. He wore horn-rimmed glasses and a Gumby tuque. I was fascinated.

Then there was Ron, a tall, handsome doctor from Australia, just fuming about life. During the cruise-missile test, he threw red paint on the police station and got a year's probation. And Adrian, an impoverished single dad. At the same time that Ron was blowing his *GQ* top, Adrian quietly painted the local bank red and got 10 bucks an hour. Some kind of yin/yang thing there.

And Julie, who was illustrating a kids' book in which the heroes were worms.

And Dan, who grew up in Vietnam. Every day was Year Zero.

And Dave, who made long lines of candles on the beach to show you where the planets would rise.

And Kal, who lived way out in the wilds even though he had a real bad back.

And Jan, who could build an up-to-code house out of driftwood, glass, and silicone.

And Val, the High Priestess of Recycling.

And Shelly, the deadly serious anthropology major. When they told her Bambi's mother was dead, she probably asked to see the body.

And Paul—man, he could talk. Clearcuts/raw logs/Brazil/his Brazilian girlfriend/why she left him/how to get permanent welfare… He downshifted through the Alps of Chitchat like a Lamborghini.

The meetings were a little chaotic. We made anarchy look like a marching band. But the basic picture was this: Fletcher Challenge Canada (actually from Down Under) had just finished tearing trees out of a highway-side spot that later became known as the infamous Black Hole. This known offender was now headed up to the Megin watershed—an untouched *Wunderland*, the place God would go fly-fishing if He knew about it—to strike again. Fletcher Challenge was blasting a logging road along the rocky shores of Sulphur Pass. If they got through the pass, it would mean the destruction of one of the last virgin watersheds on Vancouver Island. Our plan was simple: head them off at the pass.

Blockading didn't appeal to me. I'm leery of war metaphors. And, anyway, the

first thing I did out of high school was build a logging road up by Chetwynd. I got off the school bus and onto the crummy (which was an old school bus). I vaguely recall stapling a metal tag to a tree with an eagle's aerie in it and wondering where the eagle would move to. What did I know about the environment? If someone had shown up one morning and wept and hidden my tools and told me I was responsible for the hole in the ozone layer…well, let's just say it would have been the wrong way to try to reach me.

On the other hand, it seemed like an excellent idea to cause a fuss, get some TV cameras out to Sulphur Pass, and show the public what was afoot in the wilds. Remember, this was back in 1988, when most folks still thought the environment was the branch of the government that dealt with highway medians.

As the day of the blockade approached, I agonized over whether to go or not. Finally I thought, "I will go. But I won't pick a side. I'll ignore the whole war metaphor. If I feel up to it, I'll just ask the police to arrest me, so I can throw my body on the pyre of civil disobedience without getting in some logger's face."

The big day came, and I was pretty alarmed. I felt like a volcano virgin. At that point in my life, though, I was cooking in a burrito joint for $6 an hour and looking after a three-month-old all night, and I was *stressed.* At least this was a trip into the wilds.

However, when I got to the protest camp, a strange and sinister thing happened. The part of me that loved Chesterman Beach felt right at home, but the part that liked to drink at the Maquinna, watch the strippers on the big semicircular stage, and fire off handguns in my pal Barry's basement felt like a frog on a dissection plate. This caused big trouble at Head Office.

Head Office is what I call that Pentagon in my soul that guards my every move. Perhaps you have one, too. When I feel at peace with myself, Head Office is shut down, except for the occasional memo about scratching my balls in public. But when I'm stressed, depressed, or under attack, I can't even talk till my lips get the green light from Head Office. I had thought being out in the wilds would give me a sip of inner peace. In fact, the last time Head Office saw this much action was in Sunday school.

The first day was a disappointment—no one showed up. But, hey, I stuck to my guns. Three days later the cops and loggers showed up, and panic ensued.

I don't recall exactly how I went from Mr. Neutral to GI Joe, but by mid-morning I was on the cliff above the blast site with Kal and Richard, howling like a wolf in between the toots of the warning horn while down on the road someone told the police not to let the loggers blast in case we got blown up.

It was a beautiful day. It was so quiet we could hear them arguing down on the road. Hours passed. "Hey," I thought, "it's working!"

Around noon, Kal went back to the camp to get some water, and Richard and I began to argue about the Canadian government.

"They're a bad bunch of apples," he said.

Now if he'd said they were a great bunch of guys, I would have mentioned the smallpox-laden blankets they used to pass out to the Indians—or something like that. But since Richard was already running them down, I stuck up for them.

"Listen," I said, "I was just in TIBET." Always a showstopper. "In TIBET, they shoot the protesters in the head and send the bill for the bullets to their families. *Those* are the bad apples. This government won't let someone blow up some rock a hundred feet away in case we get hurt, because here in Canada..."

KA-BOOOOOOOOOM!

A ton of bedrock went up in smoke, along with my "True North, Strong and Free" speech. Richard and I hit the deck so fast we bounced off each other. Fly rock came rattling down around us. This was one hell of a war metaphor.

For the rest of the day we were chased through the bush and up and down cliffs by what appeared to be loggers with superhuman powers. Helicopters buzzed us. Cops yelled through bullhorns. It was an old-growth *Gong Show.* Then, suddenly, Vietnam Dan appeared from behind a tree and said the cops wanted to make a deal with us: we could just "come down" and they wouldn't arrest us. This did not seem likely. Dan went back down and told them he couldn't find us, and shortly afterwards five o'clock came and everyone went home. It was just like that old cartoon where the sheepdog and the wolf fight all day and then the whistle blows and they politely bid each other farewell. Sulphur Pass was silent again.

When we got back to our camp, it was deserted and there were court injunctions stapled to everything. We used them to light a fire. I huddled in my sleeping bag and let the night wrap its starry limbs around me. What a day. But at least the family fuse would reset itself by morning, and I could get the hell out of there.

The utter silence of the dawn was broken by the sound of a distant outboard. I paid it no heed until Richard went tearing past my feet, screaming: "It's the cops! Run for it!"

I sat up. Right in front of me a Zodiac hit the beach. Five cops in bright-red survival suits spilled out. Still groggy from sleep, I ran into the bush wearing only my underpants.

I had imagined the scene of my arrest very differently. Back in town, I'd pictured it this way: me and the police would talk it over, then they'd nod and slap the cuffs on me in a matter-of-fact way. Since I'd arrived at the camp, a second fantasy had eclipsed the first. In it, I was dragged from under the bumper of a huge logging truck while cameras rolled and loggers cursed and my eco-buddies sang "One Tin Soldier" in the background. But this was like nothing I'd ever imagined. I was being chased through the bush in my underpants, and not a camera in sight.

As I marvelled at the difference between fantasy and reality, I noticed Pierre, the local cop, coming through the trees. He was tracking me, just like a Mountie in some old movie. Then I thought, "Hey...he really *is* a Mountie. And I'm his man!" I was trapped in the dark underbelly of the Canadian Dream.

In terror, I slid under a huge rock and tried to become one with the earth. It didn't work. Suddenly, Pierre leaped on me from the top of the rock, yelling "Don't move!" After a brief cop/naked guy scrum, we stood up and said hello. Then we walked down to the protest camp, where he began to read me a court injunction the size of a telephone book.

Blackflies bit. The sun got hot. Tides of emotion surged through me: a desire to weep, a desire to laugh hysterically, concern that the charred remains of the court injunctions sticking out of the campfire made me look less than neutral—and Pierre was taking forever to plough through this legal mumbo jumbo in his Trois-Rivières brogue. The blackflies got intense. In desperation, I began to help with some of the bigger words.

At last, Don Lennox, the local sergeant, came over and asked me for my full name.

"Uh...John Doe?" I mumbled half-heartedly.

"No way!" exploded Pierre. "You're the one that done the funny menus at the pub! It's Andrew Sumptin!"

"Always remember—be just. And if you can't be just, be arbitrary."
—William S. Burroughs

Andrew Sumptin appeared in Supreme Court in Vancouver a few weeks later. The charge: civil contempt of court. They were trying us by the bunch, and that morning about 30 of us filed into the courtroom.

The first thing that struck me was the size of the judge's desk. It was huge. It looked like the portable in which we took Grade 10 drama, except with pens and notepads on the roof. I was quite intimidated. Also, a paranoid fantasy had sprung up regarding those burned injunctions. I see a lawyer holding up the charred remains in a plastic bag. "Exhibit A!" The judge angrily brings down his gavel. BAM! "Thirty days!" My daughter never forgives me for deserting her. We grow distant. I lose her. I become a bitter, lonely old man...

So it came as a welcome surprise when the Fletcher Challenge lawyer stood up and said he wanted to drop the charges.

To my amazement, my lawyer stood up and said, "No way."

"My Lord," he began, "my clients do not appreciate being dragged here...lost wages...expense...blah blah blah bla-blah blah blah..."

Personally, I had lost all desire to do anything except escape. But I didn't say anything, and the trial lasted two days.

The second day was worse. It started with a little rally down at the Fletcher Challenge head office. We chanted "No more clearcuts!" and handed out flyers that said "The Battle for Clayoquot" and I'm not sure what else, because Dorothy showed up with them at the last moment and I was too strung out to read.

Halfway through the morning, the prosecution rolled in the big TV and showed a tape of Ron. His year of probation had ended that morning. By noon he was riding the drill rig at Sulphur Pass as if it were a mechanical bull at a honky-tonk. There was a spontaneous burst of applause, which the prosecution cited as an example of our contempt. I guess it was. But the judge was mainly concerned with the fact that most of us were nowhere near the end of the road when we were arrested, except for C.J., who actually pitched his tent on the blast site. He decided to concentrate on C.J.

BAM! Down came the gavel. Fletcher Challenge had to cough up cash for my expenses, which my lawyer took in lieu of a fee. I didn't care. I was free!

There was an after-court soiree at Shelly's house in Kerrisdale. I got a six-pack and started pounding them back. I was so relieved to be free that the relief was like a drug. By the time the news came on, a mixture of beer, relief, and the prospect of seeing myself on TV as the White Knight of Clayoquot Sound had given me a cavalier attitude. When they showed the clip of Ron riding the drill rig, I wanted to be up there with him. "Go, Ron!" I slurred, waving my beer. Then they showed a scene from the rally at head office that morning, and I appeared in the corner of the screen for a flash—but mysteriously changed. I was roaring my head off and waving a list of demands in some pedestrian's face. "Wow!" I thought. "The Nazi Brownshirt of Clayoquot Sound."

That did it. The family fuse went nuclear. Head Office shut down completely. Energies went coursing through my brain that I had no connection with. I dimly recall leaving the party with Jan and Poole, and Spanish Banks swirling past as I clung to the dash of Poole's Volkswagen, and much later I got picked up by UBC Security, clinging naked to a totem pole somewhere near the Anthropology Museum.

War Without Winners

BY DANIEL WOOD, APRIL 28–MAY 5, 1995

She presses the needle into the back of her tattooed hand. Beneath the syringe, striped along its barrel with tiny calibrations, the skin puckers, but doesn't yield. Cindy Jackson clamps her wrist tightly between her crossed thighs, again trying to raise a bulge in her veins. This time, the needle goes in. She works the plunger and three milligrams of extra-fine heroin hit her heart, hit her cerebellum, hit her body and—

within seconds—she's tweaking, doing the smack jitterbug, shuffling and rubbing her arms like someone covered with ants, like someone possessed. Which—in a real way—she is.

"I use lethal amounts. I play Russian roulette," she says, her voice neither boastful nor sad. She studies me in an unfocused manner, trying to discern the implications of a stranger's interest, here in a sunny alley behind East Hastings' Brandiz Hotel. She has a scrape on her chin and dried blood on her tight blue jeans, and, she tells me, she is dying of AIDS. She spins back into the doorway where she's just fixed, shaking her head disconsolately, rubbing the spot where the needle went in. Among the graffiti on the wall behind her is one that reads: LIFE IS FUCKING PAINFUL. "They treat it as a crime, the drugs. Not as a sickness," she tells me. "When someone's sick, you don't send them to jail. You don't turn your back on them."

For half her 26 years, Jackson has been a prostitute; almost half her life a junkie and a thief. In jail for petty crimes, she caught AIDS from using dirty needles. She is, I tell myself, a victim, but not yet a statistic in the War on Drugs. However, her friend Morris Broeffle, a young, ponytailed Native, has—Jackson tells me—just become a statistic. He is the latest Vancouver drug death, overdosing in his hotel room three days before Jackson and I speak. One of several dozen B.C. drug deaths in 1995. Not as many, so far, as the 220 that died last year or the 355 that OD'd in the province the year before that when the potent China White hit the streets. But to Broeffle's friends, Room 26 in Gees Royal Hotel, diagonally across the street from the Vancouver Police Station, is just another place where the country's absurd laws and the reality of addiction have arrived at a dead end. It is where Broeffle OD'd. Like the current Canadian drug strategies, like the futile policing efforts, like the prisons where the addicts inevitably go, the view out the window of Room 26 is of a brick wall offering no hope of escape from the problems facing those addicted to drugs.

From his 20th-storey window in Burnaby's Metrotown, Vince Cain, 63, a man of courtly gestures and avuncular observations, surveys a vast panorama of the Fraser Valley delta. Twenty-five years an RCMP officer, seven years B.C.'s chief coroner, Cain has spent half his life trying to fathom the behaviour of people like Broeffle and Jackson. And what he recently discovered, after a year of research, has made him something of a pariah among those he once worked with: he has sided with "the sinners."

"I never, ever, ever thought I'd say this," he says. "The War on Drugs is a failure, an *expensive* failure. We should not be hiring more police. We should not be directing addicts into the courts. We should not be building more jails. Addicts don't need jails. They need *care*. What we have now is a system that's persecuting society's victims."...

An Insatiable Emptiness

BY EVELYN LAU, JULY 21–28, 1995

I no longer clearly remember the first time I forced myself to throw up. What I do remember is how inexpert I was and how long it took before I succeeded in actually vomiting instead of just gagging and retching. I began by sticking my finger down my throat and wiggling it around, but this produced few results; it wasn't until articles about bulimia appeared in women's magazines that I finally thought to use the handle of a toothbrush instead of my forefinger. It became easy after that.

In my mid-teens, I was too young to believe I was anything but immortal. It didn't occur to me that what I was doing was dangerous—instead, it seemed a smart and practical way of coping with things. I went through months of throwing up once or twice a day, then brief periods when I did not throw up at all, when I seemed to have broken the pattern. Surely this meant I was in control. But by the time I turned 18, the months of not throwing up had diminished to weeks, and when I *was* vomiting I was doing it four, five, six times a day. I had became addicted to the sensation. It was no longer a penance I had to perform after eating, but the reward at the end of a binge. I loved the feeling I had after purging, of being clean and shiny inside like a scrubbed machine, superhuman. I would rise from the bathroom floor, splash my face with cold water, vigorously brush the acid from my mouth. I would take a wet cloth, wipe off the vomit that had spattered my arms, and feel as energized as someone who had just woken from a nap or returned from an invigorating jog around the block. I felt as if everything disgusting inside me had been displaced so that it was now outside myself. Not only all the food I had eaten, but my entire past.

No one could tell me to stop, not even my friends who eventually knew what I was doing. They could not control this part of my life or any other. This was mine alone—the chemical flower smell of the blue water in the toilet, the vomit that shot out as a burning liquid, drenching the sides of the bowl. After a session in the bathroom, a certain emptiness would sing inside me, a sensation of having become a cage of bones with air rushing through it. I craved this feeling so much I no longer cared what I had to eat in order to vomit—I would cram clusters of bananas into my mouth, or tubs of ice cream that lurched back up my throat in a thin and startlingly sweet projectile.

When I left the bathroom, I felt like someone who had achieved some great thing—climbed a mountain, written a book—and survived. I was overweight by only 10 pounds or so, but when I looked in the mirror all I saw was buttery flesh covering my body. My stomach had become swollen and globular from the gorging and purging; I had earned it the way other women earn washboard stomachs and lean waists from hours of sit-ups and crunches at the gym....

The Road Never Travelled

BY SHAWN BLORE, NOVEMBER 16–23, 1995

May 1929. A young man in blue pinstripes and a jaunty bow tie glances around as he steps off the train at Canadian Pacific's waterfront station. It's his first time in Vancouver, and although he's impressed by the mountains and the harbour, by the combination of natural beauty and bustling industry, there's still something vaguely smug in the way he appraises his surroundings. His name is Harland Bartholomew. He's an American, a civil engineer from the thoroughly modern city of St. Louis, Missouri. He's come to Vancouver at the behest of the city government, which has commissioned him for the daunting task of transforming Vancouver from a provincial backwater of a city into a major world metropolis.

Over the next several months, Bartholomew created a blueprint for a modern city. He decided where to put the shops and houses, and he indicated where the city's industry should develop. The basic street grid was largely in place, so Bartholomew contented himself with selecting some of the streets to become major arterials, leaving others as quiet residential lanes. Finally, the engineer from St. Louis spread out his map of the city's streets and, after careful consideration, inked in a few red dotted lines. One of these markings began at the edge of downtown by Main and Georgia Streets, then slanted obliquely past the rail yards in False Creek flats and continued on past Boundary Road into the wilds of Burnaby, where one day there would be suburbs. Bartholomew labelled this dotted red line with neat block letters: NEW MAJOR STREET. The east-side freeway was born.

In his plans, Bartholomew explained his decision thus: "In 1926, there were 66,933 cars in British Columbia, one to every 8.6 persons; in the United States, there is, on average, one car to every five persons; and in California, one to every 2.8 persons. This is a condition that must be planned for." The century was but 29 years old, and already Vancouver had found its destiny as L.A. North.

The Depression and the Second World War prevented this blueprint from coming fully into fruition, so 18 years later, in 1947, Bartholomew was brought back to Vancouver to update his plan. In the interim, Canada had helped make the world safe for democracy and transformed itself into the world's second-wealthiest nation in the process. The city fathers were thinking big. During the same interval, American engineers had invented a new, ultramodern kind of road: the freeway. Not surprisingly, what in 1929 had been a New Major Street in 1947 became a freeway.

There is no contemporary record of how the great unwashed from Vancouver's east side felt at the time about new freeways and major streets running through their neighbourhoods. Bartholomew never asked. Alas, this lofty confidence in his own acumen proved to be the undoing of his freeway designs. East-side residents have been battling Bartholomew's New Major Street, in all its various guises, ever since.

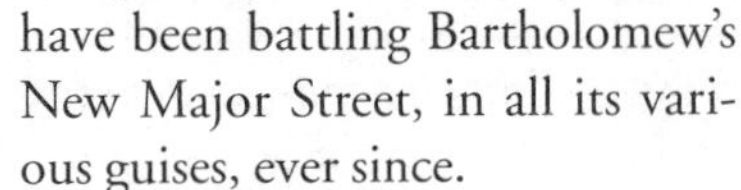

They won the first skirmish in 1967, when they stopped the Chinatown Freeway. The city won the second round, though, when it pushed through the Georgia Viaduct in 1971. City planners and politicians felt that once the viaduct was in place, the Strathcona and Quebec Street freeways would inevitably follow. As it turned out, however, the viaduct was the only segment of the Vancouver freeway system ever built. In 1972, the anti-freeway camp scored two quick victories. First, it convinced the federal government to abandon plans for a combined downtown freeway and third crossing of Burrard Inlet. Then, later in the year, it pressured the city to give up on its last plan, a six-lane freeway that ran for most of its length through the False Creek industrial flats and Grandview Cut. At the time, residents thought their victory final. But now, 23 years later, the city is gearing up for another round. So, too, are many east-side Vancouverites.

Ben Gilbert is a slightly shaggy 22-year-old. He was born 43 years after Bartholomew first inked in those red dotted lines across the face of Vancouver, 25 years after the word *freeway* entered the city's political vocabulary. Gilbert's major preoccupation at the moment—aside from completing his second year of forestry at Langara College—is ensuring that a revived version of one of Bartholomew's freeways doesn't carve its way through the Grandview Cut.... "Every few years," says Gilbert, "the city comes along with a proposal for some kind of road through the cut. First it was a freeway; now it's a truck route."

To understand the deep mistrust of city hall shown by people like Ben Gilbert, one has to look back to the Great Freeway War of the late '60s and early '70s.... The political point man during these battles was NPA mayor and Shaughnessy millionaire Tom Campbell. During the course of the freeway debate, Campbell managed to alienate just about everyone. At the public hearings over the penultimate freeway plan, Campbell declared that the only people opposed to the freeway were "rangitangs, hamburgers, pinkos, or troublemakers." (Campell's definition of "hamburger" was anyone without a university degree.)....

The deserted and decaying hearts of cities like Detroit bear witness to the destructive power of urban autoroutes. For Vancouver to re-embrace that vision now, when its disastrous results are so readily apparent, would be an act of wilful stupidity. The fanatics who fought so hard to bring a freeway to Vancouver sincerely believed that 16 lanes of concrete was just the thing to revitalize the city's downtown. They believed the "hamburgers and pinkos" who opposed it were truly the enemies of progress. We now know the opposite to be true.

American urban critic Lewis Mumford noted of the people and politicians who pushed through the urban freeways in the United States that "the most charitable thing that can be said was that they had not the faintest notion of what they were doing."

If we allow a freeway in Vancouver, we will not have even that excuse.

Infernal Voice Mail Plays Grave Reminder

BY BILL RICHARDSON, JANUARY 25–FEBRUARY 1, 1996

Truth be told, I don't know why I bother having voice mail. Don't know how I ever got seduced by it. Stupid name. Voice mail. Dumb concept, too. Just plain dumb. Trades on the myth of indispensability. I'm not here, but since neither of us can do without the other, and since our lives are so very, very chockablock with events, you can leave your message and then I'll leave one for you and then you'll leave one for me, and eventually we'll meet by chance in Starbucks and joke about it and one of us will say "phone tag" and the other will try not to gag.

Voice mail. Yeeesh. It makes me anxious. You have no control. Everything depends on memory and dexterity. You have to learn which button to push for which function. You have to be deft enough to hit the right one. Most mornings, I can't recollect where my socks are, even if I put them on the night before. Most mornings, I can't load the toaster. It doesn't necessarily get better as the day goes on. With voice mail, a single slip of the finger and everything speeds up, slows down, gets erased, repeats, gets saved for seven days, tells you what time and date the message came in. Tells you how long it is.

Voice mail. All it does is get your hopes up, incite optimism, foster the foolish notion that someone out there is thinking of you. But day after day, there are no messages, and so you feel ignored. And when there *are* messages, they're just from people who want something from you, and so you feel harassed. I mean, I don't know about you, you're reading this on the bus or some damn place and I can't see you, and you might very well belong to some oppressed group, might have every right to feel ignored and harassed, and if such is the case, believe me, I'm sorry. But as for me, I'm white. I'm middle-class. I'm male. I'm employed. The world is my oyster. Oppressed? Harassed? What have I got to complain about? Voice mail? Not fuckin' likely.

Listen, I'm not usually a cranky person. Ask anyone who knows me. Sweet and good-natured and compassionate and kind. These are the adjectives to which they will surely turn to sum me up. But voice mail! That changes everything. It's evil, as I've outlined above. What's more, it can make you try to cheat death. Case in point. Monday, December 18, I get a 37-second message from Ken. He's inviting me to a solstice party at the end of the week. It's a "drop by if you're in the neighbourhood, if you're free, if you've nothing else planned" kind of message. No urgency. No RSVP required. Even so, common courtesy should have dictated that I phone with my regrets. Especially since it was Christmas. Especially since I only ever saw Ken twice a year, at the max. Especially since I'd heard through the grapevine that he hadn't been doing very well. I should have called right then and there, like they tell you to do in time-management seminars. I should have. But I didn't. I guess I was busy. I guess I meant to get around to it. I guess I just skipped over the message, thinking I'd get to it later in the week. And I should have. But I didn't. I forgot all about the party and the message till it surfaced again in seven days' time—Christmas Day, in fact. It surfaced along with a warning from the stern timekeeping lady—who's really a computer, don't let her fool you—saying that she would delete Ken unless I gave her instructions to the contrary. Unless I saved Ken for another week by pressing 9. Which I did. So that once again I'd be reminded to call, to apologize for my shabbiness. Oh, but it was Christmas week, and I was busy, and I was fretful with my new espresso machine, and I forgot, which was too bad, because had I called early enough I might have got him before he went into the hospital. And when his message came up for deletion or renewal in another week's time, on New Year's Day, he was already dead, though I didn't know it, and I remember that I felt a little annoyed with him, irrationally, as I saved his message for a third time, wondering how long this would go on.

And now once a week he comes up for renewal, Ken who died, and it gives me an odd but not unpleasant turn to hear his impossible voice, to think of him setting his sickness to one side to plan his last party, to know that he thought well enough of me to dial my number and talk kindly for 37 seconds while I was away from home, while I was leading my busy little life, while his was winding down. And now once a week I press 9 and save him in some digitized drawer of the infernal voice-mail machine, save him because I can, because I didn't, because I couldn't, because I might as well, because there's no harm done, because it's little enough to do, now. Save him because he was sweet. Save him because I'm sorry.

EVERYTHING OLD

People Make Market Work

BY SEAN ROSSITER, AUGUST 28–SEPTEMBER 4, 1987

Crowds had a bad name in Vancouver before Granville Island. Crowds were what you ran into at the PNE, the Pacific Coliseum, or the opening of the Bay's Summer White Sale.

Until 1978 or so, the idea of actually seeking out a mob scene to join—just for kicks, as a kind of recreation—would have seemed absurd. It still does; at least, it does on paper. But by now I, and thousands of others (millions, it seems, at 2 p.m. on Sunday afternoons), do it regularly without even thinking about it. Only on Granville Island would I willingly drive into a guaranteed traffic jam.

A couple of months ago I went to the Granville Island Public Market to find some halibut. The experience reminded me of how novel it was the first few times I stepped into the market, joined the throngs, and lost myself in the sheer mass of humanity that seems to feed on itself inside the old shed. To be among so many people is to immerse yourself in life itself; to feel reconnected with all those bits of the city that the people there represent; to walk around a corner and to be face-to-face with a former lover whose name escapes you.

To tell the truth, I had forgotten what a revelation the market was at first. It has become such an accepted part of our lives—everybody's, I assume—that it's difficult to imagine a time when there was nothing like it anywhere west of Toronto's St. Lawrence Market. Not only did Vancouver not have one, we really thought we couldn't make one work. Every once in a while an open-air market would open at some godforsaken location like the foot of Main Street, fail in about six months, and lead us all to believe that somehow one of the truly civilizing elements of the great cities of the world—and even backwaters like Ottawa—just would not work here. It seemed hard to believe, but there was the evidence.

This failure was an affront to a local conceit that dates back almost as far as World War I, when the federal government dredged False Creek and dumped a million cubic yards of silt on the sandbar that became Granville Island. This conceit of ours was that Vancouver was more of a world city than a Canadian one: something of a mini-Europe all its own, with a German street, an Italian street, a French corner, some Greek blocks, and so on and so forth. As recently as 1970, the distinctly non-European Chinatown and Strathcona were civic embarrassments awaiting the bulldozer: the sooner they were gone, the *Sun* once editorialized, the better. However, we liked this idea of a mini-Europe. It fostered the illusion that Vancouver was a pretty cosmopolitan place.

But, of course, if there is any hallmark of the European way of life, at least compared with ours, it is the amount of time Europeans spend in public places, just hanging out, wasting time, watching the human comedy unfold. North Americans require good, solid reasons to gather in large crowds; reasons like county fairs or football games. We distrust doing anything in large crowds that you don't have to buy a ticket to join.

In Vancouver, at least, the Granville Island redevelopment, with the market as its centrepiece, changed all that. Offered the opportunity to sit back in the sunshine and munch fish and chips on a waterfront bench and watch Dick and Dick tell bad jokes and throw flaming torches back and forth, we seized the opportunity. We liked it. This was fun. The main attraction, though, was the other people, not some event we were all there to see or watch.

Why did this market work when none of the others had? It seems so obvious in retrospect. Allan Waisman, whose firm of architects has laid out the Whistler Village and the New Westminster waterfront, thinks that seemingly sudden advances in urban design have less to do with new ideas or breakthroughs in materials than with what he calls "the moment in architecture"—a sudden combination of elements that nobody could anticipate or create, which occurs at exactly the right time. Granville Island is the product of one of those architectural moments, where politics, an ideal site, and planning all came together.

The moment began with Ron Basford, a local cabinet minister with steadily declining vote totals, who wanted to leave some personal memorial behind before the entire Liberal house of cards collapsed. In other words, Granville Island was a pork-barrel project. There was very little public say about what should happen with the crumbling collection of corrugated-tin chairmaking shops, railcar-loading docks, and the Ocean Cement plant, all of it on government property—yours and mine. The whole wasteland was located under the especially unpicturesque Granville Street Bridge: troll territory. It was, in *Architectural Review*'s words, "an inner city dump."

The dump did have some natural advantages: it was a unique, physically isolated location only five minutes from downtown; it had character imparted by the ageing industrial buildings; and it was adjacent to a lively waterway.

Still, it took architect Norman Hotson to gaze upon this mess and see how—with some brightly coloured pipe here, a few trees there, and paving bricks laid just about everywhere—it could be turned into a model of inner-city revitalization such that Hotson himself is now in Toronto trying to breathe new life into the St. Lawrence Market....

Not that much was changed to create the showcase we see today. In fact, some kind of industrial activity is now considered essential near a market to give people something to watch. If anything, Granville Island's industrial feel and texture was intensified, with wall-to-wall paving and loading bays converted to bus shelters. The cement trucks stayed. Mulvaney's, the Arts Club Theatre, the art school, the Granville Island Hotel, and the Friday afternoon-to-sunset scene outdoors at Bridges—all those additional activities were wedged into gaps and corners, adding layers of life, extending it round the clock....

My personal theory is that the bridges have a lot to do with the way life concentrates and piles up in layers on Granville Island. Both bridges. The Burrard Bridge, which is the place to feel the pulse of Vancouver, if it has one, makes a storybook backdrop for all those encounters. As for the Granville Bridge, every bit of the character that it lost when its structure was tucked underneath stands revealed on the island, which has the bridge's underpinnings as its roof.

Seeing the bridge from below for the first time, under the influence of alcohol, was what I'd come right out and call an epiphany. It was past sundown, toward the end of one of the press previews of Mulvaney's. The atmosphere was so thick with dust by then that everybody there was complaining about it, but they stuck around just the same. I found myself alone, gazing through one of the north-facing windows, nursing my third drink, and suddenly realizing what an un-Vancouver-like scene it was. A flood-lit bridge abutment—flood-lit—and nothing else.

No mountains. No harbour. No shiny new skyscrapers. Just concrete with structural steel rising out of it, fanning out as it rose toward the deck somewhere up above. And I liked it.

Phantom Will Haunt Orpheum Birthday

BY SEAN ROSSITER, NOVEMBER 6–13, 1987

They'll be showing Lon Chaney's original *Phantom of the Opera* at midnight Saturday, November 7, as part of the Orpheum Theatre's 60th-birthday celebration, but the truth is that the phantom of this particular opera at Seymour and Smithe is there *all* the time. I know.

At least, I *sensed* his presence. It's dark down there in the basement caverns of the Orpheum. Two doors await the unwary at the bottom of the stairwell two storeys below the stage. They are unmarked now, but the one to the right used to carry the words "Organ Blower."

Whether those words were removed for reasons of taste by the civic theatres department when the City bought the Orpheum in 1973 and restored it seems to be a mystery. Not even Doug McCallum, who wrote the book on the Orpheum three years ago, knows.

But that subterranean crypt still holds the turbine that brings in outside air by suction and feeds it to the pipes of the, yes, "mighty Wurlitzer" organ. Gaylord Carter, last of the great silent movie organists, will accompany *The Phantom* on it. (When word got out that Carter would be in Vancouver Saturday night, a flood of ticket requests came from Seattle, where they know what he can do.)

Once Carter puts finger to key and foot to pedal, the magic begins, and when The Man of a Thousand Faces appears on the silver screen, the Orpheum's own phantom will manifest itself in a dozen ways. For when the Wurlitzer is pumping, the building is alive. It plays music you can feel as well as hear....

Doug McCallum is the architectural historian who researched the plaques affixed to 101 heritage buildings last year, and the author of *Vancouver's Orpheum: The Life of a Theatre*.... McCallum is giving me his insider's tour of the building. Believe me, there is no tour in Vancouver like it. There is no building that presents so many false fronts, so many illusions. Almost nothing is as it seems. The curtains, chandeliers, and loudspeaker system are so heavy they have to be suspended from braided wires which run up through holes in as many as four ceilings—and floors—and are anchored to a steel gridiron hung from the beams of the roof.

"Basically," McCallum says, "theatres were rigged like a ship. That was where they found the first stagehands—on sailing ships."

And where the two of us stand is the bilge. It is scary down here. The subterranean concrete walls, some eight feet high, others only three, are caked with soot from the early days, when the two huge boilers burned coal. Hot air circulates through these tunnels and rises through valves under the seats. It's scrubbed by cold-water sprays as it comes in, is heated, warms the auditorium, and is then ducted up through the plaster tracery of the roof and dome....

"Look..." McCallum says. I jump. Every hair on my neck jumps. The word echoes through the caverns. "...the original ticket-punching machine." It is a polished chrome-and-enamel antique, a bit like a trolley's fare bin, but more baroque. You'd have to be told what it is.

McCallum sounds like an archeologist. Other discarded items litter the dark corners. Bits of the past gleam for a moment as we pass by, then recede into the gloom. He suggests heading upstairs. We work our way up. When he says upstairs, he means *up*stairs. This is a five-storey building, although it is part of the Orpheum's mystery that, once inside, you never quite know how high you are. McCallum asks whether I'd like to see the dome *from above.* Is he kidding?

This is the Orpheum's last illusion. Or at least its uppermost one. We step through a door leading from the room where large fans exhaust the heated air as it rises through all the holes in the ceiling. Through this door, all we can see are catwalks and the top of the dome, where hundreds of wires and chains of several thicknesses make the dome look like a gigantic pincushion. Everything we see, everything in the auditorium, in fact, is hung from these wires and cables.

The dome, as we can see, was made by caking plaster on a chicken-wire form, which itself held the moulds for the gilt ornament underneath. The whole thing is held up by a forest of smaller wires attached to the steel rebar grid overhead. The chain holding the big chandelier over the auditorium rises through the dome's middle.

Through the thousands of holes in the plaster, we can see the seats four storeys below. Being up here gives me a heady feeling....

When Gaylord Carter begins to play the first silent film accompaniment in this building for half a century, all that hollow gilt plaster, all those chains, those cables and wires and the golden dome itself, will begin to vibrate.

At that moment, we will feel the phantom of the Orpheum rouse itself and shake the cobwebs from those sooty cavernous walls and move its thousands of parts like some gigantic musical instrument itself.

Which, as we know, it is.

Stadium Distorts Time-Space Continuum

BY VERNE McDONALD, JULY 28–AUGUST 4, 1989

There is a little mountain in the centre of Vancouver. It is home to a water reservoir, a park so pretty that people come from Japan to have their wedding pictures taken there, and a time machine. The time machine is cleverly disguised as a baseball stadium.

Time machines have become necessary in a post-modern world. (That's right, *post*-modern. Forget *now*, baby, it's already gone, we're way *past* now.) Punks hooked on computers, assault rifles selling over the counter, faxing birthday greetings to Grandma in Wichita, public spectacles of buildings being dynamited downtown—most people do not want to even think about how strange the world has become.

Thus the time machine, the search for warps and doorways in the time-space continuum that might take people to George Bush's "kinder, gentler nation" or some other idealized image of the past. The time-warp people are everywhere. Laissez-faire conservatives, classic rock listeners, bearded panhandlers on Robson Street who flash the peace sign at you, new romantics singing Celtic dirges—the Great Depression will probably be the next focus for a nostalgic fad.

Wreck Beach is a time machine that will take you right back to the early Bronze Age, but most people prefer to travel only a little bit into the past. They will settle for a decent bus system or humane architecture. Such folks can be seen, on warm summer nights, collecting under the shadow of Vancouver's little mountain, entering the gates of Nat Bailey stadium.

There are genuine baseball fans who attend the games at Nat Bailey, experts who can actually tell you where each Vancouver Canadians player stands in the Chicago White Sox farm-team hierarchy, who really care which team wins the Pacific Coast League pennant. They are the minority. Most of the people in the stands are not fans of Triple A professional baseball—they are time travellers who are fans of Nat Bailey.

Move the levers: set the time for 1951. After the better part of half a century,

baseball moved from Athletic Park on South Granville to a shiny new facility. There was a roof over much of Vancouver's largest grandstand, and it was named Capilano Stadium.

The "Capilano" came not from local geography but from the name of the baseball team's sponsor: Sick's Capilano Brewery. Beer and baseball have always travelled together. Sick's had already built a larger park in Seattle, and Capilano Stadium was its perfect little sister.

The stands overflowed with 7,000 fans that June day as the Capilanos thumped Salem 10 to 3. Vancouver pitcher Bob Snyder collected his 12th win of the season. The fans ate hotdogs, booed the umpire's calls, and sang "Take Me Out to the Ball Game" during the seventh inning stretch.

They still do. Nothing has changed. Baseball is the ultimate *Twilight Zone*....

Another Country Lies Across the Lions Gate

BY JAMES BARBER, AUGUST 9–16, 1991

Canadian Airlines will fly you to San Francisco three times a day: a two-hour flight, a light lunch, a glass of champagne, and there it is—ready for you to leave your heart, a couple hundred bucks, and a few more credit-card stubs than you originally intended.

A few rides on the cable car, kites and drums at Ghirardelli Square, crab on Fisherman's Wharf, drinks at the Top of the Mark—there's a fairly predictable rhythm to a San Francisco quickie. People with a bit more time get outside the city; they cross the San Mateo Bridge, and because it's not city anymore it feels like another country, even if you go no further than Carmel.

Carmel is a time machine—a time gone by coexisting with a time to come; the sort of past that comes from having a wealthy family and the sort of future that goes with winning the lottery. But there's no point in having time or money unless you have places to spend them.

Everybody in Vancouver recognizes Commercial Drive as a special neighbourhood. I've seen it described in tourist brochures as "a must-see for its street life." *Almost* everybody in Vancouver wonders why Granville Mall and Gastown are such disasters and why nobody but the most gullible of tourists would want to go there. We all explain Commercial Drive in terms of its ethnic mix and the street life and the artists, but nobody accepts the obvious: that places that are allowed to grow, without too much interference from planners and developers, are a lot more comfortable than places designed in two dimensions on a drawing board and forced upon us as "desirable" neighbourhoods.

Carmel grew out of a shanty town into a romantic-dream theme park. It was the one-night stand that became love everlasting, and if it wasn't roses round the door for everybody, it was a lot of roses in the back lanes.

But most of all and first of all, it was a place to spend time; later it developed into a place to spend money. Commercial Drive owes its popularity (and much of its mythology) to the simple fact that it has a lot of places in which to spend time, and if anybody really tries to commercialize it and organize it, then it will turn into another planning disaster.

The old men of Commercial Drive play *bocce* in Victoria Park—street-style bocce, just as they do in Sicily. Somebody in the park board office decided they should have a nice, clean, well-organized pair of bocce courts to play on—level, fenced, and free from all interference. Weeds grow on the courts, and the old men still amble all over the park, playing between dogs, puddles, small children, and enthusiastic tourists with cameras, perfectly and happily unorganized.

Carmel and Commercial Drive have a lot in common: they both just happened, even though they arrived at different destinations. West Vancouver, which has always claimed a kinship with Carmel based on the cleanliness, the bridge, the roses, and an awful lot of Ladies Who Lunch (and wear Tilley hats), actually had very little in common with it until very recently. And it never claimed even a distant relationship with Commercial Drive (where Tilley hats are *not* worn).

But West Vancouver is finally beginning to become more than a paint-by-numbers water colour. It's beginning to smell. At 15th and Marine Drive there is a coffeehouse that roasts beans, and when the wind is right, for blocks around, it's early morning, it's time to get up, it's Grandma's house, and it's coffee time.

Bean Around the World it's called, cohabiting with the Savary Island Pie Company, and the two of them make the corner the warmest, most welcoming coffeehouse I've found outside New York, fully equipped with the *New York Times Review of Books*, the *Village Voice*, the *Economist*, *Harrowsmith*, and dozens of other specialist and exotic magazines....

Round the corner, on 15th and Bellevue, is yet another luxurious smell—of fish and chips. Kings Fare, long established at the south end of Granville as the fussiest of all the fish-and-chippers (separate fryers for cod and halibut and thick, hand-cut chips), has opened a new place in the new West Vancouver. From 11 a.m. to 8 p.m., they serve the ultimate lunch on a summer's day: a Newcastle Nut Brown Ale, three pieces of halibut, brown vinegar...and if you want the maximum benefit from your warm and fragrant bundle, then the beach is just a few yards across the tracks. Up the street, at 25th and Marine, is Capers...a paradise for an ambitious stomach, the sort of place to restore your faith in the organic-food movement.

Nobody is selling kites or flying them off the pier, and there are no cable cars, but there is a genuine Italian ice-cream maker, L'Arte del Gelato, making something very favourably comparable with the ice cream you eat much too much of in Venice, and open from 9:30 a.m., a sensible time to eat ice cream on a day off.

West Van is actually worth driving to these days.

Remembering Woodward's

BY JOHN LEKICH, SEPTEMBER 3–10, 1993

As a kid, I knew the Woodward's label intimately. For years, I thought it was the only store in town where you could buy underwear. My mother, leery of camping-trip mixups or a sudden visit to the emergency room, would sew my initials above the trademark, a navy-blue logo that, set against a T-shirt Javexed as white as Pat Boone's smile, spelled out the store's brand name like frosting on a birthday cake.

It could be that I've spent too many formative years staring at Woodward's jockey shorts, but I've never been able to get over the idea that our mutual fates have been stitched together on the waistband of destiny. These days, this is not the most comforting thought. After more than 100 years, Woodward's is deader than Elvis. And, all things considered, I'm not feeling so good myself.

I was one of those kids who thought Woodward's would always be there. Like the tree in our backyard. I was vaguely aware of other stores while in primary school, but Woodward's had the kind of jingles that stuck in your mind with the staying power of that first time you were allowed to stay up late and watch a drunken relative do the hula. Long after I've forgotten the principles of physics or geometry, I can still remember the radio ad that belted out: "Woodward's is a nice department store. We have silks and laces, pillow cases, plenty of roomy parking spaces."

Unlike the Bay, whose jingles experimented with down-and-dirty blues combined with a thick coating of eastern sarcasm (remember "Stick your head in the Bay"?), Woodward's jingles were so desperately earnest that they sounded as if someone had cranked up an ice-cream truck to warp speed. They were, of course, at their best while blending urgent harmonies in homage to the red-hot mother of all local sales: "Dollar Forty-Nine Day! Tuesday! Dollar Forty-Nine Day! Woodward's!"

It should be pointed out that my mother relished the prospect of department-store sales the way some people dream about marlin fishing or a chance encounter with some beautiful stranger. She always considered $1.49 Day to be the cornerstone of shopping-bag extravaganzas. On such Tuesdays, she favoured a hat-and-gloves formality, returning home with a combination of packages that could include a bath mat, a few pillowcases, and a cheese grater that gleamed like the bumper on a brand-new Buick. After unwrapping all the purchases, she would entertain me with tales of gorgeous women who squirted her with perfume or urged her to try the latest sandwich spread.

I was always extra restless in school during those Tuesday sales. While the teacher was shuffling flash cards or making us gobble like Thanksgiving turkeys, I'd imagine standing in front of the entrance at the downtown Woodward's and bracing myself for the crush. The door would be especially heavy, like some secret entranceway to another world. It was as if everything you ever wanted to buy was folded, stacked, or draped on the other side....

The Bridge of Our Dreams

BY SEAN ROSSITER, SEPTEMBER 24–OCTOBER 1, 1993

...One of the strongest urges of the Vancouver mind-set, of our provincialism, is the wish for some man-made expression of what we are all about, one that would be recognizable anywhere. Each time some new architectural expression of our aspirations has appeared, such as B.C. Place or Canada Place, someone declared the event a certification of our status among big-league cities. *This* could be our Sydney opera house. *This* could be our Tivoli Gardens. For a long time, few of us noticed that our trademark had been there all along.

We know now. Our appreciation of the [Lions Gate Bridge] has been growing for, oh, going on 10 years. Part of this dates back to 1985, when the Lions Gate was subjected to one of those dumb beautification tricks our Social Credit uncles were constantly thinking up during those days. (Actually, it was a Socred aunt: Grace

Nothing else can do what the Lions Gate Bridge does for Vancouver.

McCarthy.) They hung lightbulbs on it. I hated the idea until they flipped the switch. It looks terrific.

The change in how we see the Lions Gate is best exemplified by the photographs taken of it in recent years. Until recently, it was almost always photographed from below, as a magnificent arc softened by the fog over the First Narrows. It was pictured from the air, but aerial photographs of the bridge made it part of a wider, more important panorama: as part of the port, as Vancouver's Gateway to the World. As Vancouver passed Thunder Bay as an outlet for Prairie grain in the early '80s—an event hardly noted when it happened—the centre of gravity of our northern part of the continent shifted west, and Mike Harcourt started talking about Vancouver as Canada's Front Door.

It was around that time that photographers began to think of looking at the world from the bridge. The most familiar result was the work of Allan Zenuk. Working for Tourism B.C. on the "Super, Natural" advertising campaign that brought Vancouver to the attention of readers of, for example, the *New Yorker*, he sought the single, essential photograph of our time and place. The photos by Zenuk and others have made the bridge a work of art in itself.

It is only now, as we contemplate the possibility that we might lose the bridge, that we see the Lions Gate Bridge as the high concept it always was. We can accept it as an intrusion on scenic Burrard Inlet.

Now that the crisis of its fate cannot be put off a moment longer, one thing about the Lions Gate Bridge seems clear. It cannot be replaced. Something else could get us to the North Shore and back again. Something else—*any*thing else—would accomplish that utilitarian task much more efficiently.

But the Lions Gate is our hourly pulse, the measure of our limits. What greater pleasure is available to us as part of our everyday routine than the view from the Lions Gate, especially at sunset with a cruise ship passing underneath? It takes us to those wonders of nature we say we live here to enjoy, and it brings us back again.

Nothing else can do all that. Nothing else can do everything the Lions Gate does for us.

Closing a Door to the Past

BY JAMES BARBER, SEPTEMBER 23–30, 1994

In the back corner of a little restaurant on Keefer Street, just east of Main, four men are sitting round a table, concentrating like poker players and, like men regretting their stock-market losses, talking intermittently.

They're business partners, doing business but not talking business. They're folding wontons—a dab of pork filling, a quick one-handed flip of the wrapper (like John Wayne rolling a cigarette), and in an hour the big bowl will be full enough for the hundred or so orders of wonton soup that the evening will bring. They've done it every afternoon for the past 30 years or so, same guys, same table, just as soon as the lunchtime trade has wiped its lips and gone back to work. The restaurant is the On On Tea Garden, an important but sadly unrecognized part of Vancouver's history.

With its Arborite tables, chalkboard menu, and particularly ugly floor of finger-paint-orange tiles, it's by no means an outstanding piece of architecture. But Trudeau has eaten there, as have Ray Charles, Buffy Sainte-Marie, and Bobbie Gentry. Most visiting showbiz people and just about every politician who ever wanted to be known as "one of the people": they've all, in their time and in their turn, been customers of the On On.

But it's not the famous who have made the little restaurant such an important cultural institution. Twenty-five years ago, there were really two Chinatowns, one east and one west of Main Street. On the east side, the wholesale produce business started about 4 a.m., and by 11 a.m. the guys who had spent the morning humping heavy sacks on and off trucks were ready for their lunch. The On On provided it. Real Cantonese food, *ga heung*-style (which means, basically, "like your mother made"): great steaming bowls of *congee* (the rice porridge that is the soul food of the Orient), strange and wonderful stews like *foo juk man ap* (fresh duck, dried rice sticks, and gingko nuts), and that lovely, addictive Chinese hamburger called *ham yee yauk pieng*, which is essentially ground pork with green onions and salt fish, not fried but steamed, with a little rice wine over top.

A sign in the window said Coffee, and the occasional timid Occidental would sit at the counter and order, but there was much better coffee in other restaurants. The bravest of the non-Chinese would point at whatever looked good on somebody else's table, and that was the beginning of the On On's devoted fan club of white folk.

It's hard to write about those times in the politically correct language of today, but Bill Yip and his partners spoke very little English, and there were, in effect, two separate clienteles: the working Chinese and the others. The others? They knew Chinese food as take-out—sweet-and-sour spareribs, almond *guy ding*, and two portions of fried rice—and the On On was a big adventure.

I got to know the partners because they didn't speak English. I had very little money and a beard, which was reason enough for them to think I was a professor and therefore able to teach. We worked out a system based on two copies of an English translation of Maupassant's *Quinze Contes*, a tape recorder, and some yellow highlighters. I would read a story per week onto the tape, they would play it back and highlight what they didn't understand, and once a week we'd go over it all. And eat. I learned a lot about Chinese food, and Bill Yip still has traces of my British accent. So.

The clientele of "others" grew. In 1968, the restaurant grew sideways to take in the vegetable shop to the east, and in 1973 it grew again, this time to the west. A printed menu took over from the chalkboard (although the chalkboard is there to this day), and in 1984 the brown paper bags and bottles of mixer were replaced by a wine list.

The word has gotten around that the On On is closing forever on October 27th, to be replaced by a bank. The faithful (most of whom don't know they're making history and consider the On On to be their own personal and private discovery) are coming from all over to take their final communion. Bill Yip taught them about Chinese food that just wasn't available anywhere else in town—vegetables like *gai choy* and *sui choy*, *gai lan* and *ong choy*. He taught them about the special combinations of simple pan-fried green beans with a fermented bean curd called *foo yee;* he showed them the season for *foo gwa*, the bitter melon, and how to eat it with beef; and he persuaded them that chrysanthemum leaves called *chuong ho* were edible, and so was *mo gwa*, the hairy cucumber. *Laup cheung yok pieng*, the lovely, homely, comforting combination of

Chinese sausage and pork chopped with two cleavers, changed their minds forever about the exotic potential of ground meat.

Bill Yip gave Chinese food a different meaning for ordinary people, and in doing so he did a great deal for racial and cultural tolerance. It's these ordinary people who have made the restaurant's reputation.

In every proper city, there is one restaurant that for some special reason embodies the essence of the city's personality, like Ben's in Montreal, Prunier's in London, and Madame Henri Berger's in Ottawa. The On On, despite its fame, has always maintained its integrity. There were no white tablecloths for Trudeau, and, in fact, when the security guys walked in a week before his visit and asked to reserve the whole mezzanine floor (with its 14 seats and 5′9″ headroom) for a special party of six, Bill Yip refused.

"Saturday night; sorry, very busy." *"But this is somebody very special..."* "I don't care; six people, not enough." So the prime minister of Canada and five others had to sit down at a table barely big enough for four, cheek by jowl with his constituents from Burnaby (their bottles of Schloss Lederhosen under the seat), and defer, like most of them, to the waiter's suggestions.

Local talent always gets a rough ride in Canada. And in Vancouver, despite having the most innovative food in the country and some of the lowest big-city restaurant prices in North America, we seem to be very reluctant to acknowledge our food folk heroes. Umberto Menghi is credited with rescuing us from a lifetime of spaghetti and meatballs, and just as it's difficult to find a baby boomer who wasn't at Woodstock, it's hard to find a Japanese-food addict in town who wasn't an intimate of Tojo when he had a five-seater sushi bar in a hole-in-the-wall on West Broadway. But we overlook the little guys who, without benefit of fashion or global trends, make changes by just hanging in.

Bill Yip will miss his restaurant, and his customers. When they ask him what he'll do, he shrugs his shoulders and grins. Not many people know about his other passion, really big classical music—Mahler, Beethoven, Tchaikovsky ("I like his cello stuff, the A-major rococo variations..."). He'll never be honorary doctor of anything, but it wouldn't be inappropriate.

The Ballroom's Modest Prince

BY JOHN LEKICH, JULY 11–18, 1996

The Commodore Ballroom inspires more loyalty, from more kinds of people, than just about any local club that I can think of. Take me, for instance. I'm the kind of guy who actually has a backup pair of fuzzy slippers. The kind of guy who wears a cardigan *off* the golf course. Still, a few years ago, I was coaxed into attending a local punk-rock reunion called Budstock at the Commodore. I wore a tie.

I made my way up the stairs, running a clammy hand along the stout brass railing. I moved past bouncers who'd torn the sleeves off their T-shirts, with absolutely no regard for stray threads, and into a throb of sound that could best be described as easy listening from hell.

I had stumbled upon an act called Hellvis. Half a dozen or so Elvis imitators wearing plastic devil's horns and singing "Viva Las Vegas." A woman onstage was happily exposing her breasts. I felt that it was appropriate to remove my tie.

I fell in love with the Commodore that night, and it was a pleasant shock to my buttoned-down soul. Like developing a sudden, inexplicable attraction to a woman with lime-green hair and safety pins through her nose—only to discover, on closer inspection, that she's actually Grace Kelly politely trying to escape terminal boredom.

Now I have something in common with my vaguely dangerous friends, the kind with tattoos that don't rub off and record collections that overlap into their kitchen cupboards. I tell them that the Commodore has good bones. And pretty soon they begin to spin tales of legendary concerts, their eyes gleaming with lost innocence.

They're like old prizefighters, recounting glorious brawls from within the secret walls of their favourite gym. And, even secondhand, it always seems as if every corner of the Commodore is blessed with the sweat of some urgent magic.

Nobody understands this better than Drew Burns, who owns everything but the walls and is preparing to leave after 27 years of making the Commodore go. Climbing up the stairs of the club, my steps sound strangely hollow, the only other sound the distant wrench of cherished things being torn from where they have always been.

Burns shakes my hand as if it really matters, his grip bearing a firmness that is the mark of a certain generation. We move toward his office, down a narrow hallway that could double for a secret passageway in some Hardy Boys mystery. He is careful not to lose me along the way. But Burns is so intimately familiar with the twists and turns of the building that, for a moment, he seems to vanish into the walls.

When I finally turn the corner to enter his office, it looks as if 27 years' worth of paperwork has been scattered by an electric fan gone berserk. His desk, a wooden slab the size of a large door, supports a loose mountain of memos, flyers, and assorted documents.

Stacks of files sit on battered sofas and chairs. The walls are lined with newer posters that have been haphazardly tacked over older posters, and there are decades' worth of genuine guy stuff poking out at odd angles: model ships, a quaintly demure girlie calendar, and clocks that have long since stopped working but are still worth having around. It's as if Burns has created the perfect boy's room, if only because there's no fussy mother around to force him outside into the fresh air.

Sensing a chance to nudge the moment into the realm of sheer bliss, Burns offers: "Sometimes I just sit here and listen to Sinatra. Anything between '63 and '67, when he was in his absolute prime."

But there have been moments, sitting in his office at a certain time of night, when Burns didn't even need Sinatra. He'd just sit there and listen. "There's something about how a good crowd builds," he says. "You can hear the buzz from my desk. The music starts, the people come in, the voices get louder and louder. That's when you know that people come here to...belong."

As he settles down to light a cigarette, there is something about Burns that seems to suggest a more generous time. His white hair, parted in the middle like that of some tenderhearted bartender in the kind of movie that only plays late at night, was darker once. At 19—desperate to see acts like the Mills Brothers at the Cave—he would touch up his temples with a sister's face powder to make himself look older.

"I used to take a mascara pencil and darken the fuzz on my upper lip," he says, grinning. "I would do anything to get where the music was."

Drew Burns sometimes appears to vanish into the Commodore's walls.

In all the years that Burns has been running the Commodore, what's the most common story he's heard from the patrons? He laughs. "It goes something like, 'Hey, Drew, did you know I saw my first concert here when I was 16?'

"We always tried to be very strict about ID here," he says, "but kids can be especially crafty." Smiling, he adds: "There's always a part of me that's glad they got in, because they saw a show they really wanted to see."

Burns has one of those seasoned voices that sound like sandpaper digging into soft wood. But what I notice the most about him is his eyes. They are the bluest I've ever seen, and decades after most of the nightspots from his boyhood vanished, they continue to give him the look of someone who is permanently underage.

It doesn't take long to notice that when Burns gets going, his eyes tend to get even brighter, shifting from a kind of cheerful, Windex blue into the kind of colour you can only get when a patient kid presses extra hard on the bluest crayon in the entire box.

Of the Commodore's success during his 27 years at the helm, he says: "Vancouver's the best city in the world, with the best people. And it's the people that make a room. There's a real sense of emotional history here.

"Sometimes, you'll get the vice-president of a record company to come out here from their glass tower in L.A. or New York," Burns says. "They always say there's nothing like the Commodore anywhere else. A music critic from the London *Times* rated it one of the top five live venues in the world."

Burns estimates that in the Commodore's 66-year history, some 15 million people have walked through its doors. "It's the glue for a lot of good memories," he says. "People used to dance here in uniform during the war. That's the kind of heritage you can't build with just a hammer and nails."

An ex-choirboy whose childhood was steeped in all kinds of music, Burns moved here from Winnipeg at the age of 11. He has so many stories about the golden age of the local club scene that the cigarette he keeps trying to ignite refuses to stay lit. Finally, after several tries, he simply cradles it in his fingers, letting thin wisps of smoke disappear into the high ceiling.

It says something about Burns that the stories he recalls with the most affection always involve some bright thread of kindness. He remembers two back-to-back shows with James Brown. "I told James to stay within certain guidelines," he laughs, noting that the second show was scheduled to start precisely at 10:30. "The first show ran an hour and a half over and the second show didn't end until 4 in the morning. When it was all over, James said to me: 'Do you think we played long enough?'

"I can remember when Bryan Adams played here," he continues. "At the end of his show, there were people lined up from the entranceway to the backstage area. They all had scraps of paper or photographs. Bryan talked to them all and signed everything."

Of course, not all of the shows were sellouts. Burns admits that his personal philosophy didn't always adhere to the bottom line, whether it came to pushing drinks or booking acts. "I could have probably changed the room around years ago and made it into a huge moneymaker," he says. "But that's not necessarily what I wanted to do. I think you should be able to listen to music even if all you choose to drink is a glass of water. So, even though we were in the business of selling alcohol, there was never the same kind of constant pressure to drink as in some other places."

When talk turns to the actual structure of the Commodore itself, Burns explains that the staircase leading to the ballroom can prove deceptive. "It doesn't really provide a clue to what you're walking into. On some nights, I'd just stand in the doorway of my office and pick out people who were coming here for the first time. You could always spot them by the surprised look on their faces."

Burns grins. "Seeing someone cross the archway for the first time and suddenly take in this massive expanse. It's always fun to watch."

Ask him what's special about the room, apart from the famous spring-loaded dance floor, and he says: "Part of it's the size. There's a lot of room to move around and schmooze." But there're also a thousand details that people miss. "A lot of thought was put into the lighting," he explains. "It's soft but not too dark. There's just enough light to throw a nice glow over the audience. The stars on the ceiling are actually patterned after the Big Dipper and the Little Dipper." When I express surprise, he grins. "You have to lie flat on your back to make out the shapes, but they're up there."

I am just about to ask Burns if he's ever spent any time flat on his back and gazing at stars on the ceiling when the phone rings.

The caller, a stranger, is someone inquiring about an AIDS benefit that's taking place at the Commodore shortly after its longtime proprietor will have vacated the premises for good. They want a contact number, and Burns spends a good minute or so happily sifting through the rubble on his desk to find it.

Unsuccessful, he reaches for a battered Rolodex. "I'm going to give you the home number of someone who has what you want," he says. "You're going to get her answering service and she talks like a machine gun, but be sure to listen for the whole message. You might have to make a couple of calls. But if you saw my desk, you'd understand."

Burns hangs up the phone and the conversation turns to acts of kindness. "There's lots of times I used to give the place over to a charity on a Saturday night," he says. "You can't just take all the time. You have to give something back. Besides, any kindness I've ever shown has been returned to me four or five times over."

That he will miss the Commodore almost goes without saying. "I've been married to it for 27 years.

"But what some people don't understand is that they were the *right* 27 years," he adds. "I was lucky enough to experience that transition period where I could still experience a Cab Calloway or a Buddy Rich. They aren't around anymore. Just like a lot of the old Delta blues guys I love so much are gone."

Burns leans forward so that his chair gives a soft squeak. "My time is done here," he says. "But even if you gave me another 27 years, how could I ever duplicate it? It was perfect."

Who will take over the club now? "I don't know," Burns concedes. "But I don't think it'll be someone like me."

He does have some advice, though. "You have to put love into a building," he says. "Because love is something that people can feel. Your staff and everybody who works in the place have to understand that instinctively. Otherwise, you could pour millions of dollars into it and all you'd get back would be bricks and mortar."

Burns looks around his office, at 27 years' worth of scattered odds and ends. "Nobody can take away a memory," he says. "It's there for anybody who ever shared it, whoever lived through it." He lets me in on a favourite saying that's been running through his head a lot lately. "Yesterday's history; tomorrow's a mystery. Today is a gift. That's why they call it the present."

Burns intends to stay in the business with a club called It's a Secret. But compared to the dismantling of his current world, that's well into the mystery of tomorrow.

We say goodbye. He shakes my hand. I am outside and halfway down the street before I realize that a single question remains unanswered. Instead of turning back, I imagine Drew Burns in the present. He's flat on his back, gazing at the Commodore's ceiling. Lost in the gift of a thousand stars, one last time.

THE HOLLY ARNTZEN
BAND

FACING PAGE:
Dan McLeod at the *Straight*'s 20th-anniversary party in 1987.

CHRONOLOGY 1986–1996

1986

JANUARY Life in Hell, by struggling Seattle artist Matt Groening, makes its *Straight* debut. "It won't be long before the 7-Elevens will have two pumps for gas and two for dinner," writes James Barber in his first *Straight* restaurant column.

FEBRUARY *Vancouver Sun* cast-off Charles Campbell replaces Bob Mercer as managing editor of the *Straight.* Abbie Hoffman and Jerry Rubin debate at the Orpheum.

APRIL "Right now, there are aircraft carriers off the coast of Libya, and there's this military flex which is really off, and I'd rather just not get involved," says Bryan Adams of turning down the job of writing for the soundtrack of *Top Gun.*

MAY Expo 86 opens in an orgy of civic self-congratulation.

JUNE The *Straight*'s John Armstrong asks Vincent Price whether he has nightmares: "Oh, yes. Being interviewed by Barbara Walters. She terrifies me." The Canadian Food Writers Awards name James Barber the community newspaper writer of the year. "Right now the problem with journalism is that it's not fun. That sounds frivolous, but you don't go into the journalism business for the money.... I remember thinking, [Nixon] is perfect. We can get him. And we did get him. That's fun."—Hunter S. Thompson in the *Straight.* The first du Maurier International Jazz Festival opens at Canada Place with consummate capitalist Jimmy Pattison on trumpet.

AUGUST Ernie Pook's Comeek by Lynda Barry is introduced to *Straight* readers. *Straight* co-founder Milton Acorn, the People's Poet, dies at 63. A brutally frank *Straight* Expo guide, first printed in May, is expanded and republished due to popular demand. "We came, drank beer, played, they pulled the plug on us, and Hamm flipped his wally."—Slow guitarist Christian Thorvaldson sums up the first (and last) concert of the Expo Festival of Independent Recording Artists. Premier Bill Bennett retires and the charismatic Bill Vander Zalm begins to lead us down the garden path.

1987

FEBRUARY The *Straight* celebrates its 1,000th issue on February 20 with a party at the Town Pump. "You were some outlaw but, hey, living smart is the best revenge," former contributor Denny Boyd writes in the *Sun.*
MARCH Bob Cummings, one of the *Straight*'s most prolific and talented writers, takes his own life. The *National Enquirer* becomes a *Straight* subscriber.
APRIL Organizers of the Stanley Park 20th-anniversary Be-in estimate that the Be-in was held from 1967 to 1974. If you can remember the 1975 and 1976 Be-ins, you weren't really there.

A celebratory bash at the Commodore features a score of performers and congratulations via video from Bob Geldof.

MAY The *Straight* publishes its 20th-anniversary issue and mayor Gordon Campbell declares May 5 *Georgia Straight* Day. A celebratory bash at the Commodore, emceed by Terry David Mulligan, features a score of performers and congratulations via video from Bob Geldof. Veteran reporter Jack Webster retires.
JUNE Carel Moiseiwitsch wins her third straight Western Magazine Award for best illustration of the year—the *Straight*'s first award for editorial excellence. The $1 coin debuts.
AUGUST Tom Berger, Farley Mowat, David Suzuki, John Denver, and 2,000 others trek to the Stein Valley for a Voices for the Wilderness conference hosted by the Lytton and Mount Currie Indian bands, who are worried that their ancestral lands are about to be logged.
OCTOBER "I tried to stop the release of *The Joshua Tree* myself. I rang our manager and I said, 'I don't think this thing is going to sell any more than three copies. I think we've made a big mistake.' But it had already gone to the pressing plant."—Bono of U2 talks to the *Straight*'s Chris Dafoe in Toronto.

1988

JANUARY Organizers estimate that the inaugural First Night on New Year's Eve attracted 50,000 people to the downtown area. Brian Mulroney and Ronald Reagan sign the North American Free Trade Agreement. The Vancouver Symphony Orchestra suspends operations after its January 26 concert.
FEBRUARY Calgary hosts the 1988 Winter Olympics.
MARCH *Straight* circulation and sales have nearly doubled in less than three years, and the paper leaves its 4th Avenue home to move downtown to Pender. The Savoy nightclub closes.
APRIL Rod Filbrandt's comic strip Wombat, late of the *Discorder*, replaces his True Life panel in the *Straight.* The Mayor's Symphony Recovery Task Force report calls for the VSO to return for the 1988–89 season.
JUNE Classical Currents columnist John Becker garners the *Straight*'s second Western Magazine Award. The Arts Club takes nine of 14 Jessie Awards, including four for *Danny and the Deep*

Blue Sea, which first surfaced at the 1987 Fringe Festival.
SEPTEMBER The CRTC gets it right for once and awards UBC radio station CiTR a proper, city-wide broadcasting licence. Ben Johnson becomes the fastest man in the world at the Olympics in Seoul. Soon after, he pees in a bottle.
OCTOBER Margaret Atwood, Timothy Findley, and Ursula K. Le Guin are the feature attractions at the first Vancouver Writers Festival.
DECEMBER The Cheese Club, by Tofino cartoonist Andrew Struthers, debuts in the *Straight*. AIDS Vancouver's Dyan Campbell appeals to bands across Canada to include an AIDS information pamphlet in their albums; only Victoria's NoMeansNo replies. Elton John gives up on his planned AIDS benefit after six months of failing to interest other artists.

1989

APRIL The opera *Aida* brings an eight-ton polyurethane Sphinx and four elephants to B.C. Place Stadium. After Capt. Hazelwood gets lost and runs aground in Prince William Sound, Matt Groening responds in Life in Hell: "To those of you who have suggested that we Hexxon executives should be forced to go to Alaska and scrub those oily rocks ourselves, not returning until the job is done, no matter how long it takes, we say simply this: *'You don't understand. We are rich and powerful beyond your wildest dreams.'*"
MAY Ken Eisner reports firsthand on an April trip to Moscow by the Scramblers and 54-40: "Laurie Mercer and Ron Allen spent the night in jail because they happened to drift into an altercation with drunks; when the police realized they were Canadians, the cops yelled 'Gretzky,' gave the latest hockey scores, and turned 'em loose." The Calgary Flames tarnish the Forum mystique and win a Stanley Cup final in Montreal.

"Why can't Bryan Adams come to my house for clam chowder?" asked CiTR personality and celebrity-phile Nardwuar the Human Serviette

---

JUNE Chinese troops and tanks crush student demonstrations for democracy in Tiananmen Square. Fox Television Network strikes a deal for 13 episodes of Matt Groening's *The Simpsons*. Veteran *Straight* production employee Brigit Goldammer becomes editorial designer.
SEPTEMBER Colin James wins seven West Coast Music Awards at Tribute '89.
OCTOBER "Rick Gibson did go through with his threat last month to eat a sandwich containing what he claimed was a slice of human testicle. This time, Gibson told us, police videotaped him, but did not charge him. A victory for the freedom of *something*, we say."—Straight Talk stands up for the freedom of something.
NOVEMBER The Berlin Wall comes down.
DECEMBER In Montreal, Marc Lepine shoots 26 female students, 14 of them fatally.

1990

JANUARY "Why can't Bryan Adams come to my house for clam chowder?" asks CiTR personality and celebrity-phile Nardwuar the Human Serviette, in an interview with Chris Wong.

SEPTEMBER The *Straight*'s Verne McDonald has nightmares before bungee jumping: "I can see my leg dangling at the end of the cord, its raw, red end sweeping back and forth as if looking for the rest of me."
NOVEMBER "People shouldn't be disheartened by the fact we're not going anymore. They shouldn't think, 'It just shows you can't be different and survive.' That's not true," says Joe "Shithead" Keithley in the *Straight*, on another (temporary) dissolution of D.O.A.
DECEMBER "This pseudo-Elizabethan half-timbered nostalgic dream of early British Vancouverites has been saved by having a large glass tower grafted onto its back."—*Straight* photographer and critic Oraf on the heritage compromise that preserved the Tudor Arms' facade on Beach Avenue. Woody Turnquist, *Straight* marketing and sales director, drives away from a seven-year record of success in a red 1967 Porsche.

1991

JANUARY James Barber proclaims: "Good sex and good food are pretty much the same thing." The Goods and Services Tax is imposed. The Gulf War brings togetherness: almost everybody agrees to bomb a large but still disputed number of Iraqis into oblivion.
APRIL Controversial Washington State Native rights activist Robert Satiacum—a fugitive from convictions on U.S. federal racketeering charges who was granted and then denied refugee status in Canada—is profiled by Martin Dunphy upon his death in police custody. News features, which have appeared sporadically in the previous year after an absence of nearly a decade, are now prominent almost every week.
AUGUST "You can't even count on *Time* magazine or the six o'clock news to tell the truth, as our most recent war showed. So how are you going to count on some rock star to teach you things?"—the Grapes of Wrath's Kevin Kane in an interview with Alex Varty. Soviet hardliners attempt coup, get stewed, now eating jail food. Gorbachev is subsequently ousted by Boris Yeltsin.
NOVEMBER June Callwood admits to Zsuzsi Gartner that she was a latecomer to feminism and once negatively reviewed Betty Friedan's *The Feminine Mystique:* "I was the second-most-frequent byline in *Maclean's* through the '50s, when I had three children. So it seemed that Betty Friedan had made a mistake. I can't believe the *stupe* I was!"

1992

MAY With issue 1272, the *Straight* celebrates its 25th anniversary.
JUNE The *Straight*'s Robin Laurence wins the arts commentary award at the Western Magazine Awards.
OCTOBER The Charlottetown Accord is defeated in a national referendum.
NOVEMBER War hero George Bush loses the U.S. election to Bill Clinton. Ross Perot captures 19 percent of the vote.
DECEMBER Classified ad: "Single white male misanthrope, 26, never has any fun, hates everything, seeks female, no major history of institutionalization, to sit around and gripe about the buffoons that inhabit the world. Also, live music."

1993

APRIL Mark Leiren-Young reports that the Vancouver Summit between Boris Yeltsin, Bill Clinton, and 2,200 journalists has also brought "incredibly inconspicuous men and women with

Spy vs. Spy trench coats, wires dangling out of their ears, and the occasional Dick Tracy–style wrist radio."
MAY The *Straight* slams city council for allowing the only heritage-designated sign in the city, the Canadian National sign at the VIA station, to be dismantled.
JUNE Vancouver theatre director Larry Lillo dies of AIDS. The *Straight* picks up four Western Magazine Awards.
JULY Dirk Beck's cover feature on Alcan's Kemano Completion Project is the media's first comprehensive look at the controversial water-diversion plan.
AUGUST The Woodward's department-store chain closes its doors.
SEPTEMBER Surrey becomes a city (of sorts).
OCTOBER Kim Campbell becomes Canada's first female prime minister, then promptly loses the election along with all but two of her party's MPs. The Natural Law Party steals a few votes by trumpeting the benefits of yogic flying.
NOVEMBER Sean Rossiter predicts that the NPA will wipe out COPE in the Vancouver civic election. It does, but not until 1996.

1994

JANUARY Nirvana plays two nights at the PNE Forum.
APRIL Hemp B.C. opens a retail outlet that openly sells marijuana seeds. The police don't bother arresting them for nearly two years. Nirvana's Kurt Cobain commits suicide.
MAY The *Straight* wins a National Magazine Award for a Terry Glavin essay on aboriginal fishing rights.
JUNE The New York Rangers beat the Canucks in Game 7 of the Stanley Cup. Vancouverites celebrate the loss with a riot on Robson.
OCTOBER The *Straight*'s Jeannine Mitchell reports on government indifference to the mentally ill on the Downtown Eastside, where the Strathcona Mental Health Team reports that 14 percent of its caseload "definitely or very likely has AIDS."
NOVEMBER A *Straight* cover feature by Ben Parfitt reports that *Cryptosporidium*, a potentially fatal parasite, has shown up in local drinking-water reservoirs. Five months later, the same story (minus a few salient details) creates a minor panic when it appears on the *Sun*'s front page and leads the six-o'clock news broadcasts.

The Strathcona Mental Health Team reports that 14 percent of its caseload "definitely or very likely has AIDS."

DECEMBER Several Fraser Valley municipal councils ban the *Straight* and gay publication *Xtra West* from local libraries. Employment classified ad: "Psychics needed. Work from home or office. 24-hour service. All shifts available." But you already knew that.

1995

FEBRUARY Phil Borsos, former *Straight* production employee and director of the landmark B.C. film *The Grey Fox*, dies.
APRIL The Federal Building in Oklahoma City is bombed.
MAY The *Straight*'s Andrew Struthers edges out Mordecai Richler and Paul Quarrington to win the National Magazine Award for humour for his "Green Shadow" serial on the

Clayoquot Sound logging controversy. The North American association of water utilities advises Vancouver water authorities to tell AIDS sufferers to boil their water to protect themselves from *Cryptosporidium*, but they don't bother. Vancouver's new public library opens.
JUNE A police siege of militant Natives takes place at Gustafsen Lake.
OCTOBER O.J. Simpson is acquitted of murdering his ex-wife Nicole and Ron Goldman.

Toronto's Garth Drabinsky says his Ford Centre will "help ensure that Vancouver never slips into the mire of banality."

NOVEMBER The Ford Centre for the Performing Arts and GM Place open. Toronto's Garth Drabinsky says his Ford Centre will "help ensure that Vancouver never slips into the mire of banality." At the first Grizzlies game, the announcer says the team will give Vancouver "a pulse."
DECEMBER Bill Richardson begins his column in the *Straight*. Vancouver's original comedy club, Punchlines, closes after 16 years.

1996

MAY The NDP is re-elected in B.C.
JULY Vancouver's beloved Commodore Ballroom closes amid legal wrangling.
AUGUST More than 10,000 Kelowna residents become ill from *Cryptosporidium*.
SEPTEMBER Issue 1500 is a record-setting 124 pages. An Angus Reid survey indicates that more than 308,000 read the *Straight* each week and about half a million read at least one of every four issues. Net circulation is over 100,000.
NOVEMBER The *Straight*'s Bruce Grierson wins the Webster award for best feature reporting in any B.C. media for his look at bone-marrrow transplants. This gives the *Straight* 31 national and regional awards from 65 nominations in three years. Bill Clinton beats Bob Dole. Conrad Black buys a controlling interest in the Southam newspaper chain, giving him 59 of Canada's 105 dailies.
DECEMBER Virgin Records opens Canada's largest entertainment-software store in the former public library building. Men to Women classified ad: "All your pictures of flame evoke your immolation. (Now your parrot talks of nothing else.) They still ask about you at the gym. Particularly the one with the freckles, the torn pupil, and the predatory grin. The days snap by like bonfires." December 25: Christmas as usual.

PHOTO & ILLUSTRATION CREDITS

Part One

viii: photo by Oraf
7: photo by Fred Davidoff
9: illustrator unknown
10: illustration of Wuxtry Man, originally by Rand Holmes
13: illustration by Rand Holmes
14: photo by Fred Davidoff
17: illustrator unknown
19: photo by Fred Davidoff
20: photo by Fred Davidoff
22: photo by Fred Davidoff
25: Acidman comic strip by Peter "Zipp" Almasy
27: illustrator unknown
29: illustration by Bob Masse
30: photo by Glen Baglo, courtesy *Vancouver Sun*
34: photo by Fred Davidoff
37: illustrator unknown
38: illustration by Rand Holmes
41: photo by Fred Davidoff
44: photo by Fred Davidoff
49: illustration by S. Seymour
52: illustration by Rand Holmes
54: photo by Fred Davidoff
57: illustration by Bruce Reifel
58: Harold Hedd comic strip by Rand Holmes
61: illustrator unknown
63: photo by Fred Davidoff
66: photo by Fred Davidoff

Part Two

75: illustration by Rand Holmes
79: illustrator unknown
81: illustration by Veronica Plewman
82: Reid Fleming comic strip by David Boswell
85: illustration by Rand Holmes
87: illustrator unknown
88: illustrator unknown
93: illustrator unknown
94: illustrator unknown
97: illustration by Rand Holmes
98: illustrator unknown
101: cartoon by David Boswell
107: photographer unknown, cover design by Bob Mercer
109: Reid Fleming comic strip by David Boswell
111: illustration by Rand Holmes
112: illustration by Jim Cummins
115: illustration by Rand Holmes, cover design by Bob Mercer
116: illustrator unknown
118: photo by Paul Little

Part Three

127: illustration by Rod Filbrandt, cover design by Brigit Goldammer
129: photo by Oraf
130: illustration by Carel Moiseiwitsch
133: Wombat comic strip by Rod Filbrandt
134: Ernie Pook's Comeek comic strip by Lynda Barry
137: illustration by Stanley Q. Woodvine
141: illustration by Stanley Q. Woodvine
142: illustration by Stanley Q. Woodvine, cover design by Brigit Goldammer
145: cartoon by Andrew Struthers
146: illustration by Otto Pfannschmidt, cover design by Brigit Goldammer
151: Life in Hell cartoon by Matt Groening
152: cartoon by Dirk Van Stralen
158: illustration by Stanley Q. Woodvine
161: photo by Art Perry
165: illustration by Andrew Struthers
170: illustration by Roxanna Bikadoroff
172: illustration by Otto Pfannschmidt
177: Wombat comic strip by Rod Filbrandt
180: illustration by Carel Moiseiwitsch
183: illustration by Rod Filbrandt, cover design by Brigit Goldammer
184: photo by Robert Kwong
189: photo by Alex Waterhouse-Hayward
192: photo by Chris Cameron

GEORGIA STRAIGHT
WUXTRY